Taming the Hacking Storm

Taming the Hacking Storm

A Framework for Defeating
Hackers and Malware

Roger A. Grimes

WILEY

For general information on our other products and services or for technical support, please contact our Customer Care Department within the United States at (800) 762-2974, outside the United States at (317) 572-3993 or fax (317) 572-4002.

Wiley also publishes its books in a variety of electronic formats. Some content that appears in print may not be available in electronic formats. For more information about Wiley products, visit our web site at www.wiley.com.

Library of Congress Cataloging-in-Publication Data Applied for:

Print ISBN: 9781394349586
ePDF ISBN: 9781394349609
epub ISBN: 9781394349593
OBook ISBN: 9781394352289

Cover Image: © elroce/Adobe Stock
Cover Design: Wiley

SKY10098920_022525

To all the Internet security practitioners who have dedicated their careers to fighting malicious hackers and their malware. Keep up the good fight!

This book, like all my others, is also dedicated to my wife, Tricia. She has supported my vision to "fix the Internet" since the day we met over 27 years ago. On our honeymoon, she sat on the beach by herself for part of each day while I toiled up in our hotel suite, thinking and writing about how to better fight hackers and malware. I know neglecting your bride on your honeymoon is not the sign of a healthy work/life balance, but the fact that she supported my efforts toward this goal without a complaint even then speaks to the great life partner she is. I would not be who I am without her.

About the Author

Roger A. Grimes, data-driven evangelist at KnowBe4, Inc., has been a computer security consultant for 36 years, as well as an instructor, holder of dozens of computer certifications, and author of 15 books and more than 1,500 articles on computer security. He has spoken at many of the world's biggest computer security conferences (e.g., Black Hat, RSA, etc.); been featured in *Newsweek* magazine; appeared on television; been interviewed for NPR's *All Things Considered*, CNBC, the *Wall Street Journal*; and been a guest on dozens of radio shows and podcasts. He has worked at some of the world's largest computer security companies, including Foundstone, McAfee, and Microsoft. He has consulted for hundreds of companies, from the largest to the smallest, around the world. He specializes in social engineering, host and network security, ransomware, multifactor authentication, quantum security, identity management, anti-malware, hackers, honeypots, public key infrastructure, cloud security, cryptography, policy, and technical writing. His certifications have included CPA, CISSP, CISA, CISM, CEH, MSCE: Security, Security+, and yada-yada others, and he has been an instructor for many of them. His writings and presentations are often known for their real-world, contrarian views. He was the weekly security columnist for *InfoWorld* and *CSO* magazines between 2005 and 2019.

You can contact the author at:

Email: roger@banneretcs.com

LinkedIn: https://www.linkedin.com/in/rogeragrimes

Bluesky: @rogeragrimes.bsky.social

X/Twitter: @rogeragrimes

Mastodon: https://infosec.exchange/@rogeragrimes

Threads: @rogeragrimes

Contents

Preface
Taming the Internet

"It is not the critic who counts; not the man who points out how the strong man stumbles, or where the doer of deeds could have done them better. The credit belongs to the man who is actually in the arena, whose face is marred by dust and sweat and blood, who strives valiantly; who errs and comes short again and again; because there is not effort without error and shortcomings; but who does actually strive to do the deed; who knows the great enthusiasm, the great devotion, who spends himself in a worthy cause, who at the best knows in the end the triumph of high achievement and who at the worst, if he fails, at least he fails while daring greatly. So that his place shall never be with those cold and timid souls who know neither victory nor defeat."

– Theodore Roosevelt (1858–1919), "Man in the Arena" speech, given April 23, 1910

I'm out to fix all of Internet security, or at least as much as I can, before I depart Earth. I know from experience that mostly what I'm doing is inviting critics to pan my ideas and tell me how I'm not that smart. It's okay. I'm a man in the arena.

At nearly the same time that I started to develop an intense interest in personal computers, I also developed a strong interest in fighting malicious hackers and their malware programs. My interest was immediately intensely passionate, religious-like, and felt life-changing. And it turned out to be exactly that, as it changed the rest of my life and became my career. I don't know why because prior to that epiphany, I had never had an interest in becoming a cop or detective in real life, even though I have always greatly admired and appreciated them. But something clicked when I got into computers.

It wasn't like malicious hacking was rampant at the time. Back in 1987, there were only a few PC computer viruses, a few on Apple computers (e.g., Elk Cloner), and a few on IBM-compatible computers (e.g., Stoned, Pakistani Brain, etc.). They were so few and generally uncommon that popular and respected early *PC Magazine* columnist John Dvorak wrote a column declaring them a hoax.

For the first decade or so after that period, even as hackers and their malware programs began to really flourish, most hackers and malware programs really didn't go out of their way to permanently harm someone or something. Back then, hacking and writing computer virus programs was more of a way for someone (usually men aged 12 to 24) to brag about their programming and hacking machismo to similarly minded online social communities. There were only a few exceptions (e.g., PC Cyborg ransomware trojan, Michelangelo virus, etc.) where a hacker program intentionally tried to harm something. But almost none stole money. And most, if they did do something harmful, really didn't intend to.

I followed an early online newsletter called *The Dirty Dozen*, so-called because it described all the currently-existing-at-time dozen malware programs to be aware of. Originally created by Tom Neff and later updated by Eric Newhouse, it quickly grew over the next few years to include many "dozens." Here's an example from 1988: https://totse.totseans.com/viruses/virus _ information/ dd.html.

I had read a 1987 book called *FluShot Plus* by Ross Greenberg, which described early malware and how to fight it. Greenberg covered how he created what he thought was a totally secure sandboxed environment and invited hackers to hack it: which they successfully did many times in a continuing cat-and-mouse game that portended today's back-and-forth antivirus battles.

The *FluShot Plus* book is such an early book on computer malware that I can't even find a mention or reference to it on the Internet. Imagine something that really existed in the real world that the Internet has no record of! Part of that reason is that the Internet wasn't really even the "everywhere Internet" as we know it now. We had a patchwork of globally connected messaging systems, but it wasn't called the Internet. The official Internet was something only privileged universities and colleges had and could afford at the time. I owned a physical copy of the *FluShot Plus* book for decades. If I had to point to a single thing that piqued my interest in fighting malicious hackers and malware the most, it was that book.

Greenberg also made an early companion antivirus program called FluShot Plus, and he eventually wrote one of the first antivirus scanning programs that could scan for multiple malware programs at the same time called Virex PC. Before then, if you thought you had a malware program on your computer, you had to hope that someone had made a dedicated "detector" program and run that specific program that looked for that one malware program. And if you learned from the detector program that you did indeed have that malware program, you had to execute and run another companion program, if you were lucky and it even existed, to remove the malware program as you crossed your fingers.

The now infamous and late John McAfee made the "virus scanner" program explode in popularity around 1988–1989 and, with it, a new mega swarm of virus writers. Before John created his VirusScan program, there were probably less than a dozen computer viruses. However, one of the weird side effects of writing a popular computer virus-eradication program was that it attracted new people who wanted to code a brand new computer virus and get their 15 minutes of fame.

I first met John in 1987 or 1988 on a computer virus fighting online group called Virus L (I think that was what it was called) on FIDONet, an early precursor of today's Internet. From that meeting, John encouraged me to learn Assembly language to disassemble viruses, and for the next few years I was disassembling and documenting DOS computer viruses for him. At first, he would send me one or two new computer viruses a month to look at, but within less than two years he was sending me dozens a day. I could not keep up. My real full-time job as an accountant was suffering. John eventually started McAfee Associates and had teams of full-time virus disassemblers. He did not need me.

But I was fully hooked into fighting malicious hackers and their malware programs by then, spending every spare hour I could on it...even neglecting my new wife and young babies more than I should have in pursuit of my new passion. I was, even back then, doing consulting services to companies hit by computer viruses. I remember dressing up in my finest brown corduroy suit and walking into the board rooms of Fortune 100 banks in distress and being paid big money to advise the U.S. Navy when they got hit by computer viruses.

It was all headed stuff, and if they knew just how scared I was inside my own young head, they would probably chased me out. But I did help them. I was even in *Newsweek* magazine in March 1992 along with John in an article about the Michelangelo boot virus that was erasing hard drives (actually only the master partition tables) around the world.

My passion was expanded past just computer malware when I read Clifford Stoll's 1989 *The Cuckoo's Egg* (`https://www.amazon.com/Cuckoos-Egg-Tracking-Computer-Espionage/dp/1668048167`) about tracking and trapping a foreign hacker using a honeypot. Not coincidentally, I later wrote a book on honeypots in 2005 called *Honeypots for Windows* (`https://www.amazon.com/Honeypots-Windows-Experts-Voice-Grimes/dp/1590593359`). I started to learn about hackers, hacking, and how to stop them.

At the time, I didn't realize cybersecurity would become my life's passion and a multidecade career. In my full-time professional life, I have worked my way from PC repair technician to network technician, to network supervisor, to regional director of networks and technology for a large healthcare organization, and finally to vice president of information services of a midsize hospitality company. But during all of that, my real passion was fighting hackers and malware. I was reading everything I could on it. I was frequently making money consulting on it. I was, for sure, neglecting my full-time job to really work on computer security. My bosses thought I was working on budgets or something like that, and really, I was researching and fighting hackers. My full-time jobs were funding my even fuller-time professional hobby. I'm not sure how I didn't get fired because I wasn't a great boss or manager.

By April 2003, I realized I had enough of doing anything that wasn't computer security related. I remember calling my wife one day out of the blue and telling her I was quitting my very well-paying job as a VP and going to start doing computer security full-time. She already knew of my passion but wasn't as gleeful as I was since we had four kids to support and a large mortgage.

She cautioned me to do general computer consulting instead and do computer security when I could until I could make it into a full-time business. And I could understand her concern. There wasn't a field called cybersecurity. There were not even a ton of malicious hackers. John's antivirus program seemed to be getting more and more accurate, and there was a real possibility that the problem of computer malware might be solved. A lot more hackers were getting arrested and put in jail...finally...including infamous early hacker, Kevin Mitnick, who decades later became my employer, friend, and supporter. It seemed like there was a real chance that the world was going to get a handle on hackers and their malware programs.

Yes, it's very funny to think about that now.

I remember thinking, "Well, we are starting to arrest the hackers and get a handle on malware programs...but there's going to be a lot more computers in the future, so even if there will be fewer of them as a percentage overall to fight, they will likely still be a big problem." With that, I went full-time to computer security in 2003 and never looked back. Fairly soon, I had a better-paying job teaching hacking to students and doing penetration testing for a cool company called Foundstone (ironically, later bought by McAfee Associates).

I mention all this because there was a time when we had computers and the Internet, and it wasn't all that clear that hackers and malware would get as bad as they are today. Hacking and malware were present, but they were not everywhere. Most people and companies didn't get hit by them. The people who got "hit" by malicious hackers and malware were just "unlucky," we thought. Most people and companies didn't suffer real damage if they were hit by hackers or malware. And we thought it was bad back then.

Boy, were we wrong!

How Bad Is It Now?

If there is one thing I'm surprised about today from being in cybersecurity for more than 36 years now, it's how bad Internet crime is today, and no one is really trying anything substantially different to fix it. I could never have imagined that we would have malware (i.e., ransomware) that is taking down thousands of companies a year, even huge conglomerates, entire cities, law enforcement, and so on…stealing billions of dollars a year…literally killing people (i.e., death rates go up when ransomware hits hospitals), info-stealing malware accessing millions of passwords and logon "cookies" a day, taking over millions of user accounts a day, exploiting hundreds of thousands of devices a day, and stealing hundreds of millions of dollars a day from people and businesses.

People's credit card information is stolen so routinely that most people don't even mind that much. It's considered just part of how life works now. Victims just wait for their new cards in the mail and then update their Amazon and other online payment accounts. My personal credit card got stolen five times in 6 months this year, and I'm still using it (well, the updated version of it with new numbers). All our personal and confidential information has been stolen so many times that any time a new hacker breaches a billion new records about our lives, it barely makes the news. And most of us, when we read about the latest breach involving our information, just give a collective sigh. I mean, everyone's personal information has been stolen so many times already; what does one more theft of it really add to our personal risk?

Even if you don't see it in your personal email inbox, most emails on the Internet are malicious (e.g., spam, phishing attacks, etc.). Most of the bad emails are filtered out before they get to your inbox, but they are there, taking up bandwidth on the Internet. A large percentage of the messages sent to our phones are malicious. Social media sites are full of scam artists and romance scammers. It's difficult to sell or buy something on the Internet without getting scammed. A kid can send a ginormous distributed denial of service (DDoS) attack and take down almost any website or service for $5 or free.

Now add to all that already existing mess, artificial intelligence-enabled deepfakes. It takes me longer to create a new account on any of the thousands of free AI-enabled deepfake services than it does to create a deepfake audio or video of you or anyone else fraudulently saying or doing anything. All I need is a picture of the victim and six seconds of their voice to create a realistic-looking and sounding fake audio or video clip that would likely fool their mother.

Out of everything I could think of about the Internet and cybercrime in the early days, I could never have imagined how bad cyberattacks would get and that the world collectively really doesn't do much to stop them.

Well, billions are spent to stop malicious hackers and malware. Every year, more money is spent trying to stop cyberattacks than in the previous year. And every year, cyberattacks just get worse. And strangely, and befuddling to me, even though how we are defending is clearly not working, we aren't really doing anything different year-to-year to change things. We literally see how bad cybercrime is, predict it's likely to be worse next year, and then don't do anything significantly different to make better defenses.

Almost nothing anyone proposes works to significantly reduce cybercrime, or if it actually could, it never ends up getting widely deployed. Well, some rare things (like DMARC, SPF, and DKIM) do work and get broadly accepted but, unfortunately, are so limited in what they impact that it's like plugging your finger in a dike that is already bursting around you. But there are a few examples of greatness and what could be.

Most Internet security fixes are temporary, whack-a-mole fixes to partially fix a very narrow, specific problem. Hackers can move around the new defenses in a day, and it then takes the Internet defense industry months to years to respond adequately. Defenders close one hole and the attackers open up a new one. It's an ever-changing game of hide and seek, and the hackers are always one step ahead and winning.

Most malicious hackers are able to steal millions of dollars and cause broad-spectrum harm without almost any fear of reprisal. To actually catch a hacker, present evidence, and have them charged, arrested, tried, and sentenced is far rarer than a lightning strike.

Imagine how good you would get if your job was to rob banks and you could never get caught, arrested, and stopped. Imagine that the worst penalty for robbing a bank was that you were stopped from robbing that particular bank, but you could drive to the next one and successfully rob it? And there was zero chance of getting arrested?

You would likely get very good at robbing banks. You would likely get very rich robbing banks. And unless you screwed up and accidentally made the wrong person mad, didn't pay the right bribe, or just got too insanely greedy, no one was ever going to stop you.

That is the story of today's Internet. It's full of crime, and nothing seems likely to change that soon.

There Is a Solution

Here's the surprising secret. There are ways to make the Internet and everyone on it significantly more resilient to malicious hacking attacks. It isn't impossible. In fact, it's far from impossible. It's do-able. And we could implement and achieve near-perfect Internet security with a modicum of change and expense in less than a year. Most people wouldn't even notice significant changes. They would just be along for the ride as we went from a very insecure Internet to a fairly secure Internet.

I've been thinking about how to make the Internet far more secure for my entire career. It's something I wake up and go to sleep thinking about. There hasn't been a day since 1987 that fixing the Internet hasn't been the majority of what I've been thinking about. It has become my life's passion.

If one day, I had been successful in helping to make the Internet a far safer place for people to compute, then my career would have been worth it. And if not, my career, as great as it has been for me and others I have helped in little ways, will have been an overall waste for humanity. I'm not here to fix the temporary little problems that fix only part of the problem. I want to fix it all.

That's the way I think about it. I feel a daily frustration because there are ways to fix the Internet and we just aren't doing them.

This book is a result of a solution I've been thinking about, refining, and promoting for more than 20 years to anyone who would listen or read.

My Early Writings on the Subject

Early on, when I first started to think about ways to solve the woes of the Internet, I was just envisioning better antivirus solutions, "next-generation" this and that, like nearly every computer security vendor was selling. But then I started to notice that all of that, version after version, the next big thing, was also failing. Nothing traditional seemed to be working. Even the new, supposedly better stuff was not working. And the reality was that each new year was worse than the last. It hasn't gotten better in more than 36 years. It just gets worse.

I started to ponder the larger underlying issues that were really causing all the other problems that I could see and experience. "Why was the Internet so full of crime?" Why aren't today's solutions working?" What would it take to make the Internet a far safer place to compute?"

About a year later, I had the beginnings of what would become my "Fix the Internet" solution. For a few years, I just posted my solution on various computer security blogs and Internet channels to anyone who would listen. Those postings are likely lost to time.

In 2005, I was made the weekly security columnist at *InfoWorld* magazine, a role I kept until 2019. I actively sought the job to broadcast my ideas about how to make the Internet a far safer place. The previous *InfoWorld* security columnists were promoting vendor ideas that were for sure not going to work. So, I claimed to be a better expert and asked for the job.

It was there that I began writing in earnest about the biggest underlying problem of why malicious hacking is so prevalent on the Internet, including this column on June 16, 2006: `https://www.infoworld.com/article/2189099/hackers-keep-hacking-because-they-can.html`. This was me finally figuring out why malicious hacking and crime were so rampant on the Internet. I finally had my answer to the first part of the problem.

With the actual problem at hand, I was able to come up with solutions. In June 2007, I wrote two *InfoWorld* columns about how to solve the problem of rampant Internet crime (`https://www.infoworld.com/article/2205234/the-security-solution-revolution.html` and `https://www.infoworld.com/article/2208906/the-security-solution-revolution-continued.html`). I wrote another on September 14, 2007 (`https://www.infoworld.com/article/2330189/trust-key-to-internet-security.html`). Six months later, in January 2008, I wrote another (`https://www.infoworld.com/article/2319151/internet-security-what-will-work.html`). The following is the headline and a bit of the article from that posting.

by **Roger Grimes**
Columnist

Internet security: What will work

Analysis
Jan 18, 2008 • 5 mins

Here's a radical plan for making the Internet safe for every legitimate user

That doesn't mean there aren't solutions. Last year, in several columns, I detailed one of the ways that a more secure Internet might be forged in the future. It's my vision. And the more I think about it, it's the only way I can see the Internet becoming significantly more secure. All other plans that I've come across break down under scrutiny or seem to rely on us becoming accustomed to a significant amount of computer crime. The other plans might reduce computer crime, but only temporarily and by a small amount.

I remember my editor-in-chief and friend, Eric Knorr, telling me to lay off writing so much about my plan to fix the Internet for a little while because I was repeating it over and over too much, perhaps boring the readers. Eric was probably right, but it didn't stop me from repeatedly re-stating an improved version of my solution several times a year for the rest of my career.

I eventually created a whitepaper and then resolved to write about and update that whitepaper every year or two. Here's a version from 2021: https://www.linkedin.com/pulse/wanna-fix-internet-roger-grimes. I sent it to industry luminaries and national cybersecurity leaders, like Bruce Schneier and Jen Easterly, director (until January 20, 2025) of the Cybersecurity and Infrastructure Security Agency (CISA). But I'm tired of writing and updating whitepapers and wanted to go a bit more formal. This book is the most recent and detailed look at my solution of how to make the Internet a far safer place for people to compute.

My solution today is far more mature and incorporates technologies that did not exist back in the early days of my articles and whitepapers, but when I look back at my original ideas from nearly two decades ago, I'm surprised that much of what they said is still the same basis of the stronger solution I promote today. Internet attacks have changed over time (not as much as you would think), but even with those changes, I didn't need to significantly update my solution. I think it's a sign of a good solution when changes in technologies and attacker methods don't mean you have to update your solution.

I've shown my "Fix the Internet" idea to thousands of people over the last 15 years. I've defended its ideas online to knowledgeable friends and industry luminaries, had its ideas covered by other publications, and even defended it in formal academic debates. All along, I've had critics poke holes and point out weaknesses. Along with debating to defend my ideas, I've always asked my

Preface   **xix**

critics one central question: "OK, you don't like my proposal. That's OK. What can you think of to better secure the Internet that is better than my idea?"

I always hear crickets.

I get it. Solving the problem of significantly securing the Internet is not an easy task. It took me 20 years to come up with a good solution, and I'm constantly re-evaluating it. If you can come up with a better solution, I welcome it. I don't care whose solution wins as long as we do something different that works to significantly reduce cybercrime. But I do think that my solution is pretty good and will work.

Why Hasn't Your Solution Happened Yet?

Many readers might be asking why, if my solution is so good, hasn't it already taken over the Internet and made it more secure? That's a great question and if I knew the answer, I would be a billionaire. How to influence enough people so that we get a far more secure Internet is the remaining big challenge of my life and career. I either do it or fail. This book is part of that fight.

Fixing Internet security will take major company support (like from Google, Microsoft, etc.), and a sizable percentage of cybersecurity-minded companies, people, and governments from all walks of life and cultures, to support it. It's hard to get the people sitting at your dinner table to agree on something, much less the entire world. People and governments are very different in different parts of the world. People very much differ on what securing the Internet really means. I'll cover how I solved that problem in Part II of the book.

I've come to the ultimate conclusion that it will likely take a tipping point event, like a digital equivalent of the 9/11 attack, to happen to the Internet, where it goes down for a day or a week or even just a sizable portion of it, like all of banking or the stock market. Without a big enough wake-up event threatening the established order, I don't think we'll see much movement toward significant progress. After all, Internet crime is pretty bad right now, and no one is really doing anything other than small, incremental fixes that will not work to significantly improve the security of the Internet anytime soon.

Pain and tipping point events make things happen. 9/11 significantly improved the aircraft passenger industry and the entire mass travel industry beyond it. We knew that hijackers could get into cockpits and fly planes into buildings or that terrorists could sneak bombs onto planes in water bottles, toothpaste tubes, and underwear long before 9/11. Our travel security experts knew all of that was a possibility prior to what happened that day.

But it took 9/11 happening so that the needed defenses and interruption to our regular lives would not only happen without people yelling and being mad, but even begged for. Now, we all pour out our liquids, make sure our toothpaste tube is only 3 ounces in size or less, throw away our sharp objects, and go through body scanners that can see our every contour. Before 9/11 happened, society simply wouldn't have tolerated it.

It took the pain happening for the needed defenses to be implemented. We, humans, are all taught to be proactive in school, but the reality is that we are mostly only reactive at scale, only implementing defenses after it's already too late, only after way more blood is on the ground than there needs to be.

Perhaps we will fix the Internet before something big happens, but I've been waiting for it for more than two decades. So, I'm not holding my breath. But I'm trying every day.

About This Book

The book is broken down with four major parts over 18 chapters. The first part defines what the problem is, part of which I've begun hinting to here in the preface. It will cover the major underlying problem that underlies all other problems. You can't solve the problem if you can't adequately define the problem. After understanding what the real Internet security problem is, Part II states the solution(s). It will do so in summary form and in more detail over individual chapters.

In Part III, I do threat modeling to find potential weaknesses and answer common questions. I'm not only open to someone finding fault with my ideas but invite it. If my ideas are good, they will withstand evaluation from smart people. Part IV covers other issues and challenges that need to be resolved in order for the Internet to be all it can be. Issues include minimizing vulnerabilities, better patching, and getting better international cooperation.

Acknowledgments

First, I want to thank KnowBe4 CEO Stu Sjouwerman and my team leader, Kathy Wattman, for their unflinching support of my goal to make the Internet a far better and safer place. They let me write, rant, and teach about it every day as my full-time job.

Special thanks to Dr. Loren Kohnfelder. If I can call anyone a mentor, it's Loren. Loren invented digital certificates in 1978 and is considered by many to be the "Father of PKI." He has never stopped trying to fix all the hardest problems in computer security. In our weekly talks, we regularly discuss how to fight hackers and improve Internet security. Loren was my sounding board for much of this project, he was my biggest constructive critic, and he always pushed me to better threat model everything I proposed.

Forever thanks to Bruce Schneier. His writings and books have impacted my thinking on how to better secure the Internet more than anyone else. He gets it better than anyone else.

I want to give special thanks to Tim Draegen, founder of Dmarcian and co-creator of DMARC. As one of the only people I know who has actually created and implemented a widespread recent Internet security standard, he has spent hours counseling me on how to be more effective and persuasive in trying to get my own solutions implemented.

Thanks to Zeke Hill, senior anti-cheat analyst at Riot Games, for educating me about how to best mitigate fake device IDs.

I want to thank Jim Minatel and Wiley for greenlighting this book. This is our sixth book together. Thanks to the rest of the Wiley team, including Ashirvad Moses and Annie Melnick.

Lastly, I strive to be as technically accurate and honest as possible. If you see a mistake in the book, it is solely mine.

Chapter Summaries

Here I summarize what is covered in each chapter.

Part I. Identifying the Problem

Part I discusses how bad Internet security is and the main underlying problem.

Chapter 1: How Bad Is Internet Security

Chapter 1 discusses how bad Internet cybercrime is, using reported statistics and figures. It shouldn't shock anyone that cybercrime involves many billions of dollars each year with millions and millions of victims. Any solution(s) to significantly improve Internet security, if successful, should significantly decrease these figures over time.

Chapter 2: How We Are Attacked and Why

This chapter covers how all Internet malicious hacking and malware exploitation happens. It focuses on the initial root access causes of hacking and the motivations of the involved cybercriminals. This chapter is a comprehensive, albeit brief, look at the cybercrime ecosystem that a good Internet security solution would mitigate.

Chapter 3: The Problem

Behind most cybercrime lies one main underlying problem that allows all the others to flourish. This chapter discusses a similar real-world crime issue and what it took to solve it. It covers the main Internet security problem we need to solve ahead of all others.

Chapter 4: Challenges

Internet security hasn't been great for decades. Everyone knows cybercrime is rampant. So why haven't better solutions been deployed for the decades the Internet has been in existence? Chapter 4 covers the big reasons why we don't yet have better Internet security. It covers these challenges that would impact any proposed solution from a strategic and tactical perspective.

Part II. The Technology Solution

Part II covers the theory and details of how to provide the solution to fix Internet security, including all its component parts and technologies.

Chapter 5: The Solution

Chapter 5 reveals the general theory of my proposed solution to better secure the Internet. It summarizes the solution and introduces the new paradigms and services, which are then covered in more detail in the following chapters. It includes a quick threat model of the general theory of the solution and how well it might work against today's Internet threats.

Chapter 6: Technology Solution Summary

Chapter 6 covers how the solution's general theory can be accomplished. It will introduce all the needed components and technologies. Then, Chapters 7–12 discuss each component in more detail.

Chapter 7: Trusted Identity

One of the central tenets of a more secure Internet is the ability for anyone to be able to trust the identity of those who are trying to connect to them. Today's Internet is the opposite of that, with pervasive anonymity and poor identity services far more common than not. Out of every part of the solution, this is the most important part. If we do it right, we have a chance to better secure the Internet. If we fail at this one thing, there is no chance.

Chapter 8: Safe and Trusted Devices

You can't have a trusted user identity without ensuring that the user comes from a trusted location and device. If an attacker can compromise a user's device, nothing else that happens on it, including identity and authentication, can be trusted. Chapter 8 covers the technologies needed to give us safe and trusted devices, including safe hardware booting and reliable device identities.

Chapter 9: Trusted OSs and Apps

The operating systems and applications users use to compute, communicate, and connect to others must have strong integrity and trustworthiness. Chapter 9 covers how trusted operating systems and applications work. We are fairly close to having trusted operating systems and applications already; we just need them to be more pervasive.

Chapter 10: Trusted Networks

Once we have trusted devices, OS, applications, and identity, we need a trusted network path to ensure that all that goodness gets from point A to Z. Chapter 10 covers trusted networks, how we create them, and how we ensure that others can trust them.

Chapter 11: Trust Assurance Service

No matter how great your trust system is end-to-end, there will always be trusted nodes that get compromised and exploited. Badness will come from trusted places. Chapter 11 covers a DNS-like service with both client and global Internet components that any participating node can use to determine a particular communicating node's trustworthiness and see if it is or isn't reported as currently compromised. This service will likely have to be supported by substantial funding.

Chapter 12: Internet Security Global Alliance

Chapter 12 covers a new needed group of security matter experts dedicated to fixing and managing the Internet's security. Today's most popular Internet standards groups aren't dedicated to security and have not proven to be able to deliver good security solutions in a timely manner. A different approach is needed; Chapter 12 discusses what that new approach should be.

Part III. Challenging the Solution

Every security defense product needs to be threat modeled. Part III covers a second threat model of the solution and answers common questions.

Chapter 13: Threat Modeling

Every cybersecurity solution should be publicly threat-modeled. Chapter 13 threat models the various types of attacks that can be attempted against the solution and technologies that were presented in Part II.

Chapter 14: Common Questions

Upon learning about my solution, which relies on verified identity, many people who believe in stronger privacy, if not absolutely anonymity, have legitimate privacy concerns about it. I've heard these questions and many others many times over the decades. Chapter 14 was written to discuss common questions and my answers.

Part IV. Other Needed Solutions

Internet security involves many big problems, not all of which are directly addressed with the solution proposed in this book. Part IV is a quick look at those other issues with other recommended solutions.

Chapter 15: Secure Coding

About one-third of all successful data breaches involve programmed software or firmware vulnerabilities and it has been this way since the beginning of computers. Chapter 15 covers the problem of insecure coding and suggests better fixes.

Chapter 16: Better Patching

Less than 2% of vulnerabilities in any given year are ever exploited by a real-world hacker against a real-world company. Still, unpatched vulnerabilities exist across the globe and large quantities, accounting for a third of all data breaches. Chapter 16 covers the problems with current patch management and recommends robust fixes.

Chapter 17: Getting International Agreements

One of the biggest problems in Internet security is the lack of legal agreement between different nations on what is and isn't allowed legally. Nation-states routinely attack each other and don't usually enforce attacks made by their own citizens on the citizens and companies of other nations. Chapter 17 discusses the history of failure in trying to get a digital equivalent of the Geneva Conventions and discusses the recently passed UN Convention on Cybercrime.

Chapter 18: What You Can Do

Every person reading this book and learning about its concepts can play a part in helping to better secure our Internet. Chapter 18 summarizes the solution and covers what you can do personally and at your organization to help make the Internet safer for everyone, from our grandparents to our grandchildren. You, too, are part of the solution.

I'm not sure if my proposed solution will be the final security solution that the Internet decides to implement. But I've thought a lot of about the problem…every day for more than 36 years, and I think that whatever does better secure the Internet…because it will eventually happen one day, will either look substantially like my solution already does or borrow heavily from many of its ideas.

I guess there is always a chance that decades from now, the Internet will be just as rife or worse with malicious hackers and their malware creations as they are today, but I just can't fathom the world accepting today's status quo. No, the Internet will finally mature past its Wild Wild West origins into a more secure, trusted platform for computing, just like every other infrastructure we use eventually did. The early electric power industry used to routinely electrocute people. Children used to work full-time in factories, often getting maimed and killed. Eventually, all these industries and services matured, became safer, and more trusted. I fully expect the Internet to be far more secure and trusted in the future, ideally before I retire.

I could be wrong. But I'm not going down without a fight.

Identifying the Problem

How Bad Is Internet Security?

As I shared in the preface, the biggest surprise of my more than 36-year cybersecurity career is just how widespread cybercrime is today and that no person, group, company, or organization is really doing anything significantly different to fix it. Most cyber defenses are just tiny incremental updates of past safeguards that did not work that well, and anything that might actually make a big impact doesn't get wide acceptance. This chapter covers some relevant current Internet crime statistics and risk factors, starting with why we have to fix Internet security.

Internet crime is so bad that many people who see the statistics I present in this chapter for the first time will likely be shocked. Internet crime is very, very common, far surpassing what most people experience in the real world. It's a hundred million of this, a billion of that, and a trillion bad things of this other thing. The numbers can be quite startling and even seem nonsensical at times, but let's get started.

Arguments for Fixing Internet Security

Cybercrime impacts nearly every aspect of modern life, from personal privacy to global economies, yet the solutions currently in place are woefully inadequate. Without significant change, the costs and risks will only continue to escalate.

The following are some arguments for why the current state of Internet security is unacceptable.

Increased Internet Criticality

When the Internet really started taking off to become what it is today, circa 1991, it was mostly a dial-up network used for email between educational facilities and government employees. Work email was just starting to become one of the "killer apps" that drove its future growth. Most of the people in the world did not yet have a personal email account. Those who did were seen as computer geeks or early adopters. The World Wide Web (WWW) was mostly a collection of static web pages, educational research portals, and early entertainment websites.

There was no globally adopted Internet search engine, like Google or Bing, being used by most Internet surfers. You couldn't type a subject inside of a box with a cursor in it, hit Enter, and get a list of every site that might pertain to your search. There weren't even enough websites to really merit a search engine; that took a few more years. Between 1995 and 1997, my brother, Richard, ran a very popular website called Cool Site of the Day, where anyone could visit and be taken to another highlighted website that the CSOD administrator thought was useful or entertaining. It was one of the most popular sites on the Internet.

Back then, in the early days, most of us could not imagine the reach of today's Internet, especially how it's critically tied to the rest of the world. I spent much of my early IT days trying to teach people how to use a mouse and how to use email. Most Internet connections, if you had one, used super slow modems that required 10 seconds to a minute for a single web page to be fully rendered on the screen. If you had to download an audio or video file . . . *fuhgeddaboudit!* You certainly could not ask your nonexistent portable cell phone to answer any obscure question you had on your mind and listen to your favorite songs and bands over the Internet.

How times have changed! We now collectively send nearly 350 billion emails and 23 billion SMS/MMS messages a day. There are more than 1.12 billion websites worldwide, and more than 250,000 new ones are added each day. The average person visits 6–10 websites with 130 separate web pages every day. Our bands and music are mostly stored on the Web and seamlessly travel with us across multiple devices.

Note: You can find some interesting global Internet statistics here:
https://www.demandsage.com/website-statistics.

For many of us, our lives are what we tell each other through our social media accounts. We make our travel reservations online (few of us use travel agents), we reserve our doctor and lab appointments online, and all our civilian critical infrastructures use the Internet to run their operations and to check on critical processes. Our 911 services and fire departments run over the Internet. Our weather forecasts are delivered on the Internet; our emails, texting, and much of our lives live and are transported on the Internet. Our meetings are made and conducted over the Internet. Our banks and stock markets run on the Internet.

Our oil pipelines run on the Internet. It's hard to think of a real-world scenario that is not critically reliant on the Internet.

The average U.S. broadband household has 17 Internet-connected devices. I have so many home systems connected to the Internet that I'm a little fearful of how to transfer their functions if I were to sell my house. The Internet helps control my power outlets, lights, alarm systems, and AC/heat systems. Every company I'm a customer of, every group I belong to, and every ongoing remote family connection happens over the Internet.

The Internet moved from a nice-to-have entertainment tool to a mission-critical platform a long time ago. It's how we get our news. It's how we communicate and coordinate. It's how we do business. It's the way we do life. A single day of downtime would be catastrophic to any country and the world. When we ask people if they would rather do without water, electricity, sewage, the Internet, or even their spouse for a day or week, most people say an Internet outage would be the most distressing event of the choices they are offered.

That's why the incredible insecurity of the Internet is so distressing to most cybersecurity professionals. As the Internet evolved from a nice-to-have to a mission-critical platform, most of us expected the security undermining the whole thing to get commensurately better. But Internet security did not get better. By almost any metric, it has gotten worse.

The question that matters most concerning Internet security is whether Internet-connected people and organizations are more or less likely to be exploited today versus the past. And the answer is that today, people and organizations are more likely to be exploited by hackers and malware than ever before. They are more likely to be exploited this year than last year, and every year before that. That's not a good thing, especially in today's Internet-connected, mission-critical world.

I Was a Average, Very Successful Hacker

For more than 20 years, I did professional penetration testing (pen testing), meaning I was paid to legally hack stuff by the owner or their agent of the thing being tested to assess its online security resiliency. I tested hundreds of software programs, hardware appliances, websites, products, and services. In every single case, I was able to break into the target in an hour or less, except for a single company, which took me three hours (because it was my second time trying after the customer had fixed things from my first successful attack visit).

Here's the kicker. As far as hackers go, I'm only average. On a scale from 1 to 10, with 10 being the highest, I'm maybe only a 5 or a 6. And I easily broke into everything. It's not like I was super smart or talented. It's just that hacking, like any other trade, is a matter of learning what things to do and with what tools. Once you learn those two things, successful hacking is as easy as being a carpenter, electrician, or plumber (all of which I find way harder than hacking).

Breaking into things, once you know what you're doing, is simply not that hard. The world is full of millions of malicious hackers. And despite everything defenders have done, we have more illegal hacking and malware year after year after year. So far, the rate and success of Internet crime, overall, has never gone down as compared to prior periods. We sometimes get temporary decreases in some areas, but then even that area accelerates and gets worse. And certainly, overall, the success rate and numbers of Internet crime has not gone down over time.

Internet Statistics and Crime

Here are some relevant cybercrime statistics.

How Often Are Organizations Compromised?

More than 40% of organizations experience a data breach each year, according to these reports:

- GetApp's 2024 *Data Security Report* states that 44% of U.S. organizations and 51% of global organizations experienced a ransomware attack over the last 12 months. `https://blog.knowbe4.com/44-us-organizations-experienced-more-ransomware-attacks-last-year`

- Ponemon Institute's *A Crisis in Third-Party Remote Access Security* report states that 52% of respondents have experienced a data breach over the last 12 months. `https://security.imprivata.com/rs/413-FZZ-310/images/IM _ Report _ Third-Party-Remote-Access-Security.pdf`

- Research suggests 40% of Fortune 1000 companies will suffer a breach every year. `https://www.bitdefender.com/en-gb/blog/businessinsights/40-of-fortune-1000-companies-will-suffer-a-breach-every-year-new-res earch-suggests`

- A 2022 Cymulate survey shows that 40% of respondents admitted to being breached over the past 12 months. After being breached once, 66% of breached respondents say they suffered additional attacks. Attacks primarily (56%) occurred via end-user phishing. `https://cymulate.com/news/breach-survey-pr-2022`

Phishing is rampant. We all get scams in our email inboxes and on our phones. Ninety-four percent of organizations had to respond to a successful phishing attack in 2023 (`https://www.infosecurity-magazine.com/news/94-firms-hit-phishing-attacks-2023`).

Here are some other eye-opening statistics:

- The Global Anti-Scam Alliance reports that scammers stole more than $1.03 trillion in 2023, much of which was due to social engineering, Internet, and phone scams. https://www.weforum.org/stories/2024/04/interpol-financial-fraud-scams-cybercrime

- The U.S. Federal Trade Commission (FTC) found that U.S. consumers lost $10 billion in the same period, which is $1 billion more than the year before, despite the number of fraud reports—nearly 2.6 million—staying the same. https://www.cnbc.com/2024/11/18/number-of-older-adults-who-lost-100000-to-fraud-tripled-since-2020-ftc.html

- The U.S. Federal Bureau of Investigation's (FBI's) 2023 *Internet Crime Report* (IC3) received a record number of U.S. complaints in 2023, 880,000, a nearly 10% increase over 2022. Reported losses exceeded $12.5 billion, a 22% increase over 2022. https://www.ic3.gov/AnnualReport/Reports/2023_IC3Report.pdf

- Microsoft's *2024 Digital Defense Report* states that their customers faced more than 600 million cyberattacks every day. https://www.microsoft.com/en-us/security/security-insider/intelligence-reports/microsoft-digital-defense-report-2024

- The Internet cable provider Comcast, in their 2023 *Comcast Business* report, states they detected 29 billion cybersecurity attacks and 9,645,028 data exfiltration events directed against their customers. https://business.comcast.com/enterprise/products-services/cybersecurity-services#threatreport

How Many Websites Are Malicious?

There are more than 1.1 billion legitimate and malicious websites. Google has stated that around 10% are intentionally malicious or are legitimate websites maliciously modified or abused for some period of time. The Anti-Phishing Working Group's 2024 *First Quarter Report* (https://docs.apwg.org/reports/apwg_trends_report_q1_2024.pdf) found 963,994 unique phishing websites over three months. Google warns browser users about 5 million malicious websites every day (https://nordlayer.com/blog/what-are-malicious-websites/).

A lot of outside observers may wonder why the cybersecurity industry cannot simply detect bad websites and prevent potential victims from visiting them. A big part of the challenge is that most malicious websites are created, used, and deleted before defenders can detect and mitigate them. According to Google, the Google Safe Browsing service detects more than 3 million potentially malicious URLs out of the 10 billion URLs and files they review every day (https://blog.google/products/chrome/google-chrome-safe-browsing-real-time). In their

2024 *Digital Trends* report, Microsoft states that 70% of malicious sites are active for less than two hours. That's perhaps being gracious. Per Google, the average malicious website exists for less than 10 minutes.

Maliciously reported or detected websites must be reported and verified before being blocked so that legitimate websites are not caught up in a wheel of unintentional misfortune. Hackers intentionally falsely report legitimate websites as being malicious so that the verification services are slowed down. The whole verification and block process is very difficult to do if the average malicious website is up for less than 10 minutes. Any Internet security solution must take this into account.

How Much of Email Is Malicious?

After its initial meager beginnings, more than 350 billion emails are now sent every day. That's more than 11,000 emails a second if I've done my math right. Unfortunately, much of or most of it is malicious—around 57% (https://dataprot.net/statistics/spam-statistics). Gmail blocks 100 million spam emails daily. Microsoft blocked 31.5 billion emails in a year, or 1,100 a second (https://www.techradar.com/news/microsoft-blocked-1000-malicious-emails-every-second-in-2021).

Note: Spam is a very popular type of malicious email, but there are many other types, such as phishing and business email compromise scams (covered later in the chapter).

What Percentage of SMS Messages Are Bad?

We collectively send more than 23 billion text messages a day (https://www.sellcell.com/blog/how-many-text-messages-are-sent-a-day-2023-statistics), or more than 84 trillion a year. Some chat services like WhatsApp are even more popular, with users sending more than 70 billion WhatsApp messages a day.

Commonly found statistics say that at least one-third of us receive a malicious SMS message each year. And, anecdotally, I find that statistic way too low. Almost everyone I know frequently receives malicious text messages. Who hasn't gotten a message from a supposed popular mail delivery service saying they could not deliver their package? I get more unwanted text messages than legitimate ones. Most people I know don't answer phone calls from unknown phone numbers and don't click any links sent to them via SMS. That's probably smart.

Globally, more than 1 billion unwanted SMS are sent per minute (https://techreport.com/statistics/cybersecurity/smishing-statistics), and at least 1 million of these are intentionally malicious. Surprisingly, not everyone knows how to spot a malicious text message. A report from TechJury (https://techjury.net/blog/smishing-statistics/) states that the percentage of people who click malicious links from fraudulent text messages varies between 8.9 and 14.5% of recipients.

How Much Internet Traffic Is Malicious?

There is a real possibility that hackers and their malware creations are most of the traffic on the Internet. Arkose Labs stated that 73% of Internet traffic is malicious (`https://www.securityweek.com/bad-bots-account-for-73-of-internet-traffic-analysis`). That figure is among the highest I can find, but even the lowest figures indicate that bad bot traffic is at least a third of all Internet traffic (`https://www.forbes.com/sites/emmawoollacott/2024/04/16/yes-the-bots-really-are-taking-over-the-internet`).

Cloudflare's 2024 *State of Application Security* report states that nearly one-third of all Internet traffic stems from bots, 93% of which appear malicious (`https://cf-assets.www.cloudflare.com/slt3lc6tev37/5naLIMtcpQ1QuuFNKFDyp9/7ba5f021de7118016ffd766ef0b2388d/BDES-5907_State-of-App-Security-2024.pdf`).

These reports do not even take into account every other possible type of malicious hacking on the Internet, including human hacker activity, malicious emails and SMS messages, and so on. If I conservatively use a third of Internet traffic being made by rogue bots and add to it malicious emails, messages, and phishing websites, it seems very likely that much of to most of the Internet's activity is malicious in origin.

Frequency of Social Engineering and Phishing

Social engineering refers to a person (or a group of people) fraudulently posing as trustworthy sender, either as someone (e.g., friend or boss), some entity (e.g., police or tax authority), or some well-known brand (e.g., Microsoft, PayPal, or your bank) trying to maliciously trick you into performing an action that would be harmful to your own interests. They want you to provide confidential information like your login details, download a boobytrapped document, run malware, etc.

Note: Although there are no "official" agreed-upon global definitions of social engineering versus phishing, most sources would agree that *phishing* is an online subset of social engineering. Social engineering can also be done in person, using physical paper mail services, and other nondigital means. The term *phishing* came about during the digital age of the Internet.

Social engineering, and email phishing in particular, has been the number-one cause, by far, of computer crime since the beginning of computers, and it doesn't seem likely to change in the near future. It plays a part in 70–90% of all Internet crime. Here are some of my articles supporting this claim:

- `https://blog.knowbe4.com/social-engineering-number-one-cybersecurity-problem`

- `https://blog.knowbe4.com/70-to-90-of-all-malicious-breaches-are-due-to-social-engineering-and-phishing-attacks`

I even wrote another Wiley book about the problem and how to solve it, *Fighting Phishing: Everything You Can Do to Fight Social Engineering and Phishing.* You can find it on `wiley.com` by searching for the title or its ISBN, 9781394249206.

It isn't just me unilaterally saying this—nearly every cybercrime report that looks at initial root causes of hacking says the same thing: Social engineering and phishing are the number-one ways hackers and their malware programs gain access to devices and networks, even if they vary in percentages. Here are some more supporting links:

- In August 2023, Comcast reported that 89.46% of attacks on their customers started with phishing (`https://blog.knowbe4.com/customer-network-breaches-phishing`). You can read the whole report here: `https://business.comcast.com/community/docs/default-source/default-document-library/ccb_threatreport_071723_v2.pdf`.

- IBM's 2023 *X-Force Threat Intelligence Index* report (`https://www.ibm.com/downloads/cas/DB4GL8YM`) had phishing at a much lower percentage but still the top cause, stating, "Phishing remains the leading infection vector, identified in 41% of incidents, followed by exploitation of public-facing applications in 26%." Their 2022 report stated much of the same but had the percentage much higher: "Phishing continued to be the most prevalent initial access vector identified. . . ." and ". . . phishing served as the initial infection vector in 78% of incidents X-Force responded to across these industries so far in 2022." `https://securityintelligence.com/posts/expanding-ot-threat-landscape-2022`

- Social engineering and phishing are a problem worldwide. The U.K.'s Official Government Statistics Cyber Security Breaches Survey 2022 (`https://www.gov.uk/government/statistics/cyber-security-breaches-survey-2022/cyber-security-breaches-survey-2022`) stated: ". . . the most common threat vector was phishing attempts (83%)."

- In 2022, Kroll's *Cyber Intelligence Report* stated that phishing was involved in 60% of all attacks. `https://www.kroll.com/en/insights/publications/cyber/threat-intelligence-reports/q1-2022-threat-landscape-threat-actors-target-email-access-extortion`

- InfoBlox's 2022 *Global State of Security Report* states: "The most successful mode of attack was phishing (58%)." `https://files.scmagazine.com/wp-content/uploads/2022/05/Infoblox-Main-Report.pdf`

If you see a report or article stating phishing was less than 40% of the problem, they usually have their taxonomy for root causes mixed up. For example, many reports claim ransomware or credential theft is the top root cause for successful hacking, but those are outcomes of initial root hacking methods, not causes.

The *2024 Comcast Business Cybersecurity Threat Report* (`https://business.comca st.com/enterprise/products-services/cybersecurity-services#threatreport`) states that 2.6 billion phishing attempts and 90% of phishing was designed to deliver malware. They detected slightly less than 5,000 phishing attacks against their customers *every minute*.

In 2023, Barracuda Networks reported (`https://www.barracuda.com/reports/ spear-phishing-trends-2023`) that while spear-phishing emails make up less than 0.1% of all email attacks, they are responsible for 66% of all successful breaches. One tactic is responsible for two-thirds of all successful attacks. Wow!

Since the beginning of the Internet, companies and organizations have been trying to design technical defenses (e.g., content filters, antimalware, anti-spam filters, etc.) to detect and stop social engineering and phishing. None has come close to being successful. How do we know? Because, as mentioned, 70–90% of all Internet crime involves social engineering and phishing, and that's only after it's made it past every technical defense put in its way.

We may not all see spam and phishing emails in our inboxes every day, but plenty of them still get by our defenses (`https://blog.knowbe4.com/as-many- as-1-in-7-emails-make-it-past-email-filters`). If social engineering and phishing were being effectively mitigated, they would not still be the top methods through which hackers and malware have exploited us for decades.

Until we come up with perfect (or near-perfect) technical defenses, we need to train everyone in how to spot the signs of social engineering and phishing, how to mitigate them, and how to appropriately report instances (if it involves a reporting requirement/recommendation).

Software and Firmware Vulnerabilities

After social engineering and phishing, software and firmware vulnerabilities are the second most common way attackers gain access to our devices and networks. Google's Mandiant, one of the most trusted names in cybersecurity defense, found that 33% of data breaches involve unpatched software and firmware (`https://www.action1.com/patching-insights-from-kevin-mandia-of-mandiant`).

There are a lot of publicly announced vulnerabilities each year. The year 2024 saw more than 40,200 separately announced (`https://www.cvedetails.com/browse- by-date.php`) vulnerabilities, and that is a new record high, just as nearly every year is a new record high for newly discovered vulnerabilities (see Figure 1-1).

We are getting warnings that more than 100 new separate vulnerabilities are found per day, day after day, year after year, and that if we have the involved product in our environment, we need to patch it. What isn't as widely known is that only 1% of all publicly announced vulnerabilities are ever used by a real-world attacker against a real-world target. The rest are just ones we talk about, demonstrate, and research. We really don't need to patch everything, just the 1%

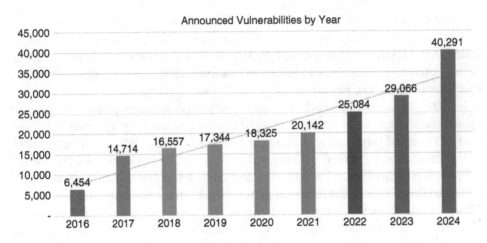

Figure 1-1: Number of known vulnerabilities by year.

Source: `https://www.cvedetails.com/browse-by-date.php/` last accessed 12/31/2024

(`https://www.cisa.gov/known-exploited-vulnerabilities-catalog`) that hackers abuse or are likely to abuse.

The fact that social engineering and vulnerabilities have been the top ways attackers break into places for decades shows you how stubbornly difficult it is to stop Internet cybercrime. There's not an IT person or company on this planet that doesn't know that social engineering and unpatched software and firmware are two of our biggest problems. We all know not to get tricked by scammers, and we all know that we need to patch our software and firmware. Companies spend billions every year to do just that. And yet these two threats, social engineering and vulnerabilities, are still our two biggest weaknesses, by far, and have been since the creation of computers. Any cyber defense solution must help to significantly mitigate these two ubiquitous threats.

Zero-Day Vulnerabilities

A *zero-day vulnerability* (or *0-day*) is a vulnerability that an unauthorized person is using to exploit a system before the vulnerability is widely publicly known, often before the involved vendor has created a patch to help potential victims avoid exploitation. Zero-days are especially troubling because they can be hard for the average customer to prevent.

It used to be that zero-days were fairly rare or uncommon and, although they existed, most organizations didn't worry about them. That has changed over the last few years. They are becoming more commonly used each year and, in 2023, according to the Cybersecurity Infrastructure Security Agency (CISA), zero-days were responsible for more exploited vulnerabilities than not (`https://www.cisa.gov/news-events/cybersecurity-advisories/aa24-317a`).

There were 97 zero-days identified in 2023, versus 62 in 2022 (https://cloud.google.com/blog/topics/threat-intelligence/2023-zero-day-trends). Most of them were developed and deployed by commercial surveillance vendors (https://storage.googleapis.com/gweb-uniblog-publish-prod/documents/Year_in_Review_of_ZeroDays.pdf). Commercial surveillance vendors are generally known as legal cybersecurity vendors who make and sell spyware (versus outright intentionally malicious hackers). Governments, law enforcement, and intelligence agencies around the world often pay them to surveil legal investigation targets.

But many of the most abused zero-days were used by nation-states and traditional hackers to illegally compromise people and organizations (https://www.cisa.gov/sites/default/files/2024-11/aa24-317a-2023-top-routinely-exploited-vulnerabilities.pdf). Many times, zero-days were initially used somewhat sparingly by their creators or users, and when publicly discovered by the masses, they were then used by thousands of other hackers and groups to compromise tens of thousands to millions of computers.

Zero-days involving software and hardware from very trusted mainstream vendors and cybersecurity vendors were often widely exploited to harm many thousands of organizations. Microsoft Exchange (https://msrc.microsoft.com/blog/2022/09/customer-guidance-for-reported-zero-day-vulnerabilities-in-microsoft-exchange-server/) and MOVEit (https://www.cisa.gov/news-events/news/cisa-and-fbi-release-advisory-cl0p-ransomware-gang-exploiting-moveit-vulnerability) zero-days are examples of this scenario.

Abuse of newly discovered zero-days seems likely to become more of a long-term norm than the exceptions of the past. Cloudflare observed an attempted real-world exploitation of a new zero-day vulnerability just 22 minutes after its proof of concept (PoC) was published on the Internet. There is absolutely no current widespread defense to mitigate zero-days, for the foreseeable future.

Account Takeovers and Password Attacks

Many millions of legitimate user accounts are compromised to come under the control of a malicious attacker. This is known as an *account takeover (ATO)*, *credential theft abuse*, or *identity attack* (among other names). ATOs usually happen when a victim is socially engineered into providing their account login credentials (e.g., passwords) or the attacker finds, steals, or guesses the account owner's login credentials.

Additionally, it is very common for someone with an already hacked- or malware-compromised device to have their "cookies" stolen. It's very common for someone to be tricked into visiting a fake or "proxy" website and have their browser "cookies" stolen that way.

A *cookie* is a text file generated by a website after a user successfully logs on and is sent to the user's browser or connecting service. A cookie is a "bearer token," meaning whoever has it is seen as the legitimate credential owner. If a hacker can obtain a user's cookie, the hacker can use it to log on to the involved site or service with the identity of the user it was stolen from without having to provide the related authentication credentials.

Egress found that 58% of organizations suffered ATOs in 2023 (`https://www.infosecurity-magazine.com/news/94-firms-hit-phishing-attacks-2023`), of which 79% came from credentials harvested through phishing. According to the *2024 Comcast Business Cybersecurity Threat Report* (`https://business.comcast.com/enterprise/products-services/cybersecurity-services#threatreport`), there were 295 million credential abuse attacks against their customers.

Microsoft has hundreds of millions of customer accounts. From the previously cited 2024 Microsoft report, Microsoft stated it blocks 7,000 password attacks per second and 600 million identity attacks per day. Microsoft stated that 29% of Internet users have now personally experienced an ATO. Internet infrastructure provider Akaimi detected more than 61 billion password attack attempts in just six months (`https://blog.knowbe4.com/18-months-61-billion-credential-stuffing-attacks`).

According to Microsoft, 1 in 250 of its user accounts are compromised each month (`https://www.microsoft.com/en-us/security/blog/2020/05/07/protect-accounts-smarter-ways-sign-in-world-passwordless-day`). This means 12 in 250, or nearly 5%, of those accounts are taken over each year. Brian Krebs reported that a single hacker gang "averages between five and ten million email authentication attempts a day and comes away with anywhere from 50,000 to 100,000 of working inbox credentials" (`https://krebsonsecurity.com/2021/09/gift-card-gang-extracts-cash-from-100k-inboxes-daily`).

Because of the volume of successful password attacks, Microsoft and nearly every other big identity vendor (e.g., Google) now recommends using multifactor authentication (MFA) instead of passwords. If the victim doesn't use a password, it's going to be hard to steal. However, hackers are increasingly targeting MFA as well as passwords and are having increasing success. From the same Microsoft report, "Over the last year, we've seen a 146% rise in adversary-in-the-middle (AitM) phishing attacks, which occur when attackers trick users into clicking a link and completing MFA on the attacker's behalf."

Hackers are very successful at finding and stealing login credentials. According to the same Microsoft report, "Between January and June 2024, we detected over 1.5 million credentials (such as passwords or certificates) discoverable by attackers in locations such as source code repositories."

There are multiple password repositories around the Internet and dark web with tens of billions of previously stolen login credentials. Here are some related stories: `https://www.forbes.com/sites/daveywinder/2024/07/05/new-security-alert-hacker-uploads-10-billion-stolen-passwords-to-crime-forum/` and `https://www.darkreading.com/vulnerabilities-threats/24-billion-credentials-circulate-dark-web-2022`.

If you've been on the Internet for more than five years, there's a good chance one of your login names and passwords is on some hacker password list.

Popular social media sites and services are also abused by attackers to create brand-new accounts, which are then used to attack other legitimate users. All the big social media sites prevent hundreds of thousands to millions of fake account attempts per day, and they are only somewhat successful. Hackers routinely create and use millions of fake accounts every day despite vendor best defenses.

Stories of various vendors finding and eradicating millions of fraudulent created and used accounts are common. Microsoft found and eradicated a gang selling access to 750 million fraudulent accounts (https://techcrunch. com/2023/12/14/microsoft-disrupts-cybercrime-operation-selling-fraudulent-accounts-to-notorious-hacking-gang/). Meta removed 426 million fraudulent Facebook accounts in Q1 2024 and another 2 million in a single fraudulent account sweep near the end of 2024 (https://www.msn.com/en-us/money/markets/meta-removes-millions-of-accounts-pushing-pig-butchering-investment-scam/ar-AA1uw5UL).

A few hundred million here, a million there, and pretty soon, we'll be talking seriously big numbers.

Most Internet crime involves stealing legitimate user identities or creating and using fake accounts. This fact will come to play an important part in the "Fix Internet Security" solution discussed in this book. If you don't solve this problem, the rest really doesn't matter.

Ransomware

Ransomware has been a top cybercrime concern for most organizations since it exploded in use in 2013 (finally taking advantage of supposedly harder-to-trace Bitcoin, which was invented in 2009). Traditional ransomware-encrypted files and asked for a ransom payment to provide the decryption key to the victim. Starting in November 2019, ransomware also began stealing passwords and exfiltrating confidential data (before the encryption event).

Today, most ransomware events also involve data exfiltration. Artic Wolf stated that 91% of ransomware attacks involve data exfiltration (https://arcticwolf.com/resource/aw/the-state-of-cybersecurity-2024-trends-report). Coveware has the number slightly lower at 75% (https://www.coveware.com/blog/2024/7/29/ransomware-actors-pivot-away-from-major-brands-in-q2-2024).

So today, if you have a ransomware event that is not also a data breach event, consider yourself lucky. In their July 30, *2024 Quarterly Report*, Coveware states that 43% of ransomware victims who pay the ransom do so purely because of the data exfiltration event, even though the victims did not have their data encrypted during the attack (https://www.coveware.com/blog/2024/7/29/ransomware-actors-pivot-away-from-major-brands-in-q2-2024).

Cryptocurrency tracking firm Chainalysis reports that ransomware took in $458 million in the first half of 2024 and seems likely on pace to have a record year (https://www.chainalysis.com/blog/2024-crypto-crime-mid-year-update-part-1).

The median ransomware payment paid by a victim, if they paid, was $1.5 million. The single largest ever recorded ransomware payment was $75 million to the Dark Angels ransomware group. Recovery costs from a ransomware attack routinely run to $4 million or more, and the victim's normal operations are often interrupted for months to more than a year.

Note: Chainalysis, which covers cybercrime involving cryptocurrencies (stolen or used as part of an illicit activity), noted that the total cryptocurrency involved in tracked illicit activity was more than $24 billion in 2023 (https://www.chainalysis.com/blog/2023-crypto-crime-report-introduction/). Much of this activity would need to be mitigated by an Internet security solution to consider a solution a success.

BEC Scams

A *business email compromise (BEC)* scam is one in which an attacker pretends to be an organization that is due a payment, usually by submitting a fake invoice. Payers are usually told to pay by wiring money to a rogue business account but may even be incentivized to pay the requested money in gift cards. It's hard to believe someone can be tricked into paying an invoice in gift cards, but it happens all the time.

The FBI states that the second-costliest type of crime (after investment scams) was BEC, with 21,489 complaints amounting to $2.9 billion in reported losses (https://www.ic3.gov/AnnualReport/Reports/2023_IC3Report.pdf). The *2024 Q2 Anti-Phishing Work Group* report (https://docs.apwg.org/reports/apwg_trends_report_q2_2024.pdf) states the average wire transfer amount requested in BEC attacks in Q1 2024 was $89,520. Google Gmail accounts were used in 72.4% of all BEC scams. Microsoft detected an average of 156,000 BEC attempts a day (5 million a year) against its customers (https://news.microsoft.com/apac/2023/05/22/microsoft-cyber-signals-report-highlights-spike-in-cybercriminal-activity-around-business-email-compromise).

Malware

Malware is short for malicious software and describes any software meant to accomplish malicious online actions. Traditionally, the term *malware* has been used to collectively summarize computer viruses, Trojan horse programs, computer worms, and other hybrid types of attack programs.

The 2024 Microsoft report stated they detected 775 million emails containing malware in one year. Malware creators generate new or evolved malware (usually just updating its encryption protection key or the involved URLs) hundreds of thousands of times per day. According to Astra, 560,000 new malware programs are detected every day, and more than 1 billion malware programs currently exist (https://www.getastra.com/blog/security-audit/malware-statistics). Independent AV-TEST Institute reports similar figures, with more than 450,000 new malware programs detected each day (https://www.av-test.org/en/statistics/malware).

Detection rates are either quite good or unusably bad, depending on how you look at it. Most studies show fairly low detection "miss rates," ranging from 1–10%. That's not bad for 450,000–560,000 new malware programs that antivirus programs are looking for each day. But the sheer volume of new malware programs means a ton of malware programs are getting through.

Personally, I've not submitted a new malware program I've come across in years that isn't missed by every antivirus engine I submitted it to. I often submit new malware samples to a Google website, VirusTotal (https://www.virustotal.com), which runs every submitted malware sample against at least 72 popular antivirus engines. Rarely do I submit a new malware program that even 1 of the 72 AV engines recognizes. I often come back weeks to months later and submit the same sample again, and even then, only a dozen or two of the AV programs recognize it. I personally don't think antivirus detection software is of much use anymore. Its glory days are long over.

I used to spend a lot of time trying to help people pick just the right antivirus program, but now it doesn't really matter. Use one. Any legitimate one. They probably won't help you avoid a malware infection. How do we know that all antivirus detection is pretty bad? Well, for one, ransomware is everywhere. And if any of the antivirus engines did a good job of detecting ransomware, everyone would buy that product . . . at a premium, and ransomware would be gone. But ransomware isn't gone. It's everywhere.

Credit Card Theft

If you have a credit card account, its information has likely been compromised, and your credit card was then used to make unauthorized purchases at some time during your adult life. Hackers literally have many millions of people's credit card information available for sale or use. Security.org states that 52 million Americans had fraudulent charges on their credit or debit cards in 2023, with unauthorized purchases totaling more than $5 billion (https://www.security.org/digital-safety/credit-card-fraud-report). Sixty percent of U.S. credit card holders have had their credit card information exploited, and 45% have had it happen two or more times.

As mentioned in the preface, I had my credit card information stolen and reused five times within six months this year. When I asked my credit card company what I was doing wrong or if I was using it at a bad place/site, they said no. I got tired of having to update my credit card information on all my monthly payment sites and Amazon, so I started using PayPal for online payments and

Google Pay for in-person payments whenever I could. Since then, and it may be a coincidence, my personal credit card information has not been used by a hacker to make an unauthorized purchase.

Today's Internet makes it way too easy to steal credit cards. Card information can be stolen anywhere in the credit card ecosystem, including by rogue merchants, compromised merchants and websites, rogue employees, directly from the victim, or anywhere the card information is used, transferred, or stored. Any solution to fix the Internet needs to address credit card crime.

Other Attacks

I could spend additional sections and pages discussing nation-state attacks, surveillance capitalism, DDoS attacks, AI deepfake attacks, and more. I could go on and on and on, but you get the idea. Internet crime is bad. It's getting worse. And nothing anyone is doing currently is making it any better.

Internet crime is a multibillion-dollar industry committed by individuals, gangs, professional corporations, and nation-states. There are tens of thousands, if not more, of groups actively trying to break into your device every day. Many are very professional and skilled. Any Internet security solution needs to understand that you're fighting against a broadly distributed industry that will work hard at making that solution fail. Whatever great solution you think you have, if it works, the bad guys will work hard to circumvent and come up with new angles you have not considered. They will work hard to use your solution against you. But this is a multigenerational fight we must win.

Why the Internet Is Not Just Fine As-Is

I'd be remiss without mentioning that I've also met many people over the years, some of whom have reviewed my plan to better secure the Internet, who tell me the Internet is just fine as it is and to leave it alone. To them, Internet security is working well enough, warts and all. And to be sure, as bad as Internet security is, our global society is muddling along just fine. We are still creating tremendously wonderful things on the Internet; we are all on the Internet every day loving it. Most businesses are doing just fine, and for the most part, it works for most of us most of the time. Sure, our credit cards get compromised every now and then, but we get a new one in the mail, update our online accounts, the stolen money gets put back into our accounts, and everything is hunky-dory. We don't appear to get as many spam and phishing attacks percentage-wise in our email inboxes as we used to, and humans are supposedly getting better at spotting online scams.

These critics are worried that too much well-meaning "fixin'" might actually harm the Internet, decrease personal privacy, and make it more expensive and slower. They believe the medicine and its unintended side effects might be more harmful than the sickness. I get it. Those are good, realistic arguments if securing the Internet is not done correctly.

It Does Cause Real Damage

To the people who think the Internet is doing just fine as is . . . Internet crime and all. I like to remind them that there is a cost in dollars, human impact, and lives.

Cost

Several respected organizations, such as RAND (`https://www.rand.org/content/dam/rand/pubs/research_reports/RR2200/RR2299/RAND_RR2299.pdf`) and the World Economic Forum (`https://www.weforum.org/stories/2023/01/global-rules-crack-down-cybercrime`) have stated that globally cybercrime at a minimum impacts worldwide GDP at 1% or greater, or close to $1 trillion annually. Some cybersecurity organizations state that the worldwide impact will be more than $10 trillion this year (2025), although I believe that number is very high (`https://cybersecurityventures.com/cybercrime-damage-costs-10-trillion-by-2025`).

TrendMicro stated email threats alone had an estimated financial impact of $3.5 billion U.S. in 2024 (`https://www.trendmicro.com/vinfo/us/security/news/threat-landscape/email-threat-landscape-report-2023`). Globally, spam email by itself is estimated to cost businesses $20.5 billion a year (`https://eftsure.com/statistics/spam-statistics`). The average cost of a single data breach initiated by phishing is $4.88 million according to IBM's *Cost of a Data Breach Report 2024* (`https://www.ibm.com/reports/data-breach`), a 10% increase over last year and the highest total ever. Whatever the reported figures are, they are large and go up year after year after year.

People Do Lose Money

Yes, funds from stolen and misused credit card information are often returned to the rightful victim, but all you have to do is use another service where that guarantee of reimbursement is not made. More and more, banks are pushing people to nontraditional fund transfer services that do not have the same protections. If you get caught in a home mortgage wire transfer fraud, you will likely not get your money back.

There are people who get scammed out of tens of thousands to hundreds of thousands of dollars who not only don't get it back but actually get taxed by the government on it (`https://www.washingtonpost.com/business/interactive/2024/ scam-elderly-tax-issues-victim-aid-congress`). Just because you may have gotten your money back, doesn't mean everyone is so lucky.

Wasted Time and Productivity

It takes unexpected time to respond to cybersecurity incidents, both for businesses and people. Ransomware, in particular, is infamous for causing business operational interruption for weeks, months, and even years. Some businesses are put permanently out of business. Getting rid of a malware program that hasn't locked up your systems or locking a hacker out of your environment can still be days to weeks of work. Meeting cybersecurity compliance guidelines and audits takes teams of people for most businesses.

People having to deal with personal issues from individual cybercrime waste hours and hours of their time. They aren't as productive as they otherwise would be for themselves, their family, or the businesses they work for. I've seen people dealing with cybersecurity attacks basically drop out of life for days to months as they deal with the outfall.

Early on in my career, I envisioned starting a business that would help people accomplish different business tasks more quickly. But as I pursued that business, I was forever helping people fight computer viruses, macro viruses, and other malware infections. Although I love my cybersecurity career, my career is helping people get back to a place where they can be more productive, only when I first get rid of hackers or malware.

Imagine the increased productivity we would all have without so much Internet crime. Imagine the great people and resources involved in cybersecurity that could be redirected to something far more beneficial and productive to society. Imagine how much faster and cheaper our Internet bandwidth would be without all the hackers and their malware creations clogging it up. Regardless, it's clear that cybercrime has a significant unproductive impact on every country and citizen that would not exist if we didn't have malicious hackers and malware.

Damage Means More Than Money

Let's not forget that malicious hacking causes real damage beyond the money, time, and resources dealing with the recovery. Malicious hacking has a real human toll. We are all emotionally impacted by it every day, whether we realize it or not. People are stressed. I worry about all of my loved ones and how safe they are or aren't on the Internet. Are my grandparents able to recognize the latest scam directed at them? Will my kids pay enough attention not to click the wrong link? Our thoughts are pervasively invaded by cybercrime worries. People are emotionally damaged and traumatized. People are fired. People are killed.

A large percentage of data breaches involve our personal data. We all worry and become more anxiety-filled when our personal information is out there for viewing and use by malicious people. Every public breach notice we receive causes additional worry. We are all worrying about whether our passwords are strong enough, whether we created enough of them, and whether we can remember them. Is this new website or service worth joining, or is it just another scam that is going to hurt me in some way? Rampant cybercrime causes an undercurrent of anxiety that permeates our online existence. It's like we are all walking through a well-known bad part of a city every day while we are just otherwise trying to live our lives.

People fall in love with fake people. Romance scams are the worst! If you've ever had a loved one involved in a romance scam, you know how utterly devastating that can be. It breaks up marriages, friendships, and family relationships, sometimes forever. I've met many people who have lost everything . . . every dollar of their retirement savings and ruined every family and friend relationship. They are utterly left with nothing but shame and being alone in every sense of the word.

People get offered fake jobs with fake employers (https://blog.knowbe4.com/job-seekers-and-employers-beware). Real employers hire fake employees. Over 50% of the résumés some companies review come from fake job applicants, often workers in other sanctioned countries (e.g., North Korea) seeking to obtain illegal payments from salaries and inside access to steal information or disrupt operations.

Note: If you're interested in more information on fake employees, see my whitepaper on the subject: https://www.knowbe4.com/hubfs/North-Korean-Fake-Employees-Are-Everywhere-WP _ EN-us.pdf.

Employees who get duped by cybercrime often face unpleasant reactions from their employers. Egress reported that, among employees who fell for a phishing attack, 51% were disciplined, 39% were fired, and 27% voluntarily left their jobs (https://pages.egress.com/whitepaper-email-risk-report-01-24.html). Most chief information security officers (CISOs) I know expect to be fired one day as a publicly known sacrificial job firing when their organization is eventually breached. They know this going into every job they take.

I am frequently contacted by people who have had their social media accounts taken over by hackers and cannot get them back. They beg me to hack into their account and take back control for them because they've lost their entire (online) lives with the theft. Every bit of content and all the photos they uploaded to the impacted site are likely gone forever. Their businesses are shut down. I had several people beg me to hack back their accounts because beloved pictures of parents who died only exist on the stolen site, and they never got around to backing them up. They almost never get them back. I've had a woman curse at me and call me terrible names because I would not help her illegally regain her account. She said I was as bad as the hackers.

The Internet is in our homes. Hackers can abuse and take over our IoT devices and systems. Hackers can take control of our Internet cameras. Parents have discovered hackers talking to their babies and children through compromised baby monitors. There is an entire subculture that exists to gain unauthorized access to people's home cameras and then sell that access to others for voyeurism.

We have unauthorized pornography. We have child pornography. We have revenge porn. We have AI-generated porn where anyone can be made into an unauthorized porn video collection. We have children caught up in sex extortion scams, where they feel forced to help the hacker scam others. They are often told they have to pay money to prevent their own naked images from being shown to friends, family members, and their school. Every year, a couple of people (usually young men and women) commit suicide rather than risk the potential reveal of what some remote hacker captured.

Hacking Kills

Hackers can initiate fraudulent shooting or hostage situation calls to local police departments, which result in an intense police response against innocent, unsuspecting victims. These attacks are known as *swatting*. I've had several friends swatted, some multiple times, and they are all still emotionally traumatized from the local SWAT team holding assault weapons and sniper rifles over them out of the blue. At least a few (innocent) people have died unwitting victims from swatting calls (`https://www.nbcnews.com/news/us-news/serial-swatter-tyler-barriss-sentenced-20-years-death-kansas-man-n978291`).

Ransomware kills. When ransomware attacks a hospital or healthcare center, it slows down and disruptions normal services. Operations and procedures are delayed. Prescriptions are delayed. Emergency patients are diverted to other, farther away, emergency rooms. Non-emergency patients are sent home (`https://www.msn.com/en-us/health/medical/uk-hospital-declares-major-cyber-incident-tells-non-emergencies-to-return-home/ar-AA1uMOAc`).

A U.S. Medicare study reported (`https://www.secureworld.io/industry-news/does-ransomware-kill-sick-people`) that during normal operations, it is expected that 3 out of every 100 hospitalized Medicare patients will die, but during ransomware events, that figure increases to 4 out of 100. It is calculated that between 42 and 67 U.S. Medicare patients died over a 5-year period due to ransomware. Considering that Medicare only covers 20% of U.S. patients, that number is likely to be far higher.

The Internet is connected to our cars, which have, time and time again, been shown to be controllable by unauthorized remote hackers. It's happening less as car manufacturers respond, but as we increasingly get more computers and the Internet in our cars, what is the chance that a hacker won't interact with our car again in the future?

Our critical infrastructures are reachable by hackers. A hacker taking down or modifying any critical infrastructure organization can potentially kill masses of people. It's already been attempted (https://www.wired.com/story/oldsmar-florida-water-utility-hack). Various nation-states have routinely been embedded in other nation's critical infrastructure. It's assumed that during any "kinetic" battle, the opponent's critical infrastructures will be taken out remotely using cyber warfare. We know it, and we still can't stop it.

This is to say that Internet crime is doing more than disrupting business operations and costing money. It causes real, lasting human harm. If we do nothing or continue to do the same types of things that do not ever work to make the Internet significantly safer as we "muddle" through life, it seems we have intentionally or unintentionally crossed a moral line. We've decided that all our cities and areas can be "bad parts of the city." I don't know about you, but that's not the life I want to live. It's not a life I want the people I love and care about to live.

Increasing Internet Crime

A big part of the rebuttal to those who think the level of Internet crime today is acceptable is that it is getting worse every new year by nearly every measure, and nothing seems on the near-term horizon to make it better anytime soon. Sure, the current level of Internet crime may be acceptable to some today, but there is strong evidence based on all past evidence that it will just keep getting worse and worse until only Internet cybercriminals will accept it.

The biggest problem, in my opinion, is that currently an Internet criminal is more likely to be randomly struck by lightning than be arrested and stopped. The World Economic Forum stated that detection and arrest rates for Internet criminals are less than 0.05% (https://www3.weforum.org/docs/WEF_Global_Risk_Report_2020.pdf). If you're making a lot of money from Internet crime what is the motivation to stop?

What Is the Goal of Fixing Internet Security?

The goal of any solution to fix Internet security should be to make the Internet a far safer place for anyone to be. It doesn't need to be perfect and stop all crime if that is even possible. I would love to defeat all hackers and malware at once, but that really isn't realistic. But make no mistake: I want to stop all Internet crime. I'm just not setting perfection with zero crime as a goal.

To stop all Internet crime, we would likely have to create an authoritarian system that is super-constrained and inflexible. And even in the most difficult, locked-down environment, it's nearly impossible to stop all crime. Think all the crime still committed within most prisons. To accomplish an environment of no crime would take an online environment akin to a Supermax prison, where prisoners are in a cell for 23 hours of the day and allowed out for only 1 hour for physical activity, and even that period of time is closely supervised.

A super locked-down Internet would likely significantly diminish Internet crime, but it's not one where most people would want to live, play, and compute. Instead, our goal should be to significantly diminish Internet crime to a level where it isn't something most of us worry about every day.

A good Internet security solution just needs to make crime somewhat comparable to the crime in today's world, where most of us are not directly impacted by it, and most of us aren't attacked on a daily basis. Most businesses are not physically robbed every day. The solution should result in an Internet where people are more often thinking about how to be more productive and have a more enjoyable experience without constantly being on the lookout for an online scam or attack. If we do it right, our grandparents and our great-grandchildren will have a better experience than we have today.

Chapter Summary

This chapter described how serious and how rampant today's Internet crime is. It covered many different types of online crime, different motivations, and different types of outcomes, including the loss of human life. It relied on facts and statistics to drive home the point that Internet crime is pretty bad, getting worse, and not acceptable. Any solution(s) to significantly improve Internet security, if successful, should significantly decrease these figures over time and still let people enjoy a relatively flexible and enjoyable Internet if it is the correct solution.

Key concepts are:

- How bad Internet crime is
- Hackers and malware
- Damaged caused
- Goals of significantly better Internet security

Chapter 2 covers the basic different types of attacks and the motivation of different types of hackers. You are going to need to understand them for the solution theory to make sense.

CHAPTER 7

How We Are Attacked and Why

This chapter covers the initial root access methods that hackers and their malware creations use to break into devices and networks and their motivations. This helps when figuring out the right defenses.

Defending Our Homes

Imagine you own a house that is constantly broken into by thieves. You love your house and neighborhood. It's perfect in almost every way. It's close to work, when you need to drive to work. The school system is great for your kids. You like the nearby stores, and you are good friends with a lot of your neighbors. You have a real sense of community. You've lived in your house for decades, and you don't want to move. It's your home.

But you've also had to put up with that beloved home being broken into, over and over again. You are never sure when a break-in will happen, only that it will definitely happen again. Imagine that the thieves steal different things every time they break in. Sometimes they steal money, sometimes art, sometimes furniture or electronics, and sometimes they are only after your car key fobs to steal your car. Sometimes, the thieves even want to burn down your home, and they aren't particularly careful in making sure you or your family are out of there first. You hate this part of your life, but every single other place you could possibly move to has the exact same problem.

You notice over time that, although there are a dozen different ways the thieves could break into your house (e.g., doors, windows, basement, garage, wall, roof, etc.), they almost consistently use the same method: the windows.

Not all the time. Sometimes, they switch it up and use another method, but 9 out of 10 times, they use the windows to break in. Sometimes, they open and enter through an unlocked window. Sometimes, they have to jimmy open the lock. Sometimes, they just break the window and enter. And this method of entry, using the window to gain entry into the house, is true of nearly every home break-in you know about.

So, to better defend your home, you decide to put a stronger deadbolt on your door. It doesn't help. You are frustrated, so you buy another, stronger door that is sure to prevent thieves from breaking through the door. And it doesn't work either. Very frustrating!

This is happening to everyone in the neighborhood, so a community meeting is planned to discuss all the crimes. They invite law enforcement with expertise in home crime to the meeting. The head law enforcement cop confirms that everyone's home is being broken into over and over again and that it is usually through the windows.

To counter that, and everyone is listening intently, he suggests that everyone buy a metal door with five locks that have a built-in alarm so that if the thieves break in through the door, it will stop them or at least give homeowners early warning of the break-in. And everyone in the audience agrees and goes out and buys what law enforcement recommended.

Not surprisingly, crime does not go down. Thieves are as successful as they had been in the past and even more so. The thieves are laughing at all the new doors. They are breaking in more often and stealing more things of value when they do. They are burning down more houses. Sometimes, they kill people. It usually starts with entry through a window.

Everyone knows this. A national law enforcement agency has been involved for decades. They know most of the crime is happening through the windows, but they, too, just like everyone else, recommend stronger door defenses. The national agency recommends that everyone hide their clocks because it seems like most criminals steal clocks when they break in. So, everyone does. Surprisingly, or not surprisingly, the crooks now more often target something else to steal, like art, instead. Everyone is shaking their head. How could anyone have anticipated that criminals would simply steal something else of value once they got in?

If this sounds insane, and it is, this allegory perfectly describes what has been going on in computer security defense for decades. We know how we are being most broken into…usually through social engineering and software and firmware vulnerabilities, but we spend almost none of our time or resources on it.

Social engineering and software and firmware vulnerabilities likely account for upwards of 90–99% of total cybersecurity exploitation. If you or your organization gets hacked, it's likely because of one of these two root causes. Everyone knows this. But there isn't an organization on Earth that spends even 5% of its cybersecurity resources (e.g., dollars, people, time, etc.) to fight it. Instead, we spend too much time focusing on the wrong threats. It is this fundamental long-time misalignment between how we are most likely attacked and how we defend ourselves that allows hackers and malware to be so long-term successful.

This chapter discusses how we are broken into—the initial root access causes. We are going to discuss all the possible ways (e.g., the online windows, doors, floors, etc.). If you want to stop thieves from breaking into your house, you have to focus more on how they break in than what they do once they are in. If you stop how they break in, you stop them from stealing all the stuff that is in the house. You stop most of the crime by stopping how they break into your house in the first place.

How All Hackers Break In

I've been explicitly following how hackers and their malware creations break into computers, devices, and networks for more than 22 years. I think everyone reading a hacking news story wants to understand how the hacker broke in, to begin with. But I had a particularly strong interest, and I began keeping spreadsheets and tallies. I wanted to understand how all the hacking happened and what the involved occurrence rates were.

I kept all sorts of spreadsheets about hacking, including what file types were used as malicious file attachments in emails. I gave up keeping that spreadsheet after 10 years when it listed more file types on it than not. It turns out that nearly every type of file can be used maliciously, including text (TXT) files. Today, I just assume it's all of them.

I created another spreadsheet to track where malware could hide and store itself on a Microsoft Windows computer to be automatically executed after the computer rebooted or some other system event. I did a fairly great job with that spreadsheet for nearly two decades, but stopped when Mark Russinovich created and released Sysinternals' Autoruns (`https://learn.microsoft.com/en-us/sysinternals/downloads/autoruns`), which helped users manage all those locations. I sent my last spreadsheet to Mark, which he incorporated into his next version of Autoruns. Now, I just use Autoruns.

The spreadsheet I maintained the longest was how hackers and their malware creations first gained initial access into a device. Every time I read a story about a new hacking event, I put it in my spreadsheet. How a company is compromised isn't always published in a news story or is miscategorized. I often emailed or called people involved in various hacking scenarios. Some wouldn't respond, and many others were not sure how the initial access happened. But many did respond and know. And when I could determine the root access method used, I wrote it down.

Over the years, the categories on my hacking list have changed slightly. I've had anywhere from 12 to 15 different categories. I've always tried to be inclusive and ask myself if this or that particular hacking attack method was accurately captured. I attempted to make each root cause category inclusive of what it describes and also not overlap with another category. If I felt that a particular hacking attack involved two or more categories at the same time, I questioned if I had the right categories. Sometimes, I didn't, and I updated my list of categories. In general, it hasn't changed much over the last two decades other than how I classified a particular attack into one category or another.

Focus on Root Causes

It's important to make sure you're discussing initial root access causes and not mixing up outcomes of initial root access causes, which is often done by most cybersecurity reports and guidelines I read that cover hacking methods.

For example, ransomware is an outcome of an initial root access method, not an initial root hacking method. The better question to ask is how the ransomware first gained initial access to a device. Was it social engineering, a vulnerability, a misconfiguration, or a physical attack? Same with credential theft. Yes, a stolen credential can be used to break into a device, but the better question is how the credential was first stolen (answer: 91% of the time through social engineering).

If someone steals your car and takes it for a joyride or steals the radio, if you want to stop your car from being stolen or your radio from being stolen again, you have to figure out how the thieves broke into the car in the first place. If you don't stop that, you'll just have thieves break into the car again. Yes, it helps to know what the thieves were targeting (e.g., the car, the stereo, car parts, etc.), but if you think removing your car's stereo will stop all the thieves in the future with different motivations, you're only going to slightly delay the next break in. If you want to best stop car thieves from breaking into your car, for any motivation, concentrate more on how thieves break into your car in the first place and not the outcome of that break-in. Most defenders focus too much time on what was stolen or done and not how it was accomplished in the first place.

Here's another way to think about it: If I discover a way to prevent all ransomware so that it never occurs again, I mitigate ransomware. If I mitigate how ransomware breaks into a device or network, I mitigate ransomware and every hacker outcome (e.g., infostealing trojan, wiperware, etc.) that could have used the same entry point. Mitigating initial root hacking causes diminishes much larger classes of attacks that all share the same entry point.

> **note** This is my 15th book, and at least 5–6 of my past books over the years have included some version of this hacking root cause method list. You can see the changes and progression of my list over time when you read the various books. Overall, I'm pleasantly surprised to see the bulk of my list has remained the same, and the changes overall have been fairly minor.

Here are the 14 different categories of initial root access methods used by hackers and their malware programs:

- Social Engineering
- Software or Firmware Vulnerability
- (Technical) Impersonation/Authentication Attack
- Intentionally Malicious Programs/Instructions/Scripting
- Human Error/Misconfiguration
- Eavesdropping/MitM
- Side Channel
- Information Leak
- Brute Force/Computational
- Data Malformation
- Network Traffic Malformation
- Insider Attack
- Third-Party Reliance Issue (supply chain/vendor/partner/etc.)
- Physical Attack

I'll cover each category in more detail below.

Social Engineering

As covered in Chapter 1, I define social engineering as someone (or a group) fraudulently posing as a more trustworthy sender, either as someone (e.g., friend or boss), some entity (e.g., police or tax authority), or some well-known brand (e.g., Microsoft, PayPal, or your bank) trying to maliciously trick you into performing an action that would be harmful to your own interests. They want you to provide confidential information like your login details, download a boobytrapped document, run malware, etc.

It's a pretty long definition that can more succinctly be stated as "someone is trying to criminally con you." Phishing is an online, digital version of social engineering. It can be accomplished using any communication channel between two people or groups, including email, messaging, websites, social media, phone calls, etc. Identity, domain, and address spoofing also fall into this category.

Disinformation postings and even maliciously intended information selection algorithms could be seen broadly as social engineering, although they are primarily trying to provoke an emotion that possibly leads to another action, which typically isn't located or instructed within the current message.

Two important points to note about this category. One, it is the most popular way hackers hack by far and has been since the beginning of computers. All the other hacking methods added together don't come close to this method. Second, it usually (although not always) heavily relies on identity fraud. The importance of this point will become clearer in subsequent chapters. If we don't solve the problem of social engineering, then the rest of everything else we could do doesn't matter nearly as much. If you solve every other problem, but not social engineering, you've basically not accomplished much of anything at all.

Software or Firmware Vulnerability

Programmers (e.g., developers) use programming, scripting, and macro languages and tools to write software and firmware (used to run hardware) programs/instructions. Most programmers intend to write something desired and considered useful by others who will knowingly and willingly use it.

Unfortunately, otherwise well-meaning programmers sometimes unintentionally write or allow an instruction or snippet of well-meaning code that can be used by other unauthorized people to inflict harm on others. Usually, this is because the programmer or tool creates an unintentional mistake (i.e., "the vulnerability") that could be exploited by others.

Most vulnerabilities come from "mistakes" and, when identified, can be fixed by correcting the error and mitigating it using an update. There are dozens, if not hundreds, of types of vulnerabilities, including buffer overflows, hard-coded credentials, SQL injection, and path traversals. Here's a recent list of the top 25 programming mistakes: `https://www.bleepingcomputer.com/news/security/mitre-shares-2024s-top-25-most-dangerous-software-weaknesses`. As previously stated, in 2024, we had at least 40,291 separately publicly announced vulnerabilities (`https://www.cvedetails.com/browse-by-date.php`).

As shared in Chapter 1, Google's Mandiant stated that 33% of successful data breaches involve unpatched software and firmware (`https://www.action1.com/patching-insights-from-kevin-mandia-of-mandiant`). This makes it the second most common initial root hacking method used by hackers and malware. After social engineering and vulnerabilities, no other root hacking method added up altogether accounts for even 10% of all successful attacks (against organizations and consumers).

(Technical) Impersonation/Authentication Attack

This category is similar to social engineering in that someone or something usually pretends to be someone else, but this is accomplished using programming instructions or actions and not purely through plaintext written and read by a person.

An example is a hacker stealing someone else's browser cookie or authentication token and using it to pretend to be someone else during another unauthorized authentication or authorization session. Another example is a hacker changing a legitimate website's DNS address so that when people type in the website's domain name to visit the legitimate website, they are instead taken to a malicious website. Another example could be a server or packet using the IP address of another server or origination point (known as *spoofing*). A *downgrade attack*, where stronger authentication is intentionally redirected or bypassed to an easier-to-abuse authentication method, also falls here.

This category could also be a hacker finding a way to technically bypass an authentication or authorization check that does not involve what most people would call a vulnerability. Programmers and reviewers will often see what others may claim is a vulnerability and respond by labeling it "as designed" and reject fixing it, at least initially (although usually they eventually do).

This category includes stolen, copied, or fraudulently presented biometric attributes. If you have my fingerprint, you might be able to impersonate me to an authentication system that relies on my fingerprint as an authentication factor. This category also includes AI-enabled deepfakes, where someone or something creates a fraudulent but realistic media experience (e.g., audio, video, image, news story, etc.) that is intended to be accepted as real and intentional to defraud the content viewers. This is one of the newest types of attacks that my previous versions of my hacking root cause list in previous books didn't consider.

Intentionally Malicious Program/Instructions/Scripting

This is the writing of programming, instructions, scripting, or macro commands to intentionally cause harm to those who are tricked into running or executing it (and/or others impacted by its execution). A vulnerability is an unintended mistake. These programs, scripts, and instructions are intended to be malicious from the start. It's why the creator created them. This category covers programs, scripts, and instructions that the creator or distributor knew were absolutely going to cause harm. Computer viruses, computer worms, and Trojan Horse programs, which pretend to be some legitimate program or tool but really intend to cause harm, fall into this category.

It also includes written/published harmful instructions that unsuspecting people could read and follow. For example, throughout the history of computers, malicious creators have written and sent fraudulent instructions to others that, if followed, will harm the recipient. A common example of this is email messages claiming to help people detect and remove some supposedly very dangerous malware program that could be on their device. Instead, if the recipients follow the instructions, they end up deleting critical operating system files, which critically halts their system until they or someone they can find with enough knowledge can recover it.

Human Error/Misconfiguration

This is an unintentional mistake or neglect of something that leads to an exploitable condition. It includes people sending confidential data to the wrong people, failing to erase data before throwing it out in publicly accessible garbage cans, and people unwittingly following a malicious hacker's request that ends up harming their organization (like a malicious password reset request). Some people include social engineering here, but I don't always agree that following a social engineering instruction is a mistake.

Some social engineering attempts are so very good that it's hard to say it was a mistake for a victim to follow it. In this category, the victim absolutely did or didn't do something that any reasonable person should or shouldn't have done. This doesn't mean that the person making the mistake is an idiot or dumb. We are humans. We make mistakes. I've made too many mistakes to count.

One of the most common misconfiguration mistakes is overly permissive access control permissions. For example, someone sets a website's file and folder permissions to Everyone Full Control/World, which allows almost anyone else visiting it to delete, add, and change files on the website. Many data breaches can be tied back to overly permissive permissions on cloud "storage buckets," where a company's confidential or customer files are stored.

Sometimes, these overly permissive permissions happen by default, depending on the service or application being used, and the administrator just doesn't realize they need to change the access control permissions to be more restrictive. Other times, a user/administrator makes a configuration mistake that unintentionally configures weak access control permissions or allows broad access without the appropriate, otherwise wanted authentication.

Bad neglect of a system, intentional or otherwise, would fit here, as well. Here are some examples:

- Someone hasn't patched a system for a long time.
- No one is completely sure whose responsibility it is to patch a particular server or device.
- No one is monitoring the event log to notice billions of ongoing password-guessing attempts.
- Poor control and tracking of a shared identity account.
- No one monitoring the expiration date of critical digital certificates.

Many types of unintentional human mistakes fit here. Some people believe that anyone falling for a social engineering scam belongs in this category, also, but those types of actions really belong in their own category because the user is being incentivized and maliciously encouraged by others to commit them. In this category, the user often makes an unintentional error without someone else intentionally motivating them to do it.

Eavesdropping/MitM

This category describes an unauthorized third party listening to and/or modifying a communication's steam or storage location between two or more authorized parties. A fairly simple example would be an intruder being able to read confidential information because it was missing encryption or the hacker inserted themselves into an HTTP/HTTPS stream between a user and a website.

As a more detailed look at this latter example, a user is sent a phishing email that tricks the user into connecting to a fake, look-alike website or proxy service, which then finishes the connection to the user's intended website. The user sees what appears to be the legitimate website. The website is connected to "what it thinks" is the legitimate user, but each side is unknowingly connected to an unauthorized website or proxy service. A hacker can use that unauthorized site or proxy service to read, capture, or modify the communications and content sent between the legitimate user and the website. This is a very common type of man-in-the-middle (MitM) attack.

note Microsoft recently relabeled MitM attacks as gender-neutral, adversary-in-the-middle (AitM) attacks.

Side Channel

This is an unintended design flaw that allows an attacker to learn about, compromise, or leverage what the designer thought was protected information using a method the designer did not initially consider or design against.

For example, smartcards are cryptographic devices that allow a user to securely store private keys and other protected confidential information. Smartcards use specialized cryptographic chips, firmware, and operating systems to keep that information safe. For decades, smart cards have been a strong and safe way to authenticate. However, attackers have learned that if they can physically monitor the smartcard's wireless emanations, the different flows of wireless electrical waves from the smartcard as it deals with different bits of information can be used to detect and reveal confidential information.

A great, unrelated, real-world side channel example is how reporters can sometimes determine when the U.S. Pentagon is going to launch a major kinetic missile or war attack against another country by tracking the number of takeout pizzas ordered by Pentagon employees late into the night. On the nights when offensive attacks start, the number of pizzas ordered is significantly higher than on other nights because more people are involved and working late.

A great hybrid example involving both people and online methods is how the U.S. military helped confirm the previously unknown location of the long-sought 9/11 mastermind Osama Bin Laden. One of the signs that the military had successfully located Bin Laden was the fact that other known Bin Laden–trusted leaders going to a particular compound would always switch off their cell phones before entering the area so they could not be actively tracked. This was a highly suspicious behavior that heightened the interest of the U.S. military and helped build confidence that Bin Laden's hidden location had been located.

Information Leak

Information leaks include intentional and unintentional displays, downloads, theft, or visibility of non-public data. An unintentional example is a legitimate website error message that displays too much confidential information or a shared storage drive in the cloud that inadvertently allows a new tenant to see an older tenant's data that was stored in the same place. A privacy event where unauthorized information was learned or disclosed to an unauthorized third party would also be an information leak. Legal surveillance that ends up collecting personal data and sending it to a database for use, aggregation, or sale by others is considered an information leak by many privacy experts. In general, the information leaks most cybersecurity professionals are most concerned with is when an attacker exploits a service or site to reveal non-private information.

Brute Force/Computational

Most hacker attacks involve some sort of unintentional design flaw or weakness that is found and taken advantage of by hackers. The Brute Force/Computational category of attack is where the hacker method doesn't use a significant vulnerability against a protective system but instead tries every potential answer possibility (i.e., brute force) or finds a mathematical "shortcut."

For example, a website may have a maximum logon password size of 12 characters. So, the hacker tries every possible 12-character password allowed by the system, often starting with more likely choices first. Another example is some early multifactor authentication (MFA) solutions sent the legitimate user a 3- or 4-digit numeric code as their authentication logon but also, unfortunately, allowed anyone any number of login attempts to guess at the same number. Hackers could simply guess all 999 (for a 3-digit code) or 9999 (for a 4-digit code) codes to exhaust all possibilities.

Most cryptographic attacks against encryption, hashing, and digital signatures fall into this category. It is not unusual for cryptographic attacks to weaken existing cryptography over time. Usually, this is a fairly slow, expected process, where small improvements in an existing cryptography attack are made that eventually weaken the protection of the targeted cryptographic algorithm so much that it must be replaced with a newer, stronger, more resilient (at least for now) cryptography algorithm. For example, we had to move from DES and 3DES symmetric encryption to AES and from MD-5 and SHA-1 to SHA-2 and SHA-3 because of improved cryptographic attacks. However, sometimes, a cryptographic attacker finds a significant mathematical "shortcut" solution that quickly and suddenly invalidates a cryptographic target.

Within the next decade (if it hasn't already been accomplished in secret), it is expected that sufficiently capable quantum computers will be able to factor large prime number equations that are used to protect most traditional asymmetric encryption far more quickly than traditional binary computers. Traditional computers might take millions of years to factor the same problems, but quantum computers are likely to be able to solve the same equations in minutes (when they are sufficiently capable).

Brute force/computational attacks can also be used in "exhaustion" denial of service (DoS) attacks. For example, years ago, attackers would try to connect to a server millions and millions of times, knowing that each connection attempt used up a little of available computer memory. With enough connection attempts, all the server's available free memory would be used up, causing the computer to slow tremendously or even lock up. Another similar type of attack is a firewall automatically blocking any IP address that sends a malicious packet. An attacker can then send enough malicious packets pretending to be originating from every possible IP address space that, eventually, all IP addresses get blocked by the firewall, and even legitimate connections will not be accepted. These sorts of "exhaustion attacks" can be classified here or as a DoS attack in the data malformation or network malformation categories.

Data Malformation

Malicious manipulation of data files is a common hacker method, either to cause some sort of unintended action, like a buffer overflow, flow control, cross-site scripting, or DoS attacks. Programs using data often don't expect the data to be malformed or be able to control the host program in an unintended way. They expect the data to have a particular format and contain only the things a legitimate data file is supposed to contain. However, hackers routinely figure out how to modify data files so that they cause an unexpected programming event, which can be used to execute new code, flow, or actions.

Data malformation also includes unauthorized tampering with data. If an attacker maliciously modifies a file, it belongs here. It can also include malicious tampering with other types of operating files that we might not immediately recognize as a data file (but they are). For example, a hacker may modify an access control list, add themselves to a privileged group, delete or corrupt a backup, or maliciously modify a log file to erase the recording of malicious events.

Timing and flow attacks could fall under this category or brute force/ computational, depending on how they are structured. Data malformation that causes a DoS or buffer overflow attacks belongs here.

Network Traffic Malformation

This category covers network packet manipulation that often leads to DoS events or malicious actions (like a buffer overflow). The manipulation can occur at the packet-level, changing bits and data within a single or multiple network packets to cause a malicious event or be the result from an attacker generating a very larger number of regular or malicious packets that overwhelm the receiving system.

An early network packet attack example, known as a *LAND attack*, involved setting a network packet's source and destination addresses to be the same address. When sent to a vulnerable receiving host, it could, depending on the operating system and version, cause the receiver to get stuck in a DoS redundancy, which halted further servicing.

This category also covers gigantic distributed denial of service (DDoS) volumetric events that use millions to billions of unneeded or malformed network packets to overwhelm the systems involved in receiving them. Sometimes, only one malformed packet is needed to break into or shut down a system; other times, it takes trillions. Reflection, relay, and MitM attacks could also be seen as network traffic malformation, but also fit into other cross-over categories, such as vulnerabilities or data malformation, depending on how the attack is performed.

Insider Attack

This generally refers to a previously trusted person within an organization performing unauthorized actions, often using the permissions and privileges given to them to perform their authorized duties. Previously trusted insiders have deleted files, locked out systems, and copied large amounts of customer data to take and use at their next employer. Insider attacks are difficult to detect and stop and often result in the largest damage and recovery costs.

Third-Party Reliance Issue

In this type of attack, which can involve a supply chain vendor, a partner, etc., the organization attacked didn't do anything wrong, other than perhaps rely on another third party they use to not get hacked or do something wrong. Many data breaches have occurred because a trusted third party or vendor was compromised, and that resulting access allowed attacks into the intended targets.

The largest and most impacting such attack to date was the Solarwinds attack (`https://en.wikipedia.org/wiki/SolarWinds#2019%E2%80%932020 _ supply _ chain _ attacks`). In this attack, Russian nation-state attackers compromised a piece of software created by a company called Solarwinds. This piece of compromised software was then unknowingly downloaded and executed by more than 10,000 Solarwinds customer companies during the normal updating process. This installed a malicious backdoor program that allowed Russian hackers to access thousands of companies, including U.S. federal government agencies, nuclear regulatory agencies, mission-critical vendors (e.g., Microsoft), and even very trusted cybersecurity vendors (e.g., Mandiant). This one attack changed vendor and supply-chain cybersecurity management forevermore.

Physical Attack

Physical attacks include anything where the hacker must be physically involved in person with a device to cause harm, such as theft, damage, or destruction of a device. It could include a hacker forcing a user to log on under the threat of physical force. It could be a hacker using physical storage media, such as a USB key or floppy disk, to launch malware or cause the same to be unknowingly used by others. A physical attack could even include using a wireless attack method, which requires the attacker to be within wireless proximity to the target device.

Physical attacks are often considered the least interesting by cybersecurity professionals because they are difficult for hackers to pull off at scale, invite far higher risks for the attacker, and can be exceeding difficult for a defender to prevent. One common way to mitigate the risk of stolen devices is encryption of the data or disk on the device so at least the attacker cannot as easily access it.

Every hacker and malware attack I can think of begins in one of these categories. I could have missed some attack types and methods, but I tried my best to come up with a good hacker attack method taxonomy that was the most inclusive and least duplicative I could think of.

> **note** MITRE Corporation's ATT&CK framework (`https://attack.mitre.org`) is the most popular taxonomy used to describe hacker attack methods. However, its coverage of "initial access" methods is not as comprehensive and inclusive as my list.

Why Hackers Hack

The initial root access methods of how hackers hack haven't changed significantly over time, but some of the motivating reasons for doing so have. Just a decade or two ago, all we had to worry about was teenagers writing mischievous computer viruses that displayed messages like "legalize marijuana" or played digital tunes like "Yankee Doodle Dandy" or individual criminals looking for bank accounts. Those impish "script kiddies" and solitary malicious hackers have been replaced mostly by organized crime gangs, corporate hackers, and nation-state-sponsored hacking groups. Oh, how I pine for the playful hackers of yesterday. Let's take a closer look at the main types of hackers today based on their motivations.

Financial Crime

The largest percentage of hacking occurs solely to financially enrich the hackers in one way or another. This category contains any hacker or malware program that exists solely to steal money or other financial instruments. It includes ransomware, financial information theft, bank account stealing Trojans, ATM skimmers, credit card number theft, phishers, spammers, buyer scams, Nigerian emails, cryptocurrency theft, stock manipulation programs, and other programs or schemes that look to somehow illegally move value from the victim to the aggressor.

In the corporate world, it often appears as either fraudulent banking transactions and money transfers or fraudulently ordered products and services. If money is the motivation for the hacking event, it falls in this category. There are no official statistics tracking how much of hacking is financial-related versus other motivations, but I think most experts would agree that 90% or more of hacking is done because of financial interests.

Nation-State-Sponsored

Any sufficiently capable country has teams of nation-state-sponsored cyber-warriors. The largest countries have tens of thousands of professional hackers and tens of thousands of contractors. Many hackers work for their military or government-aligned companies, looking for digital edges to help their country maintain an advantage in both the real and digital world. Cyberwarriors often look for and steal military-related intellectual property and projects. They spy on individuals and companies. They also assess their enemies' cyber defenses, looking for ways to disable critical functionality if their country ever needs those types of services.

What has changed over the last decade or so is that nation-state adversaries are increasingly focused on compromising any organization and business. The target no longer has to have a direct link to their nation's government or military. Any organization or individual of the other country is fair game. Nation-state attackers are routinely stealing money, cryptocurrency, and intellectual property and installing ransomware.

Corporate Espionage

Many professional groups around the world look for and steal valuable corporate secrets, regardless of whether they have military value. Competing firms often steal information from competitors. Ex-employees may steal from their previous employer.

The lines between nation-state-sponsored hackers and corporation espionage can often be very thin. For example, the 2014 hack against Sony Pictures by North Korea is one of the most damaging attacks in history (`https://en.wiki pedia.org/wiki/Sony _ Pictures _ hack`). Apparently, the sole motivation for the hack was to punish Sony financially and reputationally for the future release of a comedic movie portraying North Korean leader Kim Jong-un in an unfavorable light. The hackers accessed and publicly released hundreds of gigabytes of Sony's internal information, including very valuable intellectual property and embarrassing internal emails.

Hacktivists

Hacktivists are hackers primarily motivated by an ideology, be it political, environmental, religious, moral, or otherwise. They are out to spread their philosophy and harm others who do not share the same belief system. They can do this in a variety of ways, including DoS outages, public information campaigns, doxing (releasing potentially harmful information about a particular target publicly), embarrassment, and public misinformation campaigns. As long as it results in negative press or a financial loss for their target, they've accomplished their job.

Disinformation

Some people like to intentionally spread lies and disinformation for a variety of reasons. Some do so for political reasons to support a particular candidate or cause. Some do so to promote their point of view or to harm an opposite cause, person, or point of view. Others are simply *trolling*, trying to cause emotional and reactionary actions by making outlandish or inflammatory claims. Disinformation is often pushed by nation-states against their own citizens and against other adversarial nations. There are dozens of books written on this subject.

Adware

Adware is malware that maliciously modifies your computer to promote a particular product or service. It can do this in a number of ways, although it usually does so by intercepting your Internet search engine queries and either displaying pop-up ads or redirecting you to a web page that you would not have been directed to by a normal search engine query.

For example, say that you type in "Wicked movie promos" in your favorite search engine because you want to find video clips from the latest *Wicked* movie. Instead of being directed by your default search engine to the best movie clips, your browser is directed to mobile phone Pokémon games or erectile dysfunction pills.

Stolen Resources

Many hackers break into computers to use the computers' resources (e.g., CPU, memory, electricity, storage space) for free. Decades ago, this category was mostly used by hackers who stole digital movies and music and used other people's large hard drives to store the content for free. Today, this category is mostly represented by hackers looking to gather large pools of electricity and CPUs to help "mine" (i.e., generate) new cryptocurrencies. Mining new cryptocurrencies, like bitcoin, can cost the miners more in electricity and other resources than what they gain with the resulting newly generated cryptocurrency. Hence, if they can "borrow" someone else's resources, they can create cryptocurrencies on someone else's dime. This could be seen as a form of financial theft.

Gamer Theft

These types of hackers could be a special subcategory of financial criminals, but they are so numerous and aggressive that they deserve their own section here. They are comprised of individuals who want to have unfair advantages in a particular game or service or cause operational disruption. Often, they create malware that searches for computers that are participating in a particular game (or series of games under a single publisher). The malware then steals the victim's authentication information or maybe just game credits. Game credits can be used to purchase items in the virtual world or be resold at a discount for another type of currency. Hackers may also use DDoS and ransomware techniques to harm other gamers and services, either to benefit monetarily or to gain a competitive advantage in the games. Malicious gamers are also known to initiate swatting.

Provoke or Cause a Physical Reaction in the Real World

Some hackers initiate programs or hacks to create a physical or kinetic response in the real world. Swatting is an example of this type of attack, where a hacker fraudulent calls a target's local law enforcement agency and claims to be a mass killer or the hostage of a killer, tricking the local law enforcement agency into an enormous law enforcement response. The intent is to scare or harm the target.

Swatting and other events used to provoke physical reactions used to be mostly committed by gamers against other online gamers they were angry with, but are now frequently used by hacktivists and other people spreading disinformation. Another example, frequently used in Hollywood hacking movies, is a hacker breaking into a missile control system in order to cause the military to launch a missile attack against a mistaken adversarial event. We do have instances of nation-states breaking into an adversary's weapons of war (e.g., drones) to take over control of the weapon or cause it to crash or self-destruct.

Information or Access Brokers

This group of hackers gathers private data and sells it to other interested parties. The information could be valuable databases, legal case information, passwords, or customer lists. Information or access brokers differ from corporate espionage hackers in that they are more interested in obtaining immediate financial reimbursement for the stolen information than in the intellectual property aspect of it.

Botnet Makers

Another large group of hackers includes those who simply want to compromise your PC or device with a "bot" (short for software robot) so that it becomes a controllable node on one of their botnets. Botnets can be rented, by the hour, to whomever wants them. They can be used to steal information, compromise companies, take money, or participate in DDoS attacks. At any given moment, literally, millions of PCs and devices on the Internet are part of someone's botnet.

Insider Threat

As covered, not all employees have their employer's best interests at heart. They can be industrial spies, but they often fall under the financial theft category or, occasionally, the nation-state-sponsored category. Insiders often target a company's credit card or customer databases, hoping to supplement their income. Many steal corporate secrets and offer them to competitors. Sometimes, they steal customer lists on their way out the door. A few each year are even brazen enough to cause operational harm. Many insider threats were originally very passionate employees who previously loved the company they are now maliciously targeting but feel they have been incorrectly wronged by the company or their boss in some way. They morph that original loving passion and turn it into hate, much like a wrongly spurned boyfriend or girlfriend might.

Commercial Surveillance Vendor

There are hundreds, if not thousands, of commercial surveillance vendors (CSVs) around the globe that develop hacking tools, software, and hardware to help their customers (e.g., governments, law enforcement, intelligence agencies, etc.) to track, surveil, and gain access to the target's devices, online activity, and physical behavior. CSVs are responsible for the creation and use of most of the zero-days we discover in a given year.

An older but fairly comprehensive guide to many different CSVs is Edward Teach's *The Big Black Book of Electronic Surveillance* (independently published, 2020). It gives a great overview of many dozens of companies and the types of products they create. Nicole Perlroth's best-selling book, *This Is How They Tell Me the World Ends: The Cyberweapons Arms Race* (Bloomsbury Publishing, 2023), is an entertaining read on how the CSV industry evolved in the early days.

Traditional and Other Types of Hackers

Do not discount the traditional hackers who are hacking for their own individual needs, be it for financial gain or just to prove they can do it. Years ago, traditional hackers conducted almost all of the hacking. Most were content just to write a computer virus that printed a funny saying on the computer or played a prank at a predetermined time. However, a few of these hacks even caused real damage, like the 1992 Michelangelo boot virus did when it formatted hard drives. But most were just someone's mostly harmless vanity project, a way of saying that the hacker was smart enough to do it but didn't want to cause real, widespread harm. Unfortunately, today, this type of traditional hacker is far less prevalent. Now, talented hackers often roam in gangs or corporations with the intent to inflict real damage.

Although the motivations discussed in this chapter cover the majority of all malicious hacking, there are endless possibilities, and you have to defend against all of them.

The Importance of Understanding Hacker Methodology and Motivation

Grasping a hacker's motivation helps you understand their ultimate objectives and what value they hope to obtain from your company. That's very important, especially when creating your threat scenarios for risk evaluation.

For example, if your company is frequently compromised by Bitcoin miner malware programs, it probably means your company's intellectual property isn't the primary goal of those hackers. The potential damage calculation is limited to stolen CPU cycles and electricity. The damage from corporate espionage or nation-states can be far greater than "borrowed" computer resources. You have to understand the motivations of the main hacker groups that are attempting to break into your devices and organizations to be able to calculate potential damages in risk assessments more accurately.

A data-driven defense values hacker methodology, particularly the initial root penetration exploit, more than other defense frameworks. If you want to stop future hacks, understanding how something breaks in is as important, if not more important, than what the hacker did once they were in. A data-driven defense soldier recognizes that learning how "pesky" adware got into an environment can be as important as how some uber-password-stealing backdoor program got in because both might have used the same initial penetration technique. Stopping nearly harmless adware just might be the key to stopping the bigger and more dangerous threat.

Countering the Possibility of a Brand New Attack Type

When trying to solve a huge, complex problem, there is always the possibility you miss something…even a big something. In trying to create a threat model of how we are attacked on the Internet, I could have missed something. Some brand new hacker methods or motivations could show up after I write this book. Things do change over time. Hacking motivations changed from individuals, mostly harmless hackers, to the professional financial and nation-state crime it is today. We didn't use to have to worry about AI-enabled deepfakes, and now we do. Disinformation wasn't a huge problem years ago, and now it is one of the largest. Things change over time. Hacking changes over time.

Because of continuing change, any solution to fix Internet security must consider that there may be "unknown unknowns" and try to plan for them. A good solution, the right solution, is able to stay a good solution in the future even after brand new things that didn't exist are created and used. This doesn't mean that a good solution must be able to fight every new future threat perfectly, but a good solution should be designed so that it is still used as part of the solution, if not the main part of the solution, even in light of new threats. If your solution is rendered completely useless in the future because of something new, it probably wasn't the right solution to begin with. All solutions created to fight Internet crime should have some anticipation of new, unexpected threats and be considered in the design of the solution.

Chapter Summary

This chapter summarized malicious hacker methodology and motivations, which are key to threat modeling cyber risks and defending against them.
Key concepts are:

- Initial root access causes
- Relative occurrences of the different initial root access causes
- Hacker intent

Chapter 3 discusses the biggest problem underlying most other Internet security problems that need to be solved first before all others.

The Problem

"If I had an hour to solve a problem and my life depended on the solution, I would spend the first 55 minutes determining the proper question to ask. For once I know the proper question, I could solve the problem in less than five minutes."

– Albert Einstein

This quote describes the importance of this part of the solution: When you are trying to solve something as complex as Internet cybercrime, you better start by asking the right question(s) and defining the right problem. Get the question wrong and the solution will not work. Define the problem wrong just a little bit, and attackers will simply skirt around your defenses as though there were none in place at all. And, so far, that's what has happened to every significant cyber defense we've put in the way of hackers and malware.

This chapter will begin by discussing some of the ways to approach hard, complex problems and then reveal the broader underlying problem of most Internet cybercrime at a high level.

Hints to Solve Hard, Complex Problems

Cybercrime is a really hard, complex problem to solve. If it was easy, some company, person, or group would have done it long ago. In fact, it's cybercrime's omnipresence and nonstop continued growth, in light of the tens of billions of dollars spent each year over decades to defeat it, that proves how stubborn and complex it is. Cybercrime is so bad that most people think we have no choice but to live with it. Most people don't even know that it is even a possibility that we can significantly diminish Internet crime.

Here are some hints and ideas I've learned to help with solving very hard, persistent problems of any type.

Picking the Right Layer to Solve

There are a lot of different ways (i.e., layers, levels) to think about any complex, continuing problem. Take, for example, drunk driving. Every day in the United States about 37 people, or more than 13,000 a year, die from alcohol-induced impaired driving. Percentage-wise, it's less than it used to be in past years, although one drunk driving death is too many. Most people think the main way to fix it is education, and certainly, that has helped reduce drunk driving deaths over the years. Others think raising the drinking age (from 18 to 21) helped a lot. Others think it just increased illegal binge drinking by teenagers. Some want to continue to raise drunk driving fines, jail time, and insurance costs as a deterrent. There is evidence to show that all of this has helped deter drunk driving. Many others, seen as extreme, think that making every vehicle contain a breathalyzer to measure the driver's alcohol level before it can be started is the only real way to reduce drunk driving deaths. And now we are increasingly having to worry about the rising threat of recreational drug-involved accidents as marijuana gets legalized across more and more states. Most people rightly think multiple solutions at different levels are all needed at the same time.

Here are some of the layers of Internet cybercrime:

- Malicious hackers and malware
- Intention and motivations of cybercriminals
- Initial root access hacking methods
- Outcomes of malicious hacking
- Different types of cybercrime
- Weaknesses that encourage cybercrime

Malicious hackers, the ultimate benefactors of their malfeasance, are certainly the direct cause of our problems. If we didn't have humans causing online crime, this would all go away (at least until we have self-running AI-enabled Internet criminal implementations). We definitely need to stop cybercriminals, their malicious actions, and their software. That's what the Internet security solution is ultimately trying to mitigate—humans committing crime. That's one way to think about the problem.

The hacker's motivation is another way . . . another layer . . . to think about cybercrime. I covered hacker intent in Chapter 2. Most cybercriminal motivation boils down to financial gain, followed by, to lesser extents, psychological provocations or ideological motivations. We could describe the problem along those lines and seek to solve it by potentially decreasing those motivations. This is like people saying we can decrease real-world crime by decreasing poverty, hunger, and racial disparities.

As I mentioned in Chapter 2, there are 14 initial access root methods that hackers and their malware programs use to break into devices and networks and, consequently, exploit the digital identities and online resources owned and controlled by people. That layer ignores hackers and their motivations. It only cares about how they accomplish badness and how to mitigate their successful methods. This might be akin to reducing gun crime by reducing gun ownership.

Another layer is the technical outcomes of the initial root access methods. What technical outcome did the initial root access hacking method allow? Was it ransomware, identity theft, financial theft, or denial of service attacks? If the solution doesn't stop those types of problems, we've not really solved the problem of Internet security.

We could also tackle Internet cybercrime by looking at the technologies and implementations that unintentionally induce weaknesses, which allow Internet crime to flourish. As with real-world crime, this might be akin to people leaving their houses and cars unlocked, flashing cash, having poor security lighting, no alarm systems, and potential victims not being aware of their surroundings and accidentally putting them into higher-risk scenarios.

Nearly every Internet solution to cybercrime I've seen in my over 36-year career tries to tackle one or more of the layers above. If only we better patch . . . if only we better detected malware . . . if only used stronger default encryption . . . if only we could reduce the number of security bugs in our code . . . then Internet crime would finally get better. You get the picture. These are the things and layers we have already tried. And despite our best efforts, Internet security hasn't gotten any better. In fact, it gets worse.

If the previous and current solutions are not working, what will? Perhaps we need a new way of looking at the problem and finding solutions.

Multiple Solutions Are Usually Needed

Most hard, difficult, persistent problems are hard, difficult, and persistent because they have more than one cause and need more than one solution. Solving any long-term, ongoing, complex problem (e.g., drunk driving, gun violence, crime, poverty, etc.) will take many solutions across a range of issues to solve. No single solution will fix a complex problem, and there are many solutions, each tackling its own layer and issue. The same is true of solving Internet cybercrime.

First Principles Thinking

Many of our world's best thinkers and creators do something known as first principles thinking. *First principles thinking* is looking at a problem in a new way by first breaking down seemingly very complex problems into their simpler core issues, questioning previous assumptions, and re-examining previous requirements. It's trying to see the problem in a new light and identifying the fundamental facts and truths. It's believing that a better solution wasn't previously found because the problem wasn't being thought of in the right way.

Elon Musk famously said, "It's particularly dangerous if a smart person gave you the requirements" (`https://www.youtube.com/watch?v=Jgw-_hlFQk4`).

He meant a few things as he continued to explain. First, smart people can be as wrong as dumb people, but also that smart people will appear more knowledgeable in their incorrect support and more easily intimidate others into not questioning their authority and answers. Who among us hasn't had an "expert know-it-all" give us the wrong answer?

> **note**   There is a fine line between appropriately questioning the experts and unwittingly being part of the Dunning-Kruger effect.

Eat the Elephant One Bite at a Time

Problems can quickly get difficult, complex, and overwhelming to think about. When that happens, break them down into their simplest components and descriptions. It's easier to solve one smaller problem than ten at the same time. If you've got a problem with multiple components, address each component one at a time. You'll better solve complex problems and keep your sanity.

> *Truth is ever to be found in the simplicity, and not in the multiplicity and confusion of things.*
>
> **Isaac Newton**

Fail Fast

There is no success without failure. No truer words have ever been said. The world's smartest minds realized that failure is how you learn, and if you can fail faster, you learn faster. That's why you see SpaceX and Blue Origin rockets blowing up and the teams cheering "the success." The idea is that they are moving along so quickly innovating, intentionally not being conservative (as compared to NASA), and that they are intentionally, as a known side effect of the design, moving too fast if your goal is to be safer. But by moving faster, they can see mistakes quicker and more quickly build eventual solutions. You can't argue with their success. SpaceX alone has launched more than 138 rockets in 2024, about one launch every two to three days, and at a far cheaper price per launch than any other rocket company.

Thomas Alva Edison, holder of 1,093 patents and inventor of the light bulb, movie projector, record player, DC power generation, and so many other inventions that touched our lives, did most of his inventing through fast failure. Edison is famous for coming up with the germ of an idea and then doing thousands to tens of thousands of experiments as fast as he could to figure out what worked best. The central lesson is to figure out a way to succeed, start on the journey, and fail as fast as you can so you can use those lessons to get to final success faster.

Prioritize Problems and Solutions

It's very important when you have a multipart problem with many solutions to figure out which are the most important and go about tackling those first. Some problems and solutions will have great bearing. In fact, with most complex problems, just a few things make up most of the problem. Conversely, other things frequently have very little to do with the problem. Make sure you start with the most important stuff first.

Go for an Easy Big Win If There Is One

With that said, if you want to be given the authority and trust to solve a complex problem that will ultimately take a long time to completely fix, if there is an important priority that can be quickly solved immediately, go for it first, even if it isn't the biggest or most important priority. People like to see progress and success. If you've got something you can do fairly quickly with not a lot of negatives, it can help build trust by doing it early on. It will help you gain support and allow you to move on to the bigger, harder-to-tackle problems.

Be Curious and Childlike

Many different famous scientists, when asked how they thought of or invented great things, often responded that they kept childlike curiosity and wonderment into their adulthood. Their childlike curiosity and simple questions never went away.

"The secret of genius is to carry the spirit of the child into old age."

Aldous Huxley

"I have no special talents. I am only passionately curious."

Albert Einstein

Be a Good Communicator

Solving broad public problems requires good communication skills. If you can't clearly communicate, you will not be able to solve complex problems involving many people as easily. When trying to discuss complex problems and solutions, spend time thinking about how to best communicate them to others. Know your audience. Different types of audiences need different types and tones of messaging. I'm writing in a more relaxed way about how to solve Internet cybercrime in this book than I would in a grant application for funding or an IETF Request for Comment (RFC).

The brightest minds and best communicators can usually break down complex issues into terms that even a child can understand. Thus, a nuclear explosion could be very simply described as one atom bumping into and pushing two atoms, those two atoms bumping into and pushing four atoms, and so on. Einstein explained relativity by discussing throwing balls on a train, not by discussing complicated physics equations and space-time curvatures. A good test of whether you fundamentally understand something is if you can readily explain it to a child so they can understand the basics.

Pushing Problems Upstream

Something that has been particularly useful to me is to see if I can find a precursor cause of the problem I was first examining. Did my problem have a cause? And was that cause really the underlying problem? And I keep doing that until I can't find any more reasonable precursor causes. I call it *pushing upstream*. I'm not sure who taught me about this method or where I read it, but it's one of the most fundamental things I do when thinking about hard problems.

Here's a personal example. As previously covered, the world had at least 40,291 publicly known individual software and firmware vulnerabilities in 2024 (https://www.cvedetails.com/browse-by-date.php).

Nearly all of those were unintentionally written into programs by a programmer and not caught by any mitigation prior to being publicly released. A big part of the problem is that almost no programming curriculum in the world teaches "secure coding" to its programming students. How can we expect our programmers to type in fewer security vulnerabilities if we aren't teaching them about common security vulnerabilities and how to avoid them in the first place? Most programmers don't innately understand directory traversal path errors, buffer overflows, and understand the problem of hard-coded credentials.

Over my career, I've tried to get many university, college, and online programming courses to include secure coding skills in their curriculums—without a single bit of success. All have ignored me or actively turned me down. For a long time, besides being very frustrated, I wondered why programming courses were not automatically including secure coding education and skills in their curriculum, without my having to ask. I mean, why wouldn't programming schools and courses, after decades of continuously growing numbers of vulnerabilities, not teach secure coding to students to help stem the tide of errors?

And then I did first principles thinking about the problem and went upstream.

Programming schools and courses teach skills desired by programmers. Programmers want skills and languages desired by employers. Programming schools and courses don't teach Cobol or Pascal programming languages anymore because that's not what employers want. Today, programming schools and courses teach Python, Java, JavaScript, TypeScript, C++, PHP, Ruby, and Rust because that's what employers are programming in, and programmers need those skills.

Programming curriculums would teach secure coding skills to students if employers proactively wanted employees with them. If employers started requiring secure coding skills in programmer job descriptions, asking about them in job interviews, and hiring new programmers first who had secure coding skills over those who didn't, the programming schools would teach it.

Why don't employers proactively ask their programmers to have secure programming skills? What employer wouldn't want their incoming programmers taught to write fewer security bugs? That would save time, money, and reputational hits and better protect customers. That's a win-win. There is absolutely no downside other than trying to figure out what to squeeze out of an existing programming curriculum to squeeze in secure coding.

I realized that employers didn't know that programmers aren't taught how to securely program. It's a big disconnect. Employers must think that programmers are taught those skills and that what we have today is the best outcome of that believed training. They have no idea that almost no programmer is taught any secure coding skills.

So, I started a public relations campaign to get more employers to ask for secure coding skills and experience in their job ads (`https://www.linkedin.com/pulse/your-employer-needs-request-secure-design-skills-all-developer-roger-1by5e` and `https://www.linkedin.com/pulse/start-requiring-secure-development-skills-your-job-ad-roger-grimes-x2ore`). I've even developed and shared a summary secure code curriculum of what to teach to new programmers: `https://www.linkedin.com/pulse/heres-secure-design-curriculum-summary-example-roger-grimes-1ayje/`.

I started talking to multiple national groups about pushing new secure coding curriculums and trying to get universities, colleges, and other types of developer programs to include secure coding education. I've had a little success.

I've been assured by the CISA leaders, with whom I've been communicating about the problem, that asking programming curriculums to include secure coding education and asking employers to require secure coding skills in job requirements will be officially included in future versions of CISA's Secure By Design (https://www.cisa.gov/securebydesign) initiative. I'll cover more about secure programming in Chapter 15.

To recap my first principles thinking by pushing the question and problems upstream example:

1. I started by asking, "Why do we have so many vulnerabilities in our software and firmware code?"
2. My first answer was, "Well, of course, primarily because programmers continue to unknowingly put them in there. They don't get there by themselves."
3. My second, more upstream question was, "Why are programmers continuing to code vulnerabilities into software and firmware?"
4. The answer to that question was, "Primarily because they aren't taught not to put them in there. Almost no programming curriculum they are exposed to teaches them not to."
5. This led to a third upstream question, "Why do programming curricula not teach programmers how to code securely?"
6. My answer was, "Primarily because employers are not proactively requiring programmers to have secure coding skills."
7. This led to a fourth upstream question, "Why are employers not requiring programmers to have secure coding skills?"
8. My answer was, "Primarily because employers don't know that programmers aren't being taught secure coding skills. They must think it's already being done and what we have skill-wise, is the best we get after programmers are appropriately trained in secure coding."
9. My final answer was, "Educate employers to require secure coding skills, which will motivate programming curriculums to teach it, which will teach programmers to code more securely, which will result in few security bugs being coded into software and firmware."

If I'm correct, employers will include a secure coding requirement in programmer job descriptions, programming schools will teach it, and we'll have fewer vulnerabilities being inserted by programmers over time.

Yes, other things cause insecure coding, such as nearly nonexistent threat modeling, insecure programming languages, insecure coding tools, and so on. But at least in solving one of the main problems of so many vulnerabilities in code, one of the primary reasons is the involved programmers aren't being taught not to put vulnerabilities into their code.

Using first principles thinking and constantly re-pushing the problem upstream to the root of the issue allows us to find more basic problems and truths. And once you have that, it's easier to figure out correct solutions (at least until we have perfect code review tools to prevent bugs from ever being placed into code in the first place).

Always Be Learning

The best minds and most successful people set aside a part of every day or week for learning something new. You should do the same. The computer world changes very fast. It seems like just yesterday that AI wasn't a thing, quantum was just a fantasy, blockchain was the solution to all security problems, and there wasn't a single service that could make a deepfake of anyone else in under a day, much less in a minute. If you aren't actively learning, you will be quickly bypassed.

I've had the general idea of how to stop Internet cybercrime for two decades, but how I would technologically do it continues to evolve to this very day. Some parts of the solution have remained exactly as I envisioned them in the beginning, and others are still evolving as I write these words. In general, it's becoming easier to solve. I only know this because I'm keeping up with the technologies. I'm also constantly asking myself if some new hacker method is something brand new or just a slight change on something new. I ask myself if the solution would stop the new attack either way. Never stop learning.

Be Open to Other Solutions

This can be the most difficult ask for anyone bright who has studied and thought about a complex problem and thinks they have a solution. We all may think we are open to other solutions and facts, but most of us are pretty hardened into our own beliefs and are only open to beliefs and facts that support our already existing opinions and beliefs. There isn't a scientific study that doesn't support this fact.

Still, be aware of your own strongly held biases and try to be a little open to other's opinions and suggestions, even if they contradict your own. Ask yourself if what the other person is saying could possibly be true. Ask yourself if your belief or opinion has strongly supported facts or if you've researched those facts in a while. Be open to learning about new solutions and facts.

Personally, like most other people, I rarely change my mind or decide to believe in new facts. But at least a few times a year, I start believing a new contradictory fact or even change my overall opinion or belief on something. It doesn't happen much. Most of the time, I remain steadfast in my existing beliefs. But it does happen. I do sometimes change from what I previously believed. I also like myself better because I am open to learning something new that changes my belief system. What I learn most of the time is that the problem or solution is more complex and nuanced than I originally believed.

Try Not to Create New Problems

It's often hard to create solutions that don't unintentionally cause new problems. For example, decades ago, the world realized that people often picked weak passwords and frequently reused the same ones across multiple unrelated websites. Hackers were easily able to guess and crack these weak passwords. So, the world decided we needed to recommend/require that people use longer passwords with more complexity (i.e., both uppercase and lowercase letters, numbers, and symbols).

And over time, the recommended/required length of people's passwords went up, from 6 characters to 8, 10, and then 12 characters. And most of those newer, longer passwords also include some basic form of complexity (e.g., uppercase and lowercase characters, numbers, and symbols).

The problem is people had a hard time remembering longer, more complex passwords and hated frequently changing them, so they reused them even more across more websites and services. In the end, the early solution to supposedly fix a common password weakness turned out to cause more people to be compromised because they shared more passwords on multiple unrelated sites and services than ever before.

After two decades of pushing longer and longer passwords with complexity, the best new thinking on the subject says people should be able to use any password they want and not require any length, complexity, or forced changes. Better yet, use multifactor authentication (MFA) if you can, and if you have to use a password, use a password manager program to create, store, and use your passwords. You have to be careful that the solution doesn't accidentally make things worse.

Don't Let Perfection Be the Enemy of Getting Something Done

There are few perfect solutions. No matter what the solution is, you or someone else can probably think of one or more edge cases that invalidate the solution. Don't let perfection be the enemy of getting a solution put in place. There aren't any perfect solutions, so don't strive for it. The things that are working fairly well today are working despite not being perfect. Strive toward a more perfect or near-perfect solution, but don't require it, or you'll never get anything accomplished.

Start by Defining the Ultimate Goal of the Solution

Before you create a solution to a problem, you need to correctly define the problem. To create a good solution, you need to define the ultimate goal of the problem. What is it you hope to solve? What does solving the problem look like? Is the goal to change or improve something that already exists? Is it to add or delete something? Do you have to be perfect with the solution or just good enough? Some solutions, like preventing global nuclear war, must be perfect to be considered a success. With most other problems, "better" is good enough.

You need to define the meaning of success ahead of time. There are a lot of ways to measure success. It's easy to get it wrong. It helps if you have a metric or something quantifiable that you can put a number or percentage on. Just saying I want to fix Internet security sounds laudable but doesn't really define what success looks like. Here's a clearer definition of success:

My overall goal is to significantly and permanently secure the Internet against malicious hacking and malware as compared to current metrics.

If I do that, the solution will be considered a success. I think the security improvement needs to be significant. However, you measure that. A small security improvement for a huge change isn't worth it. If I had to put exact numbers on it, I would count any solution that reduces current Internet crime levels to $1/20^{th}$ (5%) of what they are today as a success. Another way of saying it is to reduce existing Internet crime by 95%. I'd prefer for Internet crime to be slashed to $1/200^{th}$ (0.5%) of what it is today, but you have to be careful of setting unrealistic goals as well.

The solution needs to be lasting. Who cares if you immediately put down Internet crime significantly, but it just learns a way around the solution, and in 5 to 10 years, you are back to the same level or higher of Internet crime? It would be best if Internet cybercrime stayed down significantly for multiple decades, if not the rest of eternity. But it is very difficult to predict anything beyond a few decades. Entire new paradigms will come into existence that I know nothing about.

A good Internet security solution significantly reduces Internet crime in a clearly measurable way and is long-lasting. If I was explaining my goal to a kid, I'd say, "Stop almost all Internet crime!"

To find a good solution to a complex, ongoing problem, you need to use first principles thinking, test assumptions, re-think requirements, ask the right questions, push the problems upstream as far as you can go, prioritize solutions, simplify, communicate, define the goal of the solution, don't seek perfection, and try not to create new problems.

Lack of Trust

The Internet is full of crime. This makes people not trust it as much as they otherwise could. *Trust* is an expectation of consistent, reliable, predictable outcomes based on previous behavior. In most cases, trust involves people making consistent good behaviors that others appreciate and rely on. A lack of trust is caused by inconsistent outcomes, malicious behavior, and a lack of transparency. Any solution to fix the Internet will have to create a better sense of pervasive trust all across the Internet, a *high-trust ecosystem*. More on this in later chapters.

Now for what you've been waiting for: the solution.

The Problem Underlying Most Internet Cybercrime

This section will discuss the main underlying problem of why we have so much Internet crime.

Identifying the Main Underlying Problem

Internet crime has been pretty bad for a long time. And I think pretty much everyone agrees that one of *the* biggest factors is that Internet criminals can't easily be arrested, punished, or even stopped. It all starts with the fact that we can't identify most Internet criminals to a verified human identity, which makes stopping and arresting them impossible, even if we legally could.

> **The underlying problem of most Internet crime is that we can't identify and stop Internet criminals.**

Most of the time we cannot correctly identify Internet criminals to their real-world identities. Sometimes, we can identify that someone or a consistent group of individuals is committing Internet crimes, but we don't know who they are. In those cases, lawyers, law enforcement, courts, and prosecutors have been known to get warrants for evidence, detainment, and warrants in the name of "John Doe," which is a legal pseudo-name placeholder that will be replaced with the real person's name if it ever becomes known in the future.

In a very small percentage of cases, we can identify Internet criminals by name and location (literally just a few dozen to a few hundred a year), but we can't arrest them because they reside in other nation's legal jurisdictions where our laws and courts don't apply. Unless we have a legal treaty with the other nation and an agreement for the other nation to make an arrest for us, our evidence and warrants for their citizen's arrest will not be honored. China and Russia are rarely going to arrest and punish hackers in their countries for attacking us and vice versa.

Regardless of whether we can arrest hackers, if we could at least identify them and their activity accurately, we could at least minimize their future crime. If we could accurately identify cybercriminals when they try to connect to us, we could say something like, "Hey, that email is from Dimitry Yuryevich Khoroshev of Russia, who is known to push ransomware and is wanted by the U.S. government. I shouldn't open that email."

> `note`   If interested, here is more info on Dimitry Yuryevich Khoroshev: `https://`
> `www.justice.gov/usao-nj/pr/us-charges-russian-national-`
> `developing-and-operating-lockbit-ransomware`.

Today's Internet allows criminals to make unlimited fraudulent connections to people and devices to commit cybercrime using any fake identity they want without repercussions. If you robbed banks for a living and could never be punished for doing it, you'd get pretty good at robbing banks. Your tools and methods would get better over time. You would figure out what did or didn't work. You would refine and optimize your skills. You'd get faster at robbing banks. You would get better at targeting the most likely prospects and taking more money.

As your success grew, you would probably hire others to help you and expand your business. You could target large and small banks at the same time. You would grow and plunder to your heart's content and never worry about being identified. That's today's Internet for anyone who wants to rob people online.

Robbing Banks in the Real World

It's not worth the risk for most people to rob banks in the real world. If you decided to become a real-world bank robber, you are likely to be identified, arrested, charged, tried, and punished…likely severely. There are people who despite the obvious big risks still rob banks. There are people who rob banks and get away with it. But most people who rob banks don't get a lot of money and often either get caught on their first bank robbery attempt or keep robbing banks until they are caught. It's the rare uncaught bank robber who stops before they get caught.

Here are the relevant stats involving real-world banks and robberies. There are 11,652 individual banks and credit unions in the United States, with more than 75,000 branches serving more than 200 million customers involving billions of transactions. According to the U.S. Department of Justice there were just 1,263 bank robberies in 2023 (`https://www.fbi.gov/file-repository/bank-crime-statistics-2023-091724.pdf/view`). About half were committed by lone individuals and half by multiple people. The average amount of money stolen in a bank robbery was just over $4,200. That's not even equal to the balance of the average individual bank account. Sixty percent of bank robbers are arrested. After being caught, the average bank robber faces years to decades in prison.

That's not a lot of bank and credit union robberies, thankfully. Just as telling, the number of bank robberies in the United States has gone down significantly over time since the all-time high many years ago. The number of U.S. bank robberies peaked in 1991 at 9,388 (`https://phys.org/news/2022-10-bandits-banks-crimes-longer.html`). Since then, it has steadily gone down over time to where it is today, consistently below 2000 year after year and getting lower. There are lots of reasons for this, but most of it has to do with the fact that if you rob a bank, you're likely to get caught and punished, and you aren't likely to get a lot of money. Who wants to risk years in prison and get a permanent felony record as a bank robber for the rest of their lives for $4,200? Some people obviously do, but most people don't. Most criminals don't.

By contrast, online thieves often steal that amount many times each day and almost never get caught. They can commit crimes, day after day, without significant worry of identification or arrest. It's profitable. It's low-risk. Because of this, there are tens of thousands of malicious hackers and malicious hacker groups. It's a full-time business for many of them.

It is not unusual to learn that individual hackers are making millions of dollars a year off the Internet. Some Internet criminals have boasted of stealing over half a billion dollars over their careers. An Internet criminal stealing only a few million dollars a year probably isn't on many law enforcement agency's radars. A small-time Internet criminal will usually make tens of thousands of dollars a day. They will almost never be identified, caught, go to trial, serve any time in jail, or have a prison record.

On the Internet, crime usually pays.

In the real world, laws and the threat of legal punishment help keep honest people honest. If someone is down on their luck, most people don't consider robbing a bank as something that would make their situation better. Most who do decide to rob a bank end up regretting it. People who continue robbing banks eventually get caught. People who get caught over and over for robbing banks eventually lose their freedom for a long, long time. At some point, one way or another, it's a crime that eventually prevents the criminal from trying again.

If only the Internet were like the real world, where criminals were likely to be identified, stopped, and possibly even arrested. That's our real underlying problem and the reason why Internet crime is so bad and growing. We will discuss this again in Chapter 5.

Chapter Summary

This chapter discussed ideas and hints to help solve difficult, complex problems like fixing Internet security. It then revealed the largest underlying problem, allowing most Internet crimes to occur. It is a fact that most Internet criminals are unlikely to ever be identified, stopped, or arrested. Until we fix this problem, Internet crime will continue occurring.

Key concepts are:

■ Techniques to solve hard, complex problems

■ Pervasive anonymity

■ Pervasive identity

Chapter 4 discusses the broad challenges to any proposed Internet security solution that might kill it.

Challenges

Why haven't good security solutions already been found and implemented to stop Internet crime? You would think that a massive global problem that siphons many billions of dollars from our economy and negatively impacts millions of people each year for decades would have been solved a long time ago. Especially since millions of people, tens of thousands of companies, and billions of dollars a year have been spent trying to solve it. Sadly, no company, organization, or person has come close. Internet crime is rampant and growing ever worse each year.

The answer is that solving Internet security problems is difficult and requires big changes. Any big change without a tipping point event (like the 9/11 terrorist attacks) forcing it to happen is nearly impossible. Solving global Internet security is among the world's hardest problems…right up there with solving poverty and Middle East peace. You probably can't get the people around your dinner table to agree on the same things happening in your household or country; imagine trying to get agreements across the world about how the Internet should function with so many different types of people, cultures, governments, and groups.

Chapter 4 will cover the many challenges that fight back against any solution trying to fix Internet security. The challenges are technical, strategic, and political.

Technical Challenges

Technical challenges are challenges with the technologies used to try to create a better Internet security solution. Here are some of them.

We Already Have the Technology We Need

Surprise! There really isn't a big technology hurdle we have to overcome. This isn't like quantum computing and nuclear fusion, where we still need to make significant technological advances to get to a working product. Nope, we likely already have all the major technologies and protocols we need to make the Internet significantly more secure.

> **note** In Chapters 7–12, I'm going to be discussing the various technical solutions in detail.

In most cases, all we have to do is agree on what to place where and make the technology more pervasive. Most of the technologies require, at most, small to moderate changes. I just put this fact here first so you understand that most of the needed technologies, in the sense of pure bits and bytes, already exist and are really not holding anything up. It's more of making up our minds to do them.

But with that said, let's look at some other technical issues we have to overcome.

Most Solutions Are too Limited

We need to think bigger. The biggest technical challenge we have is that, so far, most of our technical solutions have been too limited, trying to solve smaller, more specific, limited problems, like spam, phishing, malware, network attacks, ransomware attacks, password thefts, and so on. We have many good solutions that work well for a specific problem, like firewalls, virtual private networks (VPNs), encryption, etc. They just tackle one small part of the Internet crime ecosystem, and hackers just skirt to the right or the left and get around it. It's like playing a multidecade game of whack-a-mole where it takes the defender years to fix a specific problem and the attacker only needs a few minutes to get around it using a new method.

One of the best examples I can give are the recent *awesome* global anti-phishing standards, Domain-based Message Authentication Reporting & Conformance (DMARC), Sender Policy Framework (SPF), and DomainKeys Identified Mail (DKIM). Let's just collectively call them DMARC for this discussion. DMARC is one of the few Internet security standards that has not only gotten widespread global acceptance but works really well at resolving the problem it was created to prevent. DMARC allows anyone (or really, an email tool on their behalf) to verify the sending domain that an email claims to be from is really from that sending email domain. So, if you receive an email claiming it's from @microsoft.com, you can verify if it is really from @microsoft.com.

And it works great. Today, most email servers and clients check incoming emails for DMARC verification, even if you don't know it. And if an email fails those checks, it normally will automatically end up in your Spam or Junk Mail folder, or even just be blocked from your Inbox altogether. DMARC works and works well.

The problem is that attackers just quickly moved from claiming to be from legitimate domains to using look-alike domains. So instead of using @microsoft .com, they just use something like @microsoft.com.logon.securityesquire.net or @security.mikcosoftie.com/logon. Sadly, most people don't know the difference even if they looked at the involved URL, and most people don't look. The average person sees the word "microsoft.com" in the domain URL somewhere and thinks it is the same as @microsoft.com. It often isn't.

And because spammers and phishers need to meet DMARC standards in order for their malicious emails not to automatically end up in all user's Spam or Junk Mail folders, nearly all spammers and phishers enable DMARC for their rogue look-alike domains at even higher rates than legitimate companies do on their legitimate domains. Unfortunately, this makes the DMARC check pass even if the email is malicious. If you want to learn more about DMARC and how it is abused, read this article I wrote: `https://www.linkedin.com/pulse/phishe rs-abusing-legitimate-neglected-domains-pass-dmarc-roger-grimes-wrl3e.`

People Don't Understand the Technology

Continuing the DMARC example, most people who first hear about DMARC think passing DMARC verification means the email isn't malicious. And that isn't true. A passing rating just means that the email is from the sending domain it claims, and the receiver still has to verify whether the domain claimed is trustworthy or not. DMARC was a huge success from the standpoint of not allowing spam and phishing attacks to claim to be from legitimate, trusted domains (when they were not), but hackers just sidetracked that issue (as discussed earlier) and began using the system against unsuspecting victims to continue great success. Hackers learned they could just create a domain that has the targeted domain's name somewhere in the name and most people would think it really was from the targeted domain (even though it was from a completely unrelated domain).

The same thing can be said about many other technologies. For example, SSL/ TLS/HTTPS. Most websites are now HTTPS-enabled, which means they use digital certificates and the TLS protocol to verify website domain names and to encrypt the communications between client and server. But most people mistakenly think that HTTPS and the "lock icon" that often accompanies it within a browser means it's a safe website.

Nope, just like with DMARC, HTTPS just means the website domain URL you are viewing is the one you are really on. It's still up to the user to determine if that HTTPS-validated website is trustworthy. Sadly, 90% of malicious websites use HTTPS, so that is often not true. I could give more examples of many other good, misunderstood Internet security technologies like Public Key Infrastructure (PKI), digital certificates, and DNSSEC, but you get the idea. Many people misunderstand the goal and reason for the computer security solution.

I don't blame the humans. We keep wanting a comprehensive Internet security solution, and the industry and the vendors keep saying they are delivering one without going out of their way to say they are only delivering on a very, very small part of the problem. End-users just want the problem of Internet security to go away altogether. Me, too!

Usability vs. Security

People don't like any security option that bothers them even a little. Truth be told, people don't want to use passwords. They don't care if they are short or long, complex or not complex. They don't want to use them. They definitely don't like using multifactor authentication (MFA). If it takes them one second longer or a single mouse click or keystroke more, they'd rather not have it. They just want to open their app and do their thing without being bothered by security. That's the simple truth.

Unfortunately, most computer security inconveniences people to some degree. This is true in the real world as well. We have to have keys to open our front doors and cars (well, a key fob or a phone these days). We have to enter through doors and gates, walk around fences, and walk on sidewalks. Many of us have alarm systems, cameras, and luggage tags. And we'll use them as long as they don't inconvenience us too much.

Usability and security have always been a great struggle. If you inconvenience the user too much, have too many false negatives or false positives, or slow down the user even a little bit, the user will fight it or try to work around it. If they have to wait longer than a second after they type in their password or swipe their finger to log in, they don't want to use it.

Fixing Internet security will require some complexity, but that complexity must be mostly hidden behind the scenes from the end user. You can't slow them down. You can't make them make too many choices. They would prefer not making any choices and just having it work 100% of the time as expected.

Almost anyone can design a very secure computer and Internet. All you have to do is lock down the choices to only the safest ones and deny everything else. The more you lock down a system, the harder it is to hack and exploit. The old, tired canard is the safest computer is one locked in a closet without a network card . . . encased in concrete.

But no one is going to want to use a severely locked-down system. People want to use feature-rich computers and devices with a reasonable level of security.

What is that reasonable level of security? One that doesn't slow them down a second or make them click one more mouse click or keystroke more than they absolutely need to. Users don't like any security that slows them down, and when it comes to usability and speed versus security, usability and speed always win every time if the user has any say in the matter. Whatever "fix the Internet" solution anyone comes up with has to be designed with this in mind.

Legacy Issues

It's evolution and not revolution. Whatever solution someone develops, it has to work on the current Internet, with existing devices, technologies, and protocols. If the solution only works with brand-new things, it's probably dead going out of the gate. We have hundreds of billions, if not trillions, of dollars invested in our current Internet-connected software and hardware. If you make a change too big that it ends up invalidating all the old, legacy stuff, you're going to get tremendous pushback. The bigger the change, the bigger the pushback. Minor changes you think no one could care about are going to get argued against. Huge changes, if they don't support legacy devices and systems, are going to get pushback.

Whenever I see a new Internet security system discussed, I always review it to see if it is the evolution of existing technologies (something we handle better) or if it is a revolutionary technology that requires a whole new Internet or all new devices (something we don't handle well). The Internet solution in this book may look revolutionary, but it relies mostly on existing technologies that perhaps need some small tweaks.

Pervasive Cryptography

No matter what the future Internet security solution is, it will absolutely be full of cryptography: encryption (symmetric and asymmetric), public-key encapsulation mechanisms, digital signatures, hashes, random number generators, and other integrity mechanisms. It will be everywhere, including on our logins, user IDs, device IDs, networks, operating systems, applications, devices, and more. It already is. And it will be even more so in the future.

The future of Internet security will probably be more end-to-end encryption, pervasive integrity, and crypto-agility. *Crypto-agility* is any system using cryptography being designed and implemented so that the involved cryptographic algorithms and key sizes can be changed or replaced without having to replace the entire system. For example, we are getting ready to move from quantum-susceptible cryptography (e.g., RSA, Diffie-Hellman, El-Gamal, and Elliptic Curve Cryptography, etc.) to newer quantum-resistant cryptography over this decade. Our existing software and firmware systems need to be made as crypto-agile as they can to allow needed flexibility.

Lifecycle Challenges

Every object involved (e.g., users, devices, printers, servers, etc.) has to be handled from cradle to grave. There needs to be a good process for adding, changing, and removing things. Most systems do a good job of allowing people to add new objects and attributes, but less so on changing or moving things. Most systems are absolutely horrible about proactively removing things when they are no longer needed. Officially, the act of removing an object is known as *decommissioning*. Most systems with collections of objects end up with a "boneyard" of unused things that only serve to take up resources, confuse people, and add to potential vulnerabilities.

Handle Shared Things

It's a computer security doctrine that we should limit shared IDs, where two or more people share the same login ID or even the same device, if it can be prevented. Shared things make it harder to assign attribution of an action or event to a single person. But our world is full of shared IDs and shared devices. Any Internet security system is going to have to learn how to handle device and ID sharing.

Complexity Fights Security

It's a well-known maxim that complexity complicates security. The more code and features you have, the more attack vectors you will open up for a hacker to explore. If you want to be more likely to keep something secure, keep it simple and short. However, fixing Internet security will absolutely take a complex set of multiple interoperating protocols and services. It may be the most complex thing we've ever done on the Internet. That complexity might be its death knell. But if we can accomplish the exact requirement in a simpler way, let's do it using a simpler way instead of a more complex way.

Feature Creep Invites Insecurities

Some very useful technologies were appropriately built with security in mind from the start. And their security was pretty good, at least in the beginning. However, as the technology became more popular, users wanted more features, vendors responded against the risk of becoming obsolete, and more features ended up coming at the cost of security.

A prime example of that was Sun's Java, first released in 1996. The first version would not allow any Java program to save files or information permanently to local storage. This was great for security because it meant a malicious Java program or an abused legitimate Java program would have a harder time maliciously modifying the local PC. Java was one of the safest programming languages on the planet.

However, programmers and users quickly wanted the ability to save files locally and to have lots of other new features. By 1998, just two years later, Java's source code had tripled in size. Six years after that, Sun Java had been used to compromise so many victims that Cisco's 2014 Annual Security Report said 91% of all web exploits could be traced to its involvement (https://www.cisco.com/c/dam/global/en _ in/assets/pdfs/cisco _ 2014 _ asr.pdf). Within two more years, because of all the continuing security problems with Java, all major browser vendors pulled support.

Choices Creep

We humans love our choices. Just look at all the choices we have for a coffee at Starbucks. If we have something and are able to keep it limited to that exact design, it's easier to troubleshoot, secure, and update. But if that thing evolves to a bunch of other different things, it becomes harder to do all of that.

For example, Linux was created in 1991. It was quickly adopted by millions of people, and many security experts laud it for its stronger (than Microsoft Windows) cybersecurity. But different people wanted different features and components for Linux, and Linux allowed anyone to legally change it. So, today, we have thousands of different versions of Linux (called *distributions* or *distros*). And securing all of them is way harder. It's hard to get a program that should work on Linux to work on the Linux distribution you are using. Updating, troubleshooting, and resolving an issue depends on which distro you have. What is secure on one distro may not be secure on another, and so on.

Another common example is installing the same hospital information system (e.g., Epic, Cerner, etc.) at a healthcare facility. Each hospital could take the same information system and install it the exact same way. If every hospital using that system did so, it would make the system easier to install, easier to update, and easier to secure. It would be cheaper. But every hospital, after spending a lot of money on the system, wants to customize the system to better fit their needs. So, the same hospital information system is super customized, takes longer to install, is more expensive, and is much harder to upgrade and secure. Usually, it takes expensive teams of consultants to install a hospital system that otherwise could be installed faster and cheaper as-is.

This can be applied to many software and computer systems. We humans like our choices and customizations. This leads to complexity, and we already know that complexity leads to insecurity. But any Internet security solution must be designed to allow choices. It won't go far if you don't allow choices and customizations.

Even Very Secure Things Get Hacked

Anything — anything — can be hacked. But some things are more resilient than others. OpenBSD (https://www.openbsd.org/) and Qubes OS (https://www.qubes-os.org/) are considered the most secure, publicly accessible operating systems on the planet (more on Qubes OS in this book later). Anything ever coded by Dr. Daniel J. Bernstein (https://cr.yp.to/djb.html) is considered some of the most unhackable code on the planet.

Still, all of these projects have had hackable vulnerabilities. Not a lot of them, but some. Even when the very best try to make the most secure things we can invent, these things have bugs. Again, we don't need perfection. Any Internet security system that comes close to what these organizations and people have proved they could create (i.e., significantly more secure code) is going to be a major step in the right direction.

Good People and Bad Intentions

Any Internet security solution will be under full-time attack by lots of very ill-intentioned people. Some will be very smart, and even more will be unrelentingly persistent. Persistence pays off the same as being very smart. Whatever system you design will have to withstand intentional, persistent attacks by bad people.

Any system you design will also have to withstand attack from good people (i.e., penetration testers), who are just trying to find vulnerabilities before the bad people do. You will also have good people without bad intentions, just trying to do their job faster or easier, who will work around the solution the best they can. At times, it will seem as if the entire world is trying to break your solution.

Sometimes, the security bypass can be unintentional. For example, when push-based MFA came out, I thought it was a terrific solution. This is type of MFA where the user gets a message on their phone or device asking them if they are really trying to log in at this moment. The user usually gets some other information such as what physical location the logon is being made from, what operating system is being used, browser being used, etc. The user is given a chance to select "Yes" to allow that logon, or "No" to deny that logon.

What designers didn't know is that about 30% of users will approve a logon that they did not initiate. Designers thought everyone would innately know to select "No" and deny a logon someone else was doing using their identity and report the rogue login attempt to the security team or help desk, but it turns out about a third of people do not. Some people will approve every rogue login prompt even when they have been warned over and over again not to. People are quirky, frustrating animals at times.

One of my favorite all-time quotes is from Dr. Cormac Herley of Microsoft Research. He said, "You might have a model of how you think 2 billion users will behave, but 2 billion users will respond the way they are going to respond regardless of your model. You can hope that it happens the same way, but you have to measure what happens to see if there is any resemblance to what you said would happen in your model. And if your model is wrong, change it."

Transparency

Good security is usually transparent security. Good security is transparently designed, clearly communicated, and open to debate. For example, most of our cryptographic standards are the result of public contests with clear requirements where anyone can submit their algorithm for consideration. Anyone who wants to evaluate it does. Through the crucible of tough analysis and critique, a winner is chosen. Part of the strength of the cryptography algorithm is its consistent transparency during the process and after. In fact, in the cryptography world, any algorithm that is not willing to be publicly revealed for analysis is one most people won't trust.

> **note** This is not to say that there isn't value in security through obscurity for some types of computer security, but it isn't the primary or only factor you want to use to secure something. But for cryptography, it is never welcomed.

Whatever Internet security solution anyone comes up with, its ideology, protocols, mechanisms, etc., it must be openly documented, clearly communicated, and allow open debate. The strength of the solution lies in revealing it, not hiding it. With that said, transparency around cybersecurity is not guaranteed, and many entities seem to thrive on hiding things. Just try to get most hacked companies to admit all the details of what happened when they got hacked. Most of us are on a need-to-know basis, and apparently, we don't need to know much. Heck, there are multiple laws that require hacked companies to reveal to their impacted customers when they get hacked, and most companies still struggle follow the law. The more transparency, the better, but it can be a challenge to get it.

These are just a few of the technical challenges any Internet security solution will face, and they are the easiest of the challenges.

Strategic Challenges

Strategic challenges are larger, guiding challenges to any Internet security solution.

Resistance to Unexpected Change

If there is something core to the human experience, it is that we don't like change, unless we are the ones initiating the change. We change all the time, but rarely do we do so quickly and voluntarily, when the change is unexpected, even when the potential outcome might be substantially better. I rarely meet a person who is excited about getting upgraded to the newest operating system or application version. They are just happy with what they got. They don't want to learn anything new. We humans are just plain resistant to most changes. Not all, but most. Any new Internet security solution is going to have to keep that in mind. It's even better if all the technical changes are hidden and the new thing appears to work just like the old thing.

Lack of Prioritization

There are a lot of broken things to fix. We have to figure out what they are and prioritize which of them is likely to have the best bang for the buck. For example, social engineering and vulnerabilities are responsible for 90%–99% of all successful hacker attacks. Whatever solution we come up with, we have to make sure we are tackling those issues first and best. It's harder than it sounds. In fact, almost no organization or cybersecurity person does it. It's easy to get distracted. It's easy to get ordered by a superior to focus on something else, even though it is less of a priority in reducing cybersecurity risk. Always keep prioritization in mind when developing a solution.

Simply Influencing Enough People

You can have the best, perfect idea for solving the Internet security crisis and never get it seen by the right people for it to be implemented. How do you and your good idea influence enough organizations, groups, and people actually to get a solution implemented?

Traditionally, it used to be that you would submit your great Internet security idea to the Internet Engineering Task Force (https://www.ietf.org/) as a Request for Comments (RFC). If it were a good idea supported by a growing number of the members of the IETF, it would progress along through several versions and eventually become an official Internet standard. Most of the Internet security standards you know today (e.g., DNSSEC, IPSEC, HTTPS, TLS, etc.) went that route. But today, this route seems to take too long, and too many good security standards have languished without ever being implemented. For example, the great DMARC standard, which has been a de facto global anti-phishing standard for more than half a decade now, still hasn't been approved by the IETF even though it was submitted 10 years ago. It's still slowly going through the IETF standards process, and members are trying to make changes to it, which will delay its release even longer.

Many people are turning to the newer World Wide Web Consortium, or W3C (https://www.w3.org/), which is the de facto standards-making body for everything web-related. It's not perfect, but it's done a tremendous job in shaping and securing the web. The W3C seems faster than the IETF, has more support and more activity, and is delivering more new things.

Conventional thinking these days is that in order to get a new security standard passed and implemented, you have to have a huge organization, like Google or Microsoft, support it first. And certainly, even huge support isn't enough to push a good idea over the line (just ask Bill Gates and Microsoft about their failed Sender ID effort). But if a huge company loves your idea, they can help push it faster through the IETF or W3C or simply just decide to push it single-handedly, others be damned. Eight-hundred-pound gorillas can act like 800-pound gorillas. We will talk more about this in Chapter 12.

> **note** In my humble opinion, this is the hardest part of solving the Internet's security problem. I've been writing about how to fix the Internet for decades. I've written whitepapers. I've written dozens, if not hundreds, of public articles on it. I've now written this book. And doesn't translate into getting a good idea heard by the right people, much less getting it implemented across the world.

I liken it to all the world's very talented musicians struggling in near obscurity. I can go into almost any bar in the world and see a talented guitar-playing singer who could be famous if they got the right break. They've been playing in bars for years, singing and writing songs, and they just haven't met or influenced the right people to make it to that next level.

How you influence the right people to get your idea not only heard but implemented is an epic struggle. But people do it. It happens.

Some Very Large Groups Possibly Don't Want to Fix Internet Security

You have to face the fact that some large groups of people, often with competing priorities, don't want to fix the Internet. They like it as it is. You have privacy extremists who don't want anyone to be able to identify anyone better. There are real reasons for strong privacy (e.g., political protests, health conditions, protection from a dangerous ex-spouse, etc.).

There are thousands of organizations that make a living breaking into people's devices. There are a million companies and organizations that make good money and give well-paying jobs to people by letting the Internet struggle along as is. If we truly "fixed" Internet security, there could potentially be millions of people put out of work (at least in their current careers).

Government and law enforcement groups use the lack of good Internet security to their advantage. They are able to take advantage of remaining anonymous to eavesdrop and spy on their targets. If we truly fix Internet security, we make it harder for all groups to spy on other people. Many people don't think we should be making it harder for the "good guys" to catch criminals, child molesters, murderers, rapists, and terrorists. And that's a very valid point. Better securing the Internet could actually cause more harm. It's something we have to consider and grapple with.

Tragedy of the Commons

Many years ago, probably 15 or so, I first presented my "fix the Internet" idea to Bill Gates in one of Microsoft's annual "Think Week" events for the first time. Think Week is a period of time set aside each year at Microsoft when any employee could introduce any idea in whitepaper form and have it heard and evaluated by someone. I submitted some early version of my *Fix the Internet* whitepaper. I had no idea that my idea would be reviewed directly by Bill Gates, but it was. And he hated it, calling my idea "So bad it would hurt people." Ouch!

But I persisted. I knew Bill Gates wasn't a computer security expert and he just didn't understand the subject well enough. I knew I was right, and he was wrong. A year or two later, completely independent of my original Think Week paper, a well-liked and popular SVP at Microsoft submitted his idea on how better to secure the Internet as a major forward-looking Microsoft initiative. It was announced to great fanfare and made the media. Even Bill Gates was promoting it. And surprisingly, about 90% of that guy's ideas matched the ideas in my earlier paper. I approached the SVP and asked why I hadn't been given any credit. He said he didn't know about my paper, but after he reviewed my earlier paper, he admitted that there were many similarities.

With that, I emailed Bill Gates and congratulated myself on how I had out-thought one of his most beloved SVPs by a year or two. I told Bill Gates that he needed to stop what he was doing and hire me to fix the Internet. I'm not making this up. Surprisingly, Bill Gates called me a few days later and told me that was exactly what he wanted to do. He wanted me to come to work directly for him. Bill Gates then put me in contact with one of his personal assistants.

The assistant asked me what job I wanted at Microsoft. I said, "I want to fix the Internet." He replied, "We don't have a product called the Internet. Pick a product we develop." I said, "No, I want to be paid to fix the Internet." He asked me how much I thought it might cost, and I said at least $50 million, a few hundred people, a building, and other resources." I was very cocky at this time— remember, I had outthought both Bill Gates and a beloved SVP.

I remember the assistant saying they didn't even just give Ray Ozzie, who was leading Microsoft at the time, $50 million without having something they could sell and make a profit on. He said no company is going to give you $50 million to fix the Internet. Then using an example, he explained to me the Tragedy of the Commons parable. Years ago, there were tens of millions of acres of public land where anyone's cattle could roam, eat grass, and grow fat, essentially for free. It was of great benefit to the cattlemen who raised their cattle there. But so many cattlemen put so many of their cattle on the commons that the cattle ate all the available grass until the whole system failed — a tragedy of the commons. Humans are often more motivated by their own self-interests than in helping the common good. Adam Smith's "invisible guiding hand" is the same general idea.

The assistant said, "No one is going to spend $50 million to fix the commons [in this case, securing the Internet]. Roger, if you want to get the Internet fixed, you have to convince every company you need money from that it is in their own self-interests to spend that $50 million, and by spending that $50 million, they will earn many multiples back and out-compete every other company by doing it." He said, "They aren't going to spend $50 million out of their kind-heartedness just to fix the Internet."

I replied, "That's sad!"

He then told me that he would give me the $50 million I needed to fix the Internet, all the people I needed, the building, and get me in contact with a businessperson at Microsoft who would make it happen. But he had one condition: I had to give up my salary for as long as it took me to pull off my vision, but if and when I did pull off my vision, and he had faith I would, I would be a very wealthy man and never have to worry about money again.

This was fantastic to hear, but then I realized that I had four kids in school, three of them about to enter college. I had a big house, mortgage, and cars to pay off. I couldn't go without any salary for years. I had too many things for which I desperately needed the money. So, I declined his offer.

I well remember his reply: "So, even you, the person that is most passionate about fixing the Internet, won't do for the common good!"

He had me. I was thumbing my nose up at the big conglomerate companies that wouldn't spend $50 million of their own money to fix the Internet, and here I was in the exact same boat. I was no better.

That day, I learned about the tragedy of the commons and its role in combating a more secure Internet. It's a good parable to remember because it's absolutely true. Rarely will you get the world to come together in some big *kumbaya* moment to help some global good. Nope, you are far more likely to be successful if you convince all the major involved players that it is to their personal benefit, to their competitiveness against other competitors, to do something. If you're going to fix the Internet, you better make many big companies participating in a common goods solution think they can make more money by doing so versus their competitors, or you'll never get their support. I may not have liked the lesson, but it's how the world works.

Any proposed solution must overcome all these strategic challenges.

Political Challenges

Finally, we get to the most challenging part of any global Internet security solution...the involved citizens, politicians, and nation-states. Citizens don't trust their government. The government doesn't trust its citizens. Nations don't trust other nations. Everyone is interested in mostly what benefits them the most.

The world is full of many different types of people and governments. Some governments are more liberal than others. Some citizens trust their government more than others. Some cultures readily give up personal freedoms and privacy in exchange for supposed additional safety and stability. Some governments give more default privacy to their citizens. Other governments don't.

In a world where it's tough to get the people in your house to agree on the same thing, it's really hard to do so across the world. How do you get very different people and cultures, who largely distrust each other, to trust and cooperate enough that you can better secure the Internet?

Costs, How to Fund?

There is no doubt that some of the solutions I propose in this book will require substantial resources: equipment, environmental services, Internet service, dollars, and people. Part of me wants to believe that better Internet security will be part of some global community collective where lots of people volunteer their time and resources. But more than likely, a more secure Internet is going to take new organizations and services of a more professional, full-time nature.

Who funds that? How is it funded? My best guess is that it's either funded as part of what the government already does, just as it already funds the Domain Naming Service (DNS) and other Internet-related services, or a very small fee gets added to everyone's Internet bill. In the United States and most other nations, either type of funding would require passing a new law. And that's pretty hard to get done without a lot of expensive lobbying, hobnobbing, and influencing. I think it's more likely that we will have a devastating tipping point event that forces us to use better Internet security, but either way, it likely has to be funded. More on this in Chapter 11.

Chapter Summary

If you look at all the technical, strategic, and political challenges that I've covered in this chapter, they provide many of the reasons why a great Internet security solution hasn't already won out. It's hard to do. It's challenging. It's political. It may be impossible without a tipping point event.

Key concepts of this chapter are:

- Challenges to a significantly more secure Internet
- Technical challenges
- Strategic challenges
- Political challenges

Part II covers how to make the Internet significantly more secure. Chapters 5–12 will reveal the general theory of my solution, which I believe can overcome all the challenges presented in this chapter.

The Technology Solution

The Solution

"The world in which you seek to undo the mistakes that you made is different from the world where the mistakes were made."

– Cormac McCarthy

Cybercrime has definitely changed (e.g., fake SMS messages, AI-enabled deepfake videos, etc.) since I started following it in 1987, although the main underlying reason it's been so pervasive in our online world hasn't changed at all since then. In Chapter 3, I revealed the main underlying reason why Internet cybercrime is so rampant: It is hard to identify, stop, and arrest online crooks. They can operate and commit their crimes over and over with near impunity. It's been this way for decades since the beginning of the Internet.

Chapter 5 reveals my solution to that underlying problem. It will be a general theory discussion of the solution followed by the first of two threat modeling exercises. The first one, in this chapter, will threat model the theory of both the problem with a supposed perfect solution. A second, more detailed threat model examining the various involved technologies is in Chapter 13.

But for now, here's my solution to the problem of rampant Internet crime.

Proposed Solution Theory

Internet crime is abundant because online criminals are almost never stopped, arrested, or punished. It is very low risk with huge upside profit potential.

Using upstream thinking and asking why this is true, I get the answer that it ultimately has to do with a lack of verifiable, trusted identity. We cannot stop or arrest Internet criminals because we cannot readily identify them when they are committing crimes. We cannot identify them because it's too easy for a criminal to claim to be anyone else or any other entity, and potential victims have no way to easily verify one way or another. Internet criminals love that we can't easily identify them. We need to change this pervasive condition.

Require Verified Trusted Identity

If we could always readily identify who we were communicating with over the Internet, we could use that verified identity to better determine if we should be communicating with them, following their directions, or doing business with them. If we could better identify Internet criminals, we could stop them, we could arrest them, and we could decrease the number of them.

To better identify cybercriminals, we need a better way to reliably identify anyone we are actively communicating with on the Internet. It takes a verified identity system that we can all trust along with an overall higher trust ecosystem. The main solution to Internet crime:

Allow anyone to validate anyone else's true identity when they are getting ready to interact along with other supporting components of trust.

If we could always accurately identify people and entities on the Internet to their true identities when we wanted, we could decide if we want to connect, communicate, or do business with them.

Note: It's crucial that people only require or provide a verified identity when they want or agree. It isn't required for all connections and either side can decide whether to participate.

Real ID

If someone's online identity (ID) can be tied to their real-world identity, it is known as *Real ID* in identification circles. There is also a legal standard for real-world IDs in the United States and other countries known as REAL ID (https://www.dhs.gov/real-id). That isn't what we are discussing here, although the concept is very similar. Both types of Real ID want to have IDs that are reliably trackable to the real human individual. The legal definition of Real ID depends on the country or legal jurisdiction you are in, but as I use the term Real ID throughout the rest of this book, it simply means being able to verify an online ID to a person's true identity (however that is done and defined).

High-Trust Ecosystem

A Real ID alone won't solve the problem of Internet crime, but it, along with creating a comprehensive supporting high-trust ecosystem that involves other trusted components (discussed in this book), is the best way. Creating and using reliable, trustworthy user IDs actually requires a broader supporting high-trust ecosystem. A supposedly reliable user ID can't be considered reliable if the rest of the ecosystem is untrustworthy.

As a real-world example for comparison, suppose I get a travel passport. A passport requires that I submit strong proof of my real identity and undergo strong verification before it is issued. But suppose the postal system that sends the passport to me after it has been issued can't be trusted, and it's easy for criminals to get my passport sent to them instead. Or suppose that the systems that read and verify passports at the airport are easy to compromise, or the immigration guards can be easily bribed, and anyone who can use my passport at immigration control even when they don't look anything like me. A reliable ID requires that all the other involved supporting systems are also reliable and trusted by participants. The reliable ID is a necessary start, but not the only step.

But if I had to choose one single thing that would best improve the Internet, it would be the pervasive availability of a Real ID when someone or something (e.g., site, service, etc.) requires it.

With a verifiable trusted identity and a high-trust ecosystem, it would be significantly harder for Internet criminals to fraudulently pretend to be other people and entities and to trick people into doing harmful things. It would be significantly harder for a bad person or entity to send a bad packet to cause a buffer overflow or denial of service attack. It would be harder for a criminal to break into a server or listen in on protected communications. In general, it would be significantly harder for online criminals to cause harm.

Of course, most Internet criminals and entities wouldn't voluntarily agree to identify themselves. This is one of the intended favorable outcomes: to incentivize criminals use the Internet less to commit crimes. Criminals would fight, resist, hack, and bypass Real IDs the best they could. But if we could create a high-trust, reliable ecosystem with Real IDs and reliably enforce it, it would be harder for criminals to commit crimes. If we did a really good job, it would significantly diminish many forms of Internet crime. That's what this book is all about.

Not everyone would be forced to use a Real ID in every transaction and session. Only when required. But this solution would work only if someone requested that the other side provide their Real ID to continue communicating that they did so, or further communications would be stopped (or undergo additional deeper inspection). If the other party trying to connect to us doesn't want to give us their true identity (there are many valid scenarios for this) along with a minimum guaranteed level of trust, we can decide if it's worth the risk of continuing to communicate with them at all or perhaps continue to communicate with them but take additional precautions because of the increased risk.

Simple Examples

I'm running a web server that offers a web page and service that people with Real ID can use to interact. When someone attempts to connect to the web server, that web server could check to see if the incoming connection is attached to Real ID, and if not, request the incoming user to upgrade/switch their identity to Real ID to be able to use the services. If the user switches to Real ID, they can continue to communicate with the web server and use the services. If they don't, the communication attempt is ended by the web server.

Or suppose I'm running a web server that offers up a web page that anyone can connect to see the commercial service I'm offering. Anyone can connect to that web server anonymously, but if they decide to pay money to use the service, the web server can then tell the user that they need to use a Real ID to continue. Or suppose I'm running a TFTP (Trivial File Transfer Protocol) server on my personal computer where other people can upload files. I could tell my TFTP server to require Real ID before people could connect to it.

Transitive Trust and Examples

Many/most connections we attempt are to other people or entity devices. Sometimes, our connections are to ourselves, our local applications, or our own services running on our own local device (i.e., 127.0.0.1), but many/most of our connections are to other remote devices belonging to another person or an intermediate service.

Even when we are trying to communicate with a specific person, most of our connections are not directly to the other person or their device. Instead, we connect to an intermediate site/service/session/application, which connects to that person on our behalf (e.g., WhatsApp) or to which that person connects when they use it, which can be at different times than us (e.g., Facebook). Most of connections to other people aren't point-to-point, directly to them and their devices. More often, we interface with sites/services/sessions/applications that interface with other people, where we eventually see and interact with the content they placed.

The verification and use of a Real ID would need to be transitive, meaning if A trusts B, and I trust A, then I also trust B. In a high-trust Real ID ecosystem, any site/service/session/application I'm using must understand and use Real IDs, and I must trust the intermediate site/service/session/application to reliably verify and enforce the Real IDs of the other person on my behalf (if I so choose).

Here are some simple examples of transitive trust:

I belong to an email service for my personal email. I require that all emails sent to me be sent by people using their Real ID. The email service knows my identity preference and enforces it on all emails sent to me. I know when opening an email in my email client that every email I receive has been Real ID-verified. I also know that there could have been other people attempting to send emails to my email address that could not because they decided not to participate with their Real ID. Alternatively, I could get a list of related failed connections and decide if there are any I want to read and communicate with even though they did not want to provide their Real ID.

Or I log on to Facebook. I see a message from my aunt saying she needs money for an emergency. If I had previously instructed Facebook to require Real ID for all Facebook content sent my way, I could reasonably assume that my real aunt sent the message. Yes, my aunt's Facebook account and Real ID could have been taken over by a hacker (super common today), but the high-trust ecosystem that goes along with Real ID will make that a lot harder for the hacker to accomplish in the future.

Or suppose I'm connecting to a legitimate website I connect to all the time. But this time, when I connected, I got a message supposedly from Adobe telling me it was time for me to update my Adobe Acrobat client. This is a common ploy by social engineers who compromise legitimate websites and send fake upgrade messages that are then used to install malware. If I require Real ID by default for all incoming connections, if I get an onscreen message claiming to be from Adobe and it is verified as coming from Adobe using its Real ID, then I can trust the message, click on the included link, and upgrade my client. If the message did not originate from a Real ID, the message would be blocked and never end up on my screen for me to interface with.

In a high-trust ecosystem using Real IDs, transitive trust is essential. We need to trust the sites and services working on our behalf to be reliable participants. Our own connection to the site/service/session/application involves our own Real ID as we log on. The site/service/session/application does the same thing to all participants who use the same site/service/session/application. So, when I use the site/service/session/application and see shared content from other participants, I can trust that the other participants are who they say they are. If I can't trust the intermediate service to correctly verify the other participants, the whole high-trust ecosystem breaks down.

To accomplish a high-trust ecosystem, we need a new dedicated local service running on each participating client that connects to a centralized global service that is dedicated to reporting and verifying trust across various components of the high-trust ecosystem. The trust components of a higher-trust ecosystem include safe and trusted devices, trusted OS, trusted identities, trusted applications, trusted actions, and trusted networks. If I get all of that trust (or really my device and applications on my behalf)...then the person or entity whom

I'm interacting with is very likely to be the person or entity I think I'm dealing with, and suddenly Internet crime becomes much harder to do.

I know this might sound like a wishful pipe dream, but we already have most of the technology to accomplish this; we just need it to be more pervasive. And yes, we do have to extend a few technologies and invent a few new things. But none of it is impossibly hard. The biggest challenges will certainly not be technological.

With a better, more pervasive, trusted identity and a high-trust ecosystem, Internet criminals will be less able to commit Internet crimes. People, devices, and entities involved in Internet crime will be quickly identified and filtered out. People and entities not wanting to identify themselves will not be able to connect to people who want a higher level of assured identity and trust to interact.

This solution isn't coming out of nowhere. It already works in the real world.

How We Stopped Bank Robberies in the Real World

Since the beginning of banking, banks have been robbed. As infamous bank robber Willie Sutton, when asked why he robbed banks, supposedly said (but apparently did not really say), "That's where the money is." The first bank robbery to make the national news in the United States was committed in 1792 (https://www.saturdayeveningpost.com/2013/03/first-bank-robbery-in-united-states).

From there, especially in the Wild Wild West era (1865 to 1895) and into the Roaring Twenties (1920s) in U.S. territories, counties, and cities, robbing banks became a popular crime. If you needed some money and you were a ne'er-do-well, you considered robbing a bank. Some bank robbers, like John Dillinger, Baby Face Nelson, and Bonnie & Clyde, even became beloved national celebrities.

Back then, punishment for bank robberies was fairly light, criminals had more firepower than the police, banks kept around lots of cash, and all the bad guys had to do to get away during a police chase was cross county or state lines. Back then, most law enforcement agencies had a rigid requirement that if the criminal crossed the county or state lines, only the law enforcement in the new jurisdiction could chase the criminal. Most police departments did not have car radios that communicated with their neighboring districts. Because of this, most bank robberies happened very near county or state lines.

One of the biggest factors that led to bank robberies and more bank robberies is that most of the criminals could not be identified, caught, or arrested. Criminals could rob banks over and over again and get away with it. Unless you were a big-time celebrity bank robber, you were not likely to be identified. You wouldn't be identified from your past bank robberies, and you wouldn't be identified as you walked in to rob the next bank. You could rob a bank and then walk up to the next one and rob again. You could rob a bank and be unlikely to be identified, caught, arrested, or punished. Sound familiar?

Success bred copycats. Bank robberies became so frequent and damaging that eventually, bank and police tactics changed, making it harder for bank robbers to be successful and harder for them to get away. Hopefully, our Internet cybercrime solution will duplicate what happened to real-world bank robbers and, not surprisingly, for similar reasons.

Eventually, both banks and law enforcement got smarter. Banks started carrying less cash on hand, putting most of their case into time-delayed, heavy, metal-doored vaults. Bank tellers only had as much cash as they normally needed to conduct their shift's transactions. Tellers started putting dye packs in the money and had access to silent alarm systems to summon the police. Bank tellers were better protected with thick walls, bullet-proof glass, and smaller, protective transaction cubby holes. Banks started hiring armed guards. Automatic machine guns were outlawed for most people, making them much harder to get. Police got car radios that worked with nearby jurisdictions, and law enforcement was allowed to cross county and state jurisdiction lines during a chase. All of this made robbing banks less profitable.

Another big key defense improvement was the increasing use of photo and video cameras within banks. This resulted in better, complete images of the criminals than the past eyewitness testimony and pencil sketches of the past. People viewing the pictures and video could often immediately tell who it was, even if they were wearing a mask. Their clothing and hats gave them away. Bank robbers who robbed multiple banks could be identified as such. Then, when that robber was arrested, they were not only arrested for robbing the current bank where they were caught but also for all the other past ones where they could be reliably identified. It changed the game. Robbing banks became a higher risk.

Fairly quickly, a higher percentage of bank robbers were caught, identified, arrested, and prosecuted. Many were shot and killed. The ones arrested got longer and longer prison sentences. Most petty criminals no longer saw bank robbing as something worth the risk. Who wanted to get arrested and identified for the rest of their lives as a bank robber? After decades of ever-increasing bank robberies, within a few short years, the era of easy and profitable bank robberies ended.

Today, bank robbery is harder than ever. Most bank and credit union branches have never been robbed. It's getting rarer all the time. Most banks have a ton of surveillance cameras. There are likely hundreds of cameras recording a criminal going to and from the bank. They and the car they are using are likely to be videoed many times. The criminal's car's GPS records their route. Traffic cameras are recording their license plate to and from the scene. The criminal's cell phones have to be switched off, or its innate default tracking abilities can be used by police to tie the criminal to the crime. It's never been harder to successfully rob a real-world bank and get away with it.

A big part of the overall defense that works is that we are very likely to catch and identify bank robbers. Because we can figure out who they are, we are able to arrest them. Because we arrest them, we can stop and punish them. Because we punish them, often by jailing, they cannot physically rob more banks, at least during their incarceration. Most people don't want to be caught and arrested for robbing banks. Those who take the risk are eventually arrested and pulled out of the risk pool. There are no old active bank robbers, as the popular saying goes. There are old bank robbers, but they, too, get caught and put in jail. Over time, this means fewer robbers and fewer bank robberies.

That's what we need to duplicate on the Internet. It starts with a high-trust ecosystem and pervasive trusted identity.

Threat Modeling the Problem Theory and General Solution

Threat modeling is the process by which potential threats to and weaknesses of a defined scenario can be identified, evaluated, prioritized, and mitigated. All cybersecurity scenarios and defensive solutions should be threat-modeled. When designing a new product or defense, threat modeling should occur during the early design phase before the product or defense is created.

The rest of Chapter 5 will threat model the general theory of the proposed problem scenario and solution as if they existed in a perfect world. A more detailed threat model will be performed in Chapter 13 after the technological details of my defense have been revealed.

There are many ways to do threat modeling, but the best involve some sort of defined process. You can start out just brainstorming ideas and putting threats on a page, but it helps to be more inclusive by following a defined process, which, if followed, can help you find more threats and weaknesses. I've tried threat modeling many times, both ways. I've tried just to brainstorm all the ways a particular defense can be circumvented without using a defined process. At the end of that brainstorming session, I've always felt like I've thought about everything I need to be worried about. But then, whenever I followed brainstorming with a formal threat model and process, I always came up with more threats that I would have missed by brainstorming alone.

Note: The best book on threat modeling I've read is Adam Shostack's *Threat Modeling: Designing for Security* (https://www.amazon.com/Threat-Model ing-Designing-Adam-Shostack/dp/1118809998).

STRIDE Threat Modeling

I've chosen to use the STRIDE threat model created by Praerit Garg and my personal friend, Loren Kohnfelder, which was developed for Microsoft decades ago. STRIDE is a mnemonic for six categories of cyber security threats that it covers. The threats are:

- **S**poofing
- **T**ampering
- **R**epudiation
- **I**nformation disclosure
- **D**enial of service
- **E**levation of privilege

You can read more about STRIDE here: `https://en.wikipedia.org/wiki/ST RIDE _ model`.

STRIDE loosely maps to my 14 initial root access causes of hacking discussed in Chapter 2, as shown in Table 5-1.

It's not a neat, one-on-one comparison. Many of my 14 initial root access categories don't fit in a single STRIDE category, such as Insider Attack and

Table 5-1: Mapping STRIDE to 14 Initial Root Access Causes of Hacking

STRIDE TAXONOMY	INITIAL ROOT ACCESS CAUSES TAXONOMY
Spoofing	Social Engineering, (Technical) Impersonation/Authentication Attacks, Insider Attacks
Tampering	Software and Firmware Vulnerabilities, Intentionally Malicious Programs/Instructions/Scripting, Data Malformation, Network Traffic Malformation, Third-Party Reliance Issues (supply chain/vendor/partner/etc.), Insider Attacks
Repudiation	(Technical) Impersonation/Authentication Attacks, Insider Attacks
Information disclosure	Eavesdropping/MitM, Side Channel Attacks, Information Leaks, Third-Party Reliance Issues (supply chain/vendor/partner/etc.), Insider Attacks, Brute Force/Computational, Human Error/Misconfiguration
Denial of service	Physical Attacks, Insider Attacks
Elevation of privilege	Software and Firmware Vulnerabilities, Intentionally Malicious Programs/Instructions/Scripting, Data Malformation, Insider Attacks

Impersonation. Plus, the standard definition of repudiation, where someone can prove they didn't say or do something, that is in the STRIDE model, isn't in my 14 initial root access causes (because repudiation is not how someone breaks into something). Repudiation is a defense when someone accuses you of something.

You don't need to use STRIDE to do your threat modeling. I've used many different threat models over the last 30 years. But if you're developing a project or creating a security defense, you should be threat modeling it, and if you threat model, you should be using a formal threat model of some type.

Threat Modeling the Solution

Now, onto threat modeling the Internet crime solution. Again, this will just be a preliminary threat model of the general theory of the solution to see if it is capable of significantly diminishing Internet cybercrime. Chapter 13 will cover the involved technologies with a more detailed threat model.

For now, we are ignoring how we will technically accomplish the solution or even the question of what we are attempting could ever be done. Let's assume that I (or anyone else) can come up with a technical solution that absolutely identifies everyone to their true, verified identity or entity when they try to connect to us online if we choose for that verification level. Let's assume we are able to create a high-trust ecosystem that works across devices, OSs, identities, applications, actions, and networks. And this could be done, perfectly or nearly perfectly, would it significantly diminish Internet crime?

Would any of the attack types listed, STRIDE or my Initial Root Access Causes, not be mitigated by the pervasive near-perfect identity and high-trust ecosystem?

To summarize the results of my own threat modeling exercise, if we had a pervasive near-perfect identity and high-trust ecosystem, the following attack methods and how they might be mitigated (in theory) are shown in Table 5-2 below.

Substantially Mitigated means the attack method would be perfectly (100%) defeated or substantially be mitigated to 1/20th (95%) or less of its current occurrence/damage in the near-perfect solution world. *Partially Mitigated* means the attack method would be significantly mitigated down from its current levels, but not to 1/20th (95%) or below. It could also mean that some forms of the referenced attack category are substantially mitigated while others are not. *Not Mitigated* means the attack type is not even reduced to 19/20ths (5%) of what its former levels were.

Most of the mitigations provided by a verified trusted identity and high-trust ecosystem solution result from attackers not wanting to be identified and finding it hard to circumvent the type of attack they are attempting. Just like with real-world bank robbers, identifying Internet criminals and stopping them

Table 5-2: Summary of Threat Modeling a Nearly Perfect Identity Solution Against Various Attack Types

ATTACK TYPE	SUBSTANTIALLY MITIGATED	PARTIALLY MITIGATED	NOT MITIGATED
Spoofing, Social Engineering (70–90% of attacks)	X		
Software and Firmware Vulnerability Exploitation (33% of today's attacks)		X	
Insider Attacks		X	
(Technical) Impersonation/ Authentication Attacks		X	
Elevation of Privilege Attacks		X	
Intentionally Malicious Programs/ Instructions/Scripting	X		
Tampering	X		
Data Malformation	X		
Network Traffic Malformation	X		
Repudiation	X		
Information Leaks		X	
Eavesdropping/MitM	X		
Denial of Service Attacks	X		
Brute Force/Computational Attacks		X	
Human Error/Misconfigurations			X
Third-Party Reliance Issue (supply chain/vendor/partner/etc.)		X	
Side Channel Attacks			X
Physical Attacks			X
Island Hopping		X	

and/or punishing them should result in fewer attackers and a natural filtering out of Internet criminal activity. With a few exceptions (i.e., human error/mistakes, physical attacks, and side channel attacks), better identifying attackers helps secure the overall ecosystem.

I'll cover each attack method and my threat model thinking in more detail next.

Spoofing, Social Engineering

Substantially Mitigated. As previously covered, social engineering is currently involved in 70–90% of all attacks. If high-trust ecosystem were pervasive, it would be much harder for criminals to social engineer people since it almost always requires that an attacker pretend to be another more trusted person or entity to fool more victims into following the requested harmful actions. A near-perfect identity service would defeat a significant portion of these types of attacks. This would be reason alone to implement the suggested solution.

I will put two significant caveats on this attack solution type. Today's scammers often use a look-alike identity to fool people into believing they are dealing with someone or some entity they really aren't. For example, they can create an identity with the name Microsoft Solution Services, which some potential victims might not fully appreciate has nothing to do with the long-time Fortune 5 company, Microsoft Corporation, headquartered in Redmond, WA.

And with some scams, the scammer's name or entity identity really doesn't matter. For example, romance scams might still work because the fraudulent lothario could claim to be anyone, including their real selves, but lie about their success, looks, or availability. In another example, a rogue but real entity could claim to be selling some fantastic product that really isn't as good as advertised. For example, (fictitious) India Channelbox Inc. could claim to be selling a device that would let any streamer download any streaming service for free. It would be social engineering from a real entity in order to sell something that does not work as advertised. Very common.

To offset these types of threats, we would need a service where a criminal or rogue identity could be reported, confirmed, and quickly broadcasted to anyone wanting to check its reputation. The attacker couldn't use a real identity with rogue intentions for long before it got marked and known as malicious. This part of the solution will be covered in Chapter 11. But a high-trust ecosystem alone doesn't solve these two subcategories of attack. Still, I would guess that more than 95% of social engineering attacks would be put down by the solution.

Software and Firmware Vulnerability Exploitation

Partially Mitigated. Exploitation of software and firmware vulnerabilities is involved in 33% of today's successful attacks. In most cases, these exploitations occur from rogue identities or entities and would be blocked by a near-perfect high-trust system. However, these exploitations could come from verified identities or be used against the near-perfect high-trust ecosystem itself. There are likely to be vulnerabilities in any near-perfect high-trust ecosystem that will be used against the system and participants until they can be fixed. However, the vast majority of exploitations should be able to be blocked. I would guess that more than 90% of these attacks would be put down by a near-perfect high-trust ecosystem on systems that could require near-perfect identity to connect.

> **note** It is still possible for an unintended vulnerability to be unintentionally triggered by a legitimate entity and cause harm. The July 2024 Crowdstrike software update that took a large percentage of its customers down, significantly impacting entire industries, is the best example of this sort of problem.

Insider Attacks

Partially Mitigated. At first glance, it might seem like a near-perfect high-trust system would have no impact on an insider attack. In fact, insider attackers are often using their own identity with their allowed permission and privileges to cause harm. But a large percentage of insiders, hoping to avoid discipline, firing, or even arrest, might not carry out their malicious plans if they thought their actions might be traced to their identities. "Helps keep honest people honest."

Some insiders don't care if they get discovered. It might even be part of their wish so that their intense anger can be known. They could even use another coworker's identity to do bad things. But a near-perfect high-trust ecosystem would make it harder for malicious insiders to do bad things. Just guessing, I would estimate that 50% or more of insider attacks might be prevented with a near-perfect high-trust ecosystem.

(Technical) Impersonation/Authentication Attacks

Partially Mitigated. Technical impersonation and authentication attacks require that the attacker is somehow able to obtain ownership of another identity. A great example of this type of attack is an attack where the hacker is able to obtain the victim's access control token or Internet browser cookie and reuse it. If this occurs, it will look like the attacker is the stolen legitimate identity to other systems.

I think a near-perfect high-trust ecosystem can help prevent an attacker from gaining the needed initial access to steal the token or cookies in order to impersonate some other identity. Although some impersonation attacks are very simple to accomplish. For example, some sites and services use sequential account numbers to identify customers. Sometimes, all an attacker has to do to take over someone else's account is guess the victim's account number. Still, with the full high-trust ecosystem solution, an attacker doing these sorts of impersonations would be eventually discovered and blocked. I think a near-perfect high-trust ecosystem would block 80–90% of these types of attacks.

Elevation of Privilege Attacks

Partially Mitigated. Elevation of privileged (EoP) attacks could be prevented by blocking known rogue identities and devices. However, EoP attacks become more difficult to detect and stop if a legitimate user is allowed access to a site or server and can then use their legitimate access and privileges to perform the EoP attack. I would guess that more than 90% of EoP attacks could be prevented by a near-perfect high-trust ecosystem solution.

Intentionally Malicious Programs/Instructions/Scripting

Substantially Mitigated. This category of attack would be substantially mitigated because any rogue person or entity pushing out malicious content would be quickly identified and blocked. Previously trusted people could still push rogue content, but only for a short time or a limited number of attempts. I predict that a near-perfect high-trust ecosystem coupled with existing integrity verification checks would put down 99% of these types of attacks.

Tampering

Substantially Mitigated. If we had a near-perfect high-trust ecosystem, it would be much harder for people to tamper with anything digital and not be identified. I believe 99% of this attack type would be mitigated with a near-perfect high-trust ecosystem.

Data Malformation

Substantially Mitigated. If we had a near-perfect high-trust ecosystem, it would be much harder for people to tamper with data and not be identified. I believe 99% of this attack type would be mitigated with a near-perfect high-trust ecosystem.

Network Traffic Malformation

Substantially Mitigated. If we had a near-perfect high-trust ecosystem, it would be much harder for people to tamper with network traffic and not be identified. I believe 99% of this attack type would be mitigated with a near-perfect high-trust ecosystem.

Repudiation

Substantially Mitigated. Repudiation is claiming that you didn't do something or were not responsible for some content or action. If we had a near-perfect high-trust ecosystem, it would be much harder for people to maliciously deny their identity and to do false repudiation. I believe 99% of this attack type would be mitigated with a near-perfect high-trust ecosystem.

Information Leaks

Partially Mitigated. Depends on the type of information disclosure. If we had a near-perfect high-trust ecosystem, it would be much harder for people to maliciously disclose data in an unauthorized way and not at the same time be identified, leading to responsibility for the disclosure. However, unintentional disclosure where the participant's name is not a mystery or is accidental (i.e., human error) would probably still happen. I believe 90% of this attack type would be mitigated with a near-perfect high-trust ecosystem.

Eavesdropping/MitM Attacks

Substantially Mitigated. Most eavesdropping and man-in-the-middle attacks occur because the authorized participants aren't aware of the unauthorized party in their communication stream. A near-perfect high-trust ecosystem would make these sorts of attacks much more difficult to pull off because it would be easier to see the unauthorized participant. I believe 99% of these types of attacks would be mitigated.

Denial of Service

Substantially Mitigated. If we had a near-perfect high-trust ecosystem, it would be much harder for people to create and perform malicious denial of service (DoS) and distributed denial of service (DDoS) attacks. Near-perfect identity would also help anti-DoS/DDoS attack services to filter out rogue senders more quickly. I believe 99% of this attack type would be mitigated with a near-perfect high-trust ecosystem.

Brute-Force/Computational Attacks

Partially Mitigated. If we had a near-perfect high-trust ecosystem, it would be much harder for people to perform online brute-force attacks and not be identified. The most common type of online brute-force attack is password guessing against an online authentication portal, like an email login screen or API. A near-perfect high-trust ecosystem would prevent a much larger percentage of these sorts of attacks.

However, offline brute-force and computation attacks where the attacker has already gained access to the necessary data and can perform the attack in the privacy of a separate environment would be difficult to stop. For example, if an attacker has gained access to a user's password hash, they can crack the hash back to the victim's plaintext password at their convenience, and it would be difficult for a near-perfect high-trust ecosystem to stop. Where a near-perfect high-trust ecosystem might still be useful is that unauthorized use from a new location or device might still be detected and stopped. But if the attack was offline and someone brute-force breaking an encryption key by obtaining and using protected encrypted data, it might not be stopped or detected. I'm predicting that 70% of these attacks could be stopped with a near-perfect high-trust ecosystem.

Human Error/Misconfigurations

Not Mitigated. An error or misconfiguration mistake by an authorized person or entity would likely not be detected or prevented by a near-perfect high-trust ecosystem. The only impact might be that the error or misconfiguration might not be abused because anyone taking advantage of it might be better identified or prevented from accessing the vulnerability. I predict that 95% or more of these types of attacks would not be prevented.

Third-Party Reliance Issues (Supply Chain/Vendor/Partner/etc.)

Partially Mitigated. These types of attacks are difficult to prevent with a near-perfect high-trust ecosystem because the flaw allowing malicious hackers access occurs to a person or entity the user trusts. The mistake or compromise is transitive. For example, perhaps a consultant's device is unknowingly compromised by malware and the consultant plugs their device into your network to do legitimate work. The consultant doesn't know that his compromised device is now attacking your network.

Or perhaps software you trust (e.g., Solarwinds) is compromised by a Russian backdoor trojan, and you unknowingly download and run the compromised program. Perhaps an air conditioning vendor's remote login to your managed HVAC system is compromised by an attacker. The reason I have marked this with Partial Mitigation instead of Not Mitigated is that a near-perfect high-trust ecosystem should make it harder for our trusted third parties to be compromised in the first place, so there should be less of them. I think a near-perfect high-trust ecosystem could prevent 70% or more of these types of attacks.

Side Channel Attacks

Not Mitigated. These types of attacks, often requiring physical access of some sort, are especially difficult to block. By their very definition, the involved vulnerability was something no one was expecting or designing for. Side channel attacks usually don't involve bypassing traditional defenses, like identity and access controls. A good example is one rogue program or process monitoring a CPU during crucial parts of a security process (e.g., encryption/decryption) and being able to determine a decryption key from the power/cycle fluctuations in the CPU.

Online remote side channel attacks may be more preventable only in that it may be easier to block or prevent them using a near-perfect high-trust ecosystem. Offline, physical side channel attacks, such as detecting micro-vibrations on an office window being used to determine speech inside the office, would be very difficult to stop using near-perfect high-trust ecosystem. I bet less than 5% of these types of attacks could be blocked.

Physical Attacks

Not Mitigated. A physical attack where someone obtains unauthorized physical access to a device to hack it or physically damages, destroys, or steals the device cannot be stopped by a near-perfect high-trust ecosystem. A near-perfect high-trust ecosystem may prevent unauthorized users from using the stolen device in the future, but that's about all that can be done. I expected less than 1% of physical attacks would be blocked by a near-perfect high-trust ecosystem.

Island Hopping

Partially Mitigated. Island hopping, a special type of spoofing, is when an attacker uses or breaks into another third-party device or service and uses that point to then launch their attack. Some hackers chain together multiple islands before doing their malicious hacking. Usually island hopping is done for two reasons. First, if the attacker's malicious activity is detected and monitored, the tracing usually stops at the involved island and is not able to be traced all the way back to the hacker's true origination point. Second, many originating hacker locations and devices have been previously identified and are blocked from communicating with other legitimate devices and networks. For example, many U.S. companies block all connections to their network originating from Russia or China.

I give this a Partially Mitigated rating because it should be harder for attackers to gain that initial island access in a near-perfect high-trust ecosystem.

Note: I readily admit I don't have the data to back up my guesses on how much a near-perfect, high-trust ecosystem might mitigate various threats. There isn't any type of data like this, and I don't have the time or money to conduct that research. Readers will just have to live with my best guesses or make their own. At worst, my estimations can serve as broad categories of approximations (e.g., completely mitigated, partially mitigated, not mitigated) and ignore the mentioned percentages. You can also use them as your own starting point for additional discussion. I realize I could be wrong.

Is The Solution Worth It?

As discussed previously, a pervasive identity and high-trust ecosystem is not a perfect solution. Substantial Internet crime is still possible. However, a near-perfect high-trust ecosystem such as this could significantly mitigate the most popular type of Internet attacks (i.e., social engineering/spoofing) and partially mitigate many of the others. There are only three types of attacks (e.g., Human Errors, Side Channel Attacks, and Physical Attacks) that are not significantly mitigated at all. If implemented, a near-perfect, high-trust ecosystem would likely significantly permanently diminish many forms of Internet cybercrime if it could actually be created and pervasively implemented.

Chapter Summary

This chapter revealed the largest underlying problem, allowing most Internet crimes to occur, and provided a general threat model of the solution theory. Most Internet attacks happen because the criminal cannot be identified, stopped, or punished, so they keep doing it. After reviewing all the different types of attacks, it was determined that the proposed solutions of a high-trust ecosystem would significantly and permanently diminish many types of Internet crime.

Key concepts are:

- Solution is a high-trust ecosystem and pervasive trusted identity
- Verified Trusted Identity
- Real ID
- Threat modeling
- STRIDE threat model

Chapter 6 describes in more detail how a pervasive identity and a high-trust ecosystem might work along with other needed support systems. Chapters 7–12 go into detail about how each of the involved systems will function.

Technology Solution Summary

This chapter summarizes the solution to significantly improve Internet security by describing the various methods and technologies involved. Chapters 7–12 go into even more detail about each major component.

Internet crime, malicious hacking, and malware are far too prevalent, with significant consequences for individuals and organizations alike. To address this, the goal is to significantly and permanently reduce the occurrence and impact of malicious hackers and their malware programs, thereby enhancing overall Internet security and safeguarding digital environments from these persistent threats.

Proposed Solution Theory

As covered in Chapter 5, the main reason online criminals commit Internet crimes is they cannot be easily identified, stopped, and punished, at least in significant percentages. The solution to significantly reduce Internet crime: **Allow anyone to validate anyone else's true identity when they are getting ready to interact along with other components of trust, if they so desire.**

Right now, anyone on the Internet can claim to be anyone else. I can claim to be Bill Gates or anyone else, and there is no good and easy way to confirm whether I am or am not Bill Gates or whether I do or don't work for Microsoft (except on a few services with varying levels of success, such as X with verified identities). It's far too easy for anyone to anonymously connect to anyone else and claim to be anyone else. I could be claiming to be Bill Gates in an email sent from Russia and the average person wouldn't know how to tell. I could say I'm an employee of Google even though I've never worked for Google. Anybody can be anybody. I call this *pervasive anonymity*.

We need to replace the Internet's pervasive anonymity with pervasive identity and a high-trust ecosystem. We need to create and deploy the ability, when wanted, to accurately identify who we are connecting to over the Internet. If we could always accurately identify people and entities on the Internet to their true identities *when we wanted*, we could better decide if we want to connect, communicate, or do business with them. If the other party trying to connect to us doesn't want to give us their true identity (there are many valid scenarios for this), we can decide if it's worth the risk of continuing to communicate with them or perhaps continue to communicate with them, but take additional precautions.

An Internet of pervasive identity would require a comprehensive high-trust ecosystem of:

- Verified identities
- Trusted devices
- Device identities
- Trusted operating systems and applications
- Trusted actions
- Trusted networks
- Trust Assurance Service
- Internet security global alliances

The general scenario would be something like this: Users would log on to their trusted devices and applications using a desired level of identity (more on this coming up), trusted device identities are automatically provided, a trusted OS would be used, trusted applications would be used, trusted actions would be allowed, and communicating parties would communicate with others across trusted networks — creating and using a particular *trust channel*.

Each participant would indicate the minimum level of accepted or required identity and trust each side must use before they begin to communicate. A DNS-like service, the Trust Assurance Service, would function as a real-time trust-reporting service indicating what levels of trust someone should have in a particular connection at a particular moment. Figure 6-1 summarizes a basic high-trust ecosystem.

I'll describe the basic components.

Verified Identities

Allow anyone to require or allow on a per-site/service/session/application basis to require or allow one of three basic types of identities from the user on the other side of the connection:

- Real ID
- Pseudo-identity
- Attempted anonymity

Both users (and their apps) on each side of a connection must agree ahead of time on the minimum or allowed levels of identity before a full-service trusted connection is granted. Since most connections between two or more parties are made through shared services, identity must be transitive, meaning the intermediate service is able to verify the identity and trust to be given when it is connecting to the other user and pass along that information to the other participant.

Real ID

Real ID is the highest confidence in this pervasive identity system and means the online identity being claimed is tied to a single real-world human identity or a verified agent of an entity and is assured to be the person or entity claimed. For example, if I state I am Roger Grimes, I really am Roger Grimes.

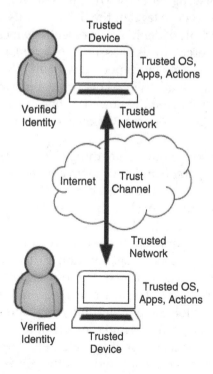

Figure 6-1: Basic high-trust ecosystem.

Of course, a name alone would likely not be enough to verify someone. Most names are not unique in the world. For example, using an online search service, I'm able to confirm there are more than a dozen different people named Roger Grimes in the United States, each with different identity information. There are at least a few Roger A. Grimes. There are at least two Roger A. Grimes who lived at least part of their life in Virginia Beach, VA (including me). However, there is only one Roger Anthony Grimes, who was born in 1966 and lived in Virginia Beach, VA. There definitely is only one Roger Anthony Grimes working for KnowBe4, Inc., now. There is only one Roger A. Grimes living where I currently live. Each Real ID would include the necessary identity *attributes* needed to confirm that each side was communicating with the person or entity you thought you were communicating with. Ultimately, every Real ID would be tied to a unique identity identifier from a trusted identity provider.

Assurance Levels

With a Real ID, a mutually trusted identity provider verifies that I am who I say I am with a strong level of assurance and confirms that I own or control the unique identity label being used. A Real ID is authenticated using strong authentication (i.e., phishing-resistant MFA, etc.) during user logins. Real ID is the strongest and most secure level of the three identity choices.

Assurance is an IT technical identity term essentially meaning verified. Online identities can have different levels of assurance or *confidence levels*. An identity that requires a person to register in person with an official ID and other legal documents to obtain the identity would be considered a strongly assured ID (or *high assurance*). Identities that require no verification or weak verification (such as a valid email address) are considered weakly assured (or *low assurance*). Medium assurance is anything in between, such as perhaps your work ID as verified at work. Some work locations require something akin to a real ID; others only care that you showed up in person and gave them a name — any name. In general, a strongly assured identity will be trusted more than a weak assured identity. Different levels of assurance have long been used in the identity management and public key infrastructure (PKI) spaces.

Either side of a trusted connection can require other related validated identity attributes for the connection (e.g., location, birth location, age, job, Social Security number, bank account number, middle name, home address, etc.) for the connection to be a success. The attributes required to be part of a verified identity during a transaction can be determined and agreed upon ahead of time by both parties. Either side can also make an attribute request of the other and/or submit it to the other side, where it is evaluated. If approved, the identity's attributes can also be viewed by both sides of the connection. In general, both parties should strive to share the minimum number of attributes required as part of the identity transaction (to protect privacy).

Pseudo-Identity

A *pseudo-identity* is an identity much like we use on the Internet today for most sites and services, where we identify ourselves with some sort of chosen identity label (e.g., roger@banneretcs.com, rogerg/knowbe4, @rogeragrimes, frogman32, etc.). The pseudo-identity may or may not be strongly assured, although usually they are not. A pseudo-identity could be tied to a particular site or service (e.g., Twitter, Facebook, etc.) we trust or self-supplied by the user/entity.

A pseudo-identity might be tied back to a Real ID, which some trusted service (e.g., Twitter, Facebook, etc.) or identity service knows but for which other participants relying on the ID may not know. But when we interact with this pseudo-identity, we know that it likely belongs to one person or entity and should exist only once within the site/service being used. Most identities we interact with on today's Internet fall here. For example, when I send an email to you from rogerg@knowbe4.com, you can be reasonably assured that it is me, Roger Grimes, working for KnowBe4, Inc.

Attempted Anonymity

Attempted anonymity identity is where the person communicating does not want to be identified in any way, especially not to a real-world person or entity. I added the prefix "Attempted" to the anonymity label to recognize that true, verified anonymity is very difficult to achieve for a variety of reasons (and is beyond the scope of this book). The Attempted anonymity label recognizes that the person and identity involved do not want to be identified or tracked to a real-world identity, whether or not true anonymity can be actually achieved.

Any participant can choose, require, or allow any of the three identity levels when interacting with any other participant on a per-connection, per-site/service, per-application, or per-session level. Both sides of a connection must agree ahead of time on which levels can be used, required, or allowed before the initial session is started.

Personas

Participants can be different identities (*personas*) to different participants and services at different times. For example, when I am connecting to my main bank, perhaps they require that I provide my verified identity in all connections. I have to prove I'm Roger Andrew Grimes born in Virginia Beach, VA. But if I connect to my cancer support group or a cryptocurrency bank, perhaps they are okay with pseudo-identity or attempted anonymity. Perhaps I connect to my bank as myself, Roger A. Grimes, with my Real ID, to do regular banking but use a different persona to donate to a charitable cause.

Real IDs or pseudo-identities should ultimately be traced back to a person or entity/company/organization/group the person works for if being used in a business context. If someone claims to be from Bank of America, you should be able to verify if they are an agent for Bank of America. If they claim to be from the IRS, you can confirm if they really are an IRS agent. Their work organization could be part of the identity's attributes.

Entity Identities

Many connections will not be verified to a person but instead only to an entity the user involved in the connection is affiliated with. For example, if I'm launching an email ad campaign for my company and sending it out to thousands to millions of people, usually that email should appear as belonging to the company, or use a pseudo-identity (e.g., press@knowbe4.com), but not carry my specific personal name or email address. But receivers would still want to know if the identity on the ad really was or wasn't affiliated with the organization claimed.

Many companies and entities may desire a Real ID or pseudo-identity to be tied to an entity identity instead. For example, many bill collectors use false names to avoid getting personal harassment from angry customers. A sex worker may not want to reveal their true name for a variety of reasons. In this instance, a pseudo-identity tied to the company/entity could be used instead.

Each user could decide what level of assured identity is acceptable and whether that choice is just valid for a single connection, single session, or something more permanent. The identity choice could be made by default, without any input from the end-user, based on the user's allowed policy or application settings. The less interaction from the user, the better, as long as the appropriate, safest, most reasonable choices for the scenario are being made.

Identity choices could be updated by either party at any future time (and possibly have to be periodically renegotiated to continue). Connections could continue at previously agreed-upon levels by default or expire at some preset occurrence metric (e.g., time, number of sessions, data usage, etc.). The idea is that each participant on each side of the connection can decide, on a per site/service/session/application-basis, what level of identity/personas they want to provide, and the other side indicates which level of identity/personas they wish to accept before the next connection packet of the connection/session is accepted between either party.

For example, perhaps I require at least a medium-assured pseudo-identity before allowing someone to send an email to me. A person connecting to my email service to send me an email can decide if that level of identity requirement is acceptable (or it could be accepted or denied by policy defaults). If they don't want to meet the minimum trust requirements, then my email service doesn't allow them to connect further (unless they or I later change their mind).

We will cover verified identities in more detail in Chapter 7.

Safe and Trusted Devices

Each device would be designed to check itself against unauthorized changes, both in hardware and firmware sequences, before further booting is handed off to the active operating system. A safe and trusted device ensures that it has integrity and will function as intended. This will be covered in Chapter 8.

Device Identities

A key part of a more assured, trusted identity in a high-trust ecosystem is verifying if someone is using or connecting using a device they are known to regularly use when performing trusted transactions. All other factors considered equal, connections from people using devices they are previously known to use to make trustworthy connections are trusted more, and vice versa.

Many sites and services (e.g., Google, Microsoft, banks, etc.) have been tracking what devices and types of devices (e.g., operating system, versions, browser version, location) you have been connecting from for a long time.

If you connect from a new device or a device with a single new attribute (say, updated operating system, new location, etc.), the vendor will usually assign a higher risk score to that connection. A new device or attribute increases the risk that your login information has been stolen and is now being used by an unauthorized party to do malfeasance. When you connect to sites and services over the web, if those sites and services want, they can query your device to see what information they can learn about it. There are hundreds of demonstration sites on the Internet that reveal what information they can collect on you and your device simply by connecting to it. Here is one query site you can test with: https://www.deviceinfo.me. You can see in Figure 6-2 some of the information that can be collected (i.e., enumerated).

Although Figure 6-2 shows only a handful of pieces of information, that site actually reveals dozens of different pieces of information. We will cover this in more detail in Chapter 8.

Because many sites and services will track which devices you visit them from and assign higher risk ratings to your connection when you seem to come from new devices or new attributes, many attackers fraudulently claiming to be you have started to do *device emulation*, where they query information from your legitimate device and then use device emulation software or a service to mimic the information that is provided by your device when you visit a legitimate site/ service. That way, the attacker can pretend to be using your legitimate device and be treated with higher trust than if it appears as if you were coming from a brand new device. Thus, our solution to Internet crime needs a way to assure any site/service/session/application that the device they are dealing with is or isn't being emulated. We need a trusted device identity.

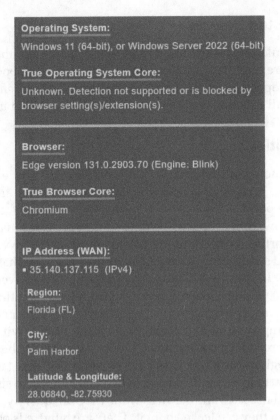

Operating System:

Windows 11 (64-bit), or Windows Server 2022 (64-bit)

True Operating System Core:

Unknown. Detection not supported or is blocked by browser setting(s)/extension(s).

Browser:

Edge version 131.0.2903.70 (Engine: Blink)

True Browser Core:

Chromium

IP Address (WAN):

▪ 35.140.137.115 (IPv4)

Region:

Florida (FL)

City:

Palm Harbor

Latitude & Longitude:

28.06840, -82.75930

Figure 6-2: Device enumeration.

The industry that has been doing the most to figure out a reliable and trustworthy device ID is the gaming industry. In the online gaming world, lots of players are banned from playing games because they have been caught cheating, harassing, or breaking the terms of service multiple times. Cheaters will often create new logon accounts with new names in an attempt to be allowed to game again, but those new logon accounts will still appear as if they are coming from the same device the cheater previously used. Hence, gaming cheaters often do device emulation to fake being different devices and attributes (even though they are using the same device) so they can appear as different users coming from different devices. It's a never-ending battle between the gaming companies and the cheaters. But it's also made the gaming industry very adept at device ID and spotting fake emulated devices. If you're going to do device ID better, you probably need to pay attention to what is and isn't working for the gaming industry.

The gaming industry has figured out that the best indicator of a particular device is its unique identifier, which is stored and provided by a hardware-based chip that is an integral part of the device, such as a Trusted Platform Module (TPM) chip. We will cover this more in Chapter 8.

Trusted Operating Systems and Applications

The operating systems (OSs) and applications we use can be maliciously modified by attackers to cause harm to ourselves or others. We need operating systems and applications that do self-integrity checks to make sure they have not been maliciously modified. On top of that, we need to make sure our identities and personas are persistent throughout operating systems and applications so that our claimed identities are held true from source to destination when connecting to someone else.

Many operating systems and applications already do self-integrity checks, including Microsoft Windows and Microsoft applications. For example, Microsoft Windows has Secure Boot and Trusted Boot (`https://learn.microsoft.com/ en-us/windows/security/operating-system-security/system-security/trusted- boot`) to protect the OS during and after the boot process. Then, Microsoft Hypervisor-Protected Code Integrity (HVCI), when enabled, makes it difficult for malicious programs to modify the operating system after using hardware-based hypervisors.

Qubes OS (`https://www.qubes-os.org/`) is even more of the type of operating system needed to pull off pervasive identity and a comprehensive high-trust ecosystem. It provides OS and application protection using a hardware-based hypervisor to provide virtual machine isolation between different security boundary isolations (known as *qubes*). It essentially allows different applications to work alongside each other in what looks like the same operating system and desktop but have hardware-enforced security separation. The complexity is mostly hidden from the user.

A user could create an identity, log on, and tie it to one or more qubes, thus better guaranteeing strong identity assurance starting at the OS and application level, which then carries through to the other side of the connection if there is one. A trusted OS and trust apps would have both self-integrity checking and hardware-enforced security isolation. We'll cover this more in Chapter 9.

Trusted Actions

Some actions are considered higher risk than others. If I'm buying a $5,000 television and shipping it to a new mailing address that the merchant does not currently have associated with me, that's riskier for the vendor and me than if I'm buying a $10 T-shirt. If I'm connecting to a server in my corporate environment that does not normally get client connections, that's riskier than if I connect to the same servers I connect to every day. Even if all the other components involved (e.g., device, user ID, OS, application) are trusted, a new risky action is something that should require additional, stronger, authentication before it is completed. Chapter 9 will cover trusted actions in more detail.

Trusted Networks

Some networks are more trustworthy than others. But, today, receivers have no way of knowing if a network connection originated from a more or less trustworthy network. Many cybersecurity vendors are aware of locations, IP address spaces, and domain names that are often associated with frequent maliciousness. To complete the circle of trust between source and destination, we need a way to define, measure, and indicate the trustworthiness of a network. We need to make it easy for someone to verify if an incoming connection is coming from a network of high or low trustworthiness so they can make their ultimate trust decision.

Trust Assurance Service

It is not uncommon for previously trusted nodes and networks to be compromised and suddenly be used to accomplish malicious hacking or send malware. We need a global DNS-like service, I call the *Trust Assurance Service*, that can be queried by participating nodes and essentially ask different versions of the same question, "Is this incoming connection trustworthy?" based on the connection's identity type, device identity, whether it came from a trusted OS and application, is using a trusted action, and over a trusted network.

Each participating client would run a client version of the service. I'll name the client version the *local Trust Assurance Service* for the remainder of the book. The global service version that all clients connect to will be named *global Trust Assurance Service*.

Clients would send one-packet queries asking for the other side's current trust assurance level. The global Trust Assurance Service would respond with a single packet containing a trust rating for each involved component and the overall trust rating, from 0 (No trust) to 5 (Highest trust). Table 6-1 shows *trust assurance level* rating labels that would be communicated by the Trust Assurance Services.

Table 6-1: Trust Assurance Level Rating labels

TRUST ASSURANCE LEVELS	DESCRIPTION
5	Highest trust
4	Higher
3	High trust
2	Medium trust
1	Low trust
0	No trust

Trust assurance levels 0–3 are essentially what's already available on today's Internet. Levels 4 and 5 involve using the technologies and methods described in this book to have a better-trusted Internet ecosystem. This will be discussed more in the forthcoming chapters.

Each participating node receiving a trust level rating can then decide how to handle the potential incoming connection, whether to block it from the start, allow it to communicate with increased mitigations, or simply allow it to flow without any special connections.

The global Trust Assurance Service would have a database service tracking, registering, and monitoring the trustworthiness of participating nodes and components. It would interface with other trusted vendors and information providers. It allows people, through their local Trust Assurance Service, to report suspected untrustworthy nodes, confirm their trustworthiness, and have appeals heard on a timely basis.

The global service will have to be governed and staffed by each participating country (and/or their allies) as the top level of trust. This is because few adversarial countries would trust other adversarial countries to determine the trustworthiness of a connection. More on this service in Chapter 11.

Example of a High-Trust Ecosystem Scenario

To demonstrate what operating in a high-trust ecosystem might look like, consider the following example scenario:

1. The device hardware and firmware boots up and checks itself for unauthorized modification, using hardware-enforced (e.g., TPM) values.

2. After the hardware and firmware pass the integrity, the boot sequence would be passed off to the BIOS/UEFI process. All of that process would be hardware-enforced as well.

3. Once passed, the boot process is handed off to the active OS. The OS Secure Boot sequence would be processed and confirmed.

4. The user would log in using a phishing-resistant form of MFA (or other similar strength type of authentication) associated with a trusted identity. This would become the default identity associated with each service/application unless otherwise instructed by policy or the user. Users can use different identities/personas for different sites/services/sessions/applications.

5. Trusted applications would be launched, each to their own hardware-enforced security domain, managed by an application control program, using security-bound access control token cookies (if involved).

6. Secure configurations of the OS and applications would be confirmed by local agents.

7. Actions taken by the user within the trusted application would be accessed by the application or service.

8. The trust of the network would be assessed, confirmed, and reported.

9. All of these statuses would be queried by the local Trust Assurance Service and optionally reported to the global Trust Assurance Service as part of the user's Trust Stack channel values.

10. When the user initiates a new connection/session, it will be tied to a particular minimum required Trust Assurance Service level (0–5) and trusted identity combination. The other side of the connection must meet or exceed the user's requirements and vice-versa in order for the connection to succeed.

11. If another user/device/site/service/session/application attempts to connect to the user to initiate a new connection, the same rules apply. Both sides of the connection will set minimum trust assurance levels that must be met or exceeded before the connection can continue.

12. When the user connects to a site/service/session/application to interact with shared content/event/transaction, the user can see what other users were involved with the shared content/event/transaction and make a decision of how and whether to interact.

13. All identity and trust assurance level transactions are handled by the user's local Trust Assurance Service, working in coordination with the global Trust Assurance Service.

Ideally much of this would happen without any end-user interaction, based upon defaults and previous policy settings. If the user needs to be involved or make a trust decision, the user's local Trust Assurance Service will visibly display the decision to the user and ask for a decision.

Internet Security Global Alliances

Lastly, because the top level of a high-trust ecosystem ultimately ends at the nation-state level (and/or its allies), we need an official group full of subject matter experts to allow the different nation-states to communicate and make decisions. This body would also agree to use and enforce new Internet security standards, ideally reviewing, approving, and implementing faster than today's current methods. More on this in Chapter 12.

Solution Summary

My high-trust Internet solution comes down to allowing the Internet to become a place of pervasive verified identity within a high-trust ecosystem instead of pervasive anonymity, at least where there might be higher levels of risk. Each person can choose what level of assured identity is right for them on a per-site/service/session/application basis. It starts with the user's assured identity, with them logging on to a trusted device, trusted OS, trusted apps, trusted actions, and communicating across a trusted network. The Trust Assurance Service can help any participant quickly determine if the other person trying to connect to them is as trustworthy or not.

All of this runs over the existing Internet and can be made fairly seamless or user-friendly to most users. Users, devices, sites/services/sessions/applications can choose whether to participate in each new connection and, if so, how to participate. If anyone doesn't want to participate in any of this for any reason, they can choose not to participate in any individual site/service/session/application or all of it. Internet service will change only for participants desiring/requiring participation.

Internet criminals will be less able to commit Internet crimes as more and more people and entities require verified high-trust identities in a high-trust ecosystem. People and devices involved in Internet crime will be more quickly identified and filtered out. People and entities not wanting to identify themselves will not be able to connect to people who want some higher level of assured identity and trust to interact.

Figure 6-3 summarizes how different clients and servers might handle different trust assurance levels between them in a high-trust Internet ecosystem. It starts with a pervasive, trusted identity and a high-trust ecosystem.

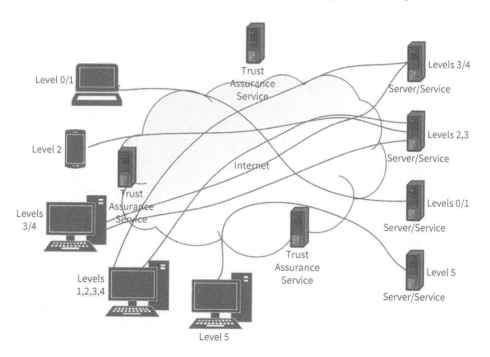

Figure 6-3: Internet high-trust ecosystem logical overview.

Chapter Summary

This chapter described the various components needed to create verified trusted identities and a high-trust ecosystem. It includes verified identities, safe devices, trusted OS, trusted apps, trusted actions, trusted networks, and a Trust Assurance Service. Chapters 7 through 12 cover those components in more detail.

Key concepts are:

- Verified identity
- Real IDs
- Pseudo-identity
- Attempted anonymity
- Safe and trusted devices
- Trusted OS
- Trusted apps
- Trusted actions
- Trusted networks
- Trust Assurance Service
- Internet Security Global Alliance

Chapter 7 starts with covering Trusted Identities.

Trusted Identity

Who we are, our individual identities, are pretty crucial to human existence. When we move past our family and close peer group, we often have to prove who we say we are using various forms of verified identification, such as birth certificates, driver's licenses, and work badges. The entity asking for our identity has to not only trust the identity document we are providing and make sure it wasn't faked or altered but also specifically trust the service that issued the identity document.

Creating a high-trust ecosystem must be based on trusted, verified identities that can be easily and reliably shared between connections. This chapter starts by defining identities and global identity high-trust ecosystem components as they are discussed in general Internet security. Then, it covers how identity needs to work specifically in our high-trust solution to significantly reduce Internet crime.

Identity Basics

This section covers identity and identity systems in general, introducing many technical concepts that are integral to any identity system. You'll need to understand them so that when we start discussing the solution and what goes where, things will make sense.

note The best authoritative coverage on identity basics is NIST's Digital Identity Guidelines (https://csrc.nist.gov/pubs/sp/800/63/3/upd2/final). Over 4–5 lengthy documents, you'll learn a lot about identity and identity systems. I encourage readers who are strongly interested in cybersecurity and identity in particular to take a day and read those documents. They are good stuff.

After food, water, and shelter, there is very little more important to the human experience than our identity and who we "are" (i.e., how we identify ourselves to others). Our identity usually involves our name, although our names are rarely unique. Humans started assigning first names early on, millennia ago, to identify people they recognized, although adding family surnames as last names didn't come around until much later.

Today, we have all sorts of different identities, which may be in one or more names (e.g., marriages, divorces, shortened names, etc.). For our more serious uses (e.g., marriage, driving, passports, etc.) we have to use Real IDs. For certain groups, our identity could be a role and not a name, such as mom or grandpa to our children and grandchildren or tax collector to a taxpayer. It's the same with the online world. We all have multiple identities that we use for certain times and tasks.

Identity Attributes

Depending on the identity system and documents we are using, our identity data could also include a lot of other identity-related information (known as *attributes*, *claims*, or *assertions*). For example, our driver's licenses include all sorts of other information that the Department of Motor Vehicles (DMV) and the police think is important besides our full name and picture, such as our home address, date of birth, and whether we need to wear vision correction to drive. All of those things are considered attributes of our driver's license identity.

Each attribute should have been verified before being added to the driver's license. Attributes need to be verified at the same level of assurance as the identity itself. In some systems, attributes are used as part of authentication during logon. Self-asserted attributes, where the user simply states a particular attribute without any verifiable evidence, should be allowed only in the lowest and no-trust environments.

At the same time, privacy concerns tell us to be skimpy with what attributes we share with other people. For example, few of us would willingly share a copy of our birth certificate or Social Security number with a bunch of complete strangers. That's just asking for trouble. We only want our identities to have the bare minimum number of attributes that are needed for the identity to do its job, and we don't want to even share all of the included attributes, if any, in every transaction unless it's needed. We should only present the required attributes when they are needed. No more, no less.

We should avoid oversharing information about ourselves and our identities, although it's tough to do at times. For example, when buying something in the real world that requires us to be 18–21 or older, such as alcohol or cigarettes, the store vendor will often ask to see our ID. They will check our date of birth on our ID, from which they then calculate our age. That's okay. But really, if we were trying to minimize attribute sharing, all the store vendor really needs is a field that says something like, "Yes, this ID holder is older than 21." But we don't have that sort of versatility in the real world with our IDs . . . and so we are often forced to overshare. But in the online digital world, identities can more easily enforce the minimum level of attribute needed to perform the job, and no more or less. Or at least that is the goal of most identity systems.

Identity Labels

The most common attribute shared with our real-world identities is our name. It's the same in the digital online world. All identities are tied to an *identity label*, which is the character representation of how the identity is tracked and indexed within a particular identity ecosystem. Identity labels could be related to our real name (i.e., rogeragrimes, rogerg, rogergrim48, etc.). It could be our email address (e.g., rogerg@banneretcs.com). Most of us have many different email addresses, and we can choose which to use when. At work and when doing work-related things, my identity is my work email account (rogerg@knowbe4.com). An identity label could be a number (like a Social Security number) or a series of bits (1s and 0s), such as when using a digital certificate.

Identity labels must be unique within the identity system and the systems relying on the same identity system. For example, our email addresses must be globally unique across the Internet, or our email will not be correctly routed. However, my login account (roger/knowbe4) at work only has to be unique for my work systems. My identity label on LinkedIn only has to be unique for LinkedIn (`https://www.linkedin.com/in/rogeragrimes/`) and can be completely different for any other service.

The more globally unique an identity label is, the better. If two or more identity systems end up having the same identity label, it can cause problems if those systems or the systems relying on them ever come into conflict.

Identity Service Providers

An *Identity Service Provider* is a system or service that creates and provides identities (IDs) that can be used for authentication by one or more users or systems. You'll see this identity system component with many other names, including *password* provider, identity *provider, credential service provider, credential provider, issuing authority, identity manager*, etc. In a high-trust identity ecosystem, the Identity Service Providers are one of the most crucial components. They must do their job well, or the whole thing collapses.

Identity Service Providers can be linked to a single service running on a single system or a single or distributed system available for use to multiple services. If an Identity Service Provider provides identity services to other sites and services, it can, in general, be considered *centralized*.

Identities can also be self-created and managed by the user. In general, these types of identities are known as *decentralized*. Users can also self-create identities and then hand them over to centralized authorities for management.

This book is more concerned about centralized identity management, but if you want to learn more about de-centralized identities, see `https://www.linked in.com/pulse/its-good-time-understand-decentralized-ids-roger-grimes`.

> **note** Identities are often linked to and discussed as only belonging to people but can be linked to any "subject" such as a computer, device, site, group, service/daemon account, network, etc. We'll also discuss them in this book as mostly belonging to people and devices because that's the forms that most people and identity systems are concerned with. Just know there are more types of identities than user and device identities, and we need them all to be trustworthy in a high-trust ecosystem.

Authentication

We are asked to prove that we have ownership and/or control over an identity/identity label in a process called *authentication*, where we are challenged to provide one or more *authentication proofs* (or *factors*) that supposedly only the authentication system and identity holder should know.

Traditionally, authentication proofs can be one of three types:

- Something you know (like a password, PIN, pattern, etc.)
- Something you physically have (like a USB key, a phone app, etc.)
- Something you are (i.e., biometric or behavioral traits)

Many mature, large-scale, authentication systems can look for and include hundreds of other factors, such as the device being used, physical location, requested actions, the origination of login versus last time, etc.).

The most common method of online authentication is using a login name (i.e., identity label) and a password. Perhaps, and I'm just making this statistic up, 98% of all logins request or accept password authentication. Conversely, again, I'm just making this up; every other form of authentication added up together would work only on 2% of the world's sites and services. This is and has been a majority password-based world since the beginning of computers. This is changing, albeit slowly, due to increasingly more secure forms of online authentication, including multifactor authentication (MFA) being available and/or required.

Supplied authentication factors are known as *authenticators*, although the word *authenticator* may also refer to the digital package containing the authentication factors themselves. An authenticator can be many things, including the user's combination of a username (i.e., identity label) and password, some type of MFA, a digital certificate, a private key, or a physical token. When a user wants to log in, they supply their authenticators, and they are evaluated during authentication.

Authentication is usually required when a subject wants to access protected resources (e.g., files, folders, sites, services, etc.) for which the owner requires authenticated identities. After successful authentication, the subject can access the protected resources in the way defined by that system's *access control* policy settings. The authenticated identity's movements and actions can be tracked, audited, and stored.

Today, authentication is usually done only once before a subject accesses protected resources for the first time in a new session. Once authenticated, the subject can do anything allowed by the access control system. Users usually don't have to re-authenticate each time they go to interact with a protected resource within the same system and session. It's like a person being stopped at a concert entrance door, asked to provide their ticket, and once having done that successfully, being able to roam nearly anywhere in the concert hall where they are allowed.

There is a growing movement known as *continuous authentication*, where a subject is continuously evaluated for trust depending on their current actions. Depending on what they are doing, they may be asked to re-authenticate or re-authenticate at a higher level of assurance. This would be more like someone being able to enter a concert hall with a ticket but being asked for their backstage pass if they want to go backstage. Or a bank allowing a user to deposit money without an ID but be asked to provide an ID to withdraw money. In the future, it is hoped by most computer security experts that continuous authentication will be more popular than one-time authentication.

Applying/Enrolling

Every subject, or an agent on their behalf, must apply for a particular identity/identity label with the involved Identity Service Provider. This process is officially known as *enrollment* (or *registering*), and the subject at this stage is known as the *applicant*. In most online web enrollment scenarios, this means the user simply goes to the Identity Service Provider's enrollment webpage, clicks the Create New Account button, inputs requested information (such as name and email address), and follows the online prompts to supply the newly used authentication factors (usually twice).

Identity proofing is the process of a subject (or a trusted agent on their behalf) providing the necessary documents, claims, and actions to officially prove their identity (and other attributes) to the Identity Service Provider and the Identity Service Provider verifying the supplied information before issuing the related ID. In most general enrollment processes, the identity proofing process is very casual and really not very trustworthy. I could claim to be Bill Gates from

Redmond, Washington, and the process would accept and "verify" me as long as my email address is good. They don't check to see if I supplied my real name or if the email address is truly related to my identity.

However, depending on the importance of the ID, identity proofing can mean providing other more reliable and trusted forms of identification (such as a driver's license, government ID, birth certificate, picture, etc.), passing background checks, and even possibly showing up to be verified in person. Identity proofing is a major part of an Identity Service Provider's job. They are essentially verifying and attesting to the enrolling person being who they say they along with any included attributes are before handing the user the requested ID.

Any enrollment process should take into account someone supplying false identification and attributes as part of the enrollment process and take steps to mitigate those occurrences. The process must also take into account a verified identity being "repudiated" by the subject it is attached to, with the subject essentially saying, "I didn't ask for that identity. It isn't mine!"

An enrollment process with strong controls and mitigations will be more trusted than one that does not do strong identity proofing. Once a user has passed identity proofing steps and has been issued the identity, they are now officially considered a *subscriber*.

Identity Assurance Levels

Are you who you say you are? That is the pinnacle identity question. As a subject applicant is increasingly asked to submit and pass stronger and stronger levels of identity proofing tied to their real-world identity, the *assurance* of that identity goes up when the claims are verified. Having to submit just a name, an email address, or anything *self-asserted* is considered low assurance. Having to show up in person with all sorts of official documents is considered high assurance. Submitting identity-proofing documents remotely is considered less secure than if they have to be submitted in person to a person of authority.

The concept of assurance is important to trust and identity. We must trust that the Identity Service Provider did their due diligence when proofing an identity before handing someone a new identity. For example, in the real world, police officers want to trust that the DMV did a good job in confirming someone's name before issuing them a driver's license. For the most part, DMV does do a great job, but scammers do get by, and DMV employees are bribed. Law enforcement knows that a driver's license is a fairly good identity document, but it isn't 100% perfect. At the same time, if someone hands law enforcement an official U.S. government ID or passport, it likely has even higher level of assurance because the identity proofing requirements are more extreme.

Here is great coverage on identities, identity proofing, and identity assurance levels: https://nvlpubs.nist.gov/nistpubs/SpecialPublications/NIST.SP.800-63a.pdf.

In general, the higher the assurance involved in identity proofing, the more reliable the identity will be. In a high-trust Internet ecosystem, there will be different types of identities with different levels of assurance. In general, identity system assurance levels should flow from lower levels of assurance to higher levels of assurance. How you label the different levels of assurance is up to leaders or participants. But whatever the assurance levels are, they should be clearly labeled, defined, communicated, and enforced.

Relying Parties

Relying parties are the people, sites, services, applications, and entities that rely on identities. A subject goes to a site or service they want to authenticate with and provides their identity label and authenticators. They are known as the *claimants* at this point in the process.

A *verifier* is the process or entity that substantiates the authentication. A verifier can be a single process for a single site/service or be shared or distributed among many different sites and services. If the claimant submits the correct authenticators and meets all the other requirements, the subject should be successfully authenticated.

At this point, most authenticated online identities are given what is known as an *access control token* (on the web, it's usually in the form of an Internet browser cookie), which is essentially a digital bearer token that the subject has (or can submit) to the relying relevant sites and services to show they have been successfully authenticated and don't need to be re-authenticated until some new session or condition occurs.

note   Bearer tokens are like real-world bearer bonds, where the holder of the bond or stock paper is considered the owner and can collect the value at will. Owning bearer bonds is considered risky because if you lose them or they are stolen from you, you can lose all ownership, and someone else can collect the value. It's the same with access control token cookies.

Access Control

Once authenticated, the subject can access protected resources according to the permissions and methods allowed by the access control system's permissions. When connecting to a protected resource, the subject need only present their access control token to the access control system, to be granted or denied particular access. This part of the process is known as *authorization*. Of course, this is all being handled "behind the scenes" by the operating system and applications (often the user's Internet browser and the vendor's website). The user's identity is used to track events and activities. Figure 7-1 illustrates the identity basics so far.

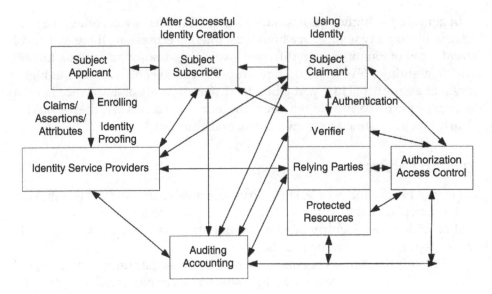

Figure 7-1: Identity system basics.

Personas

Personas are identities tied to the same or different systems, which belong to the same unique individual. Each persona can be tied to different identity/ identity labels, have different assurance levels, have different attributes, and be used with the same or different systems. It's similar in the real world, where a woman can be the CEO of a Fortune 500 company, a lawyer when she signs legal documents, a wife to her husband, and a mother to her children. We can be different things to different systems. The system administrators for most companies have at least two different accounts, one for doing personal tasks and one for doing system administrative stuff.

Personas are a much less used term in the field of identity systems. Most discussions of identity systems don't discuss them at all, primarily because most identity systems are focused on authenticating a subject to a single identity. Having the same person with two or more identities in the same identity system could be seen as a design flaw in some systems. However, in a globally designed and high-trust Internet ecosystem, people will need to have different types and levels of identity, depending on how they want to present themselves to that system. The Identity Service Provider would track all the related and issued personas to a single identity. Any high-trust ecosystem must understand the concept of personas and not see them as undesirable flaws. They are a feature.

In the perfect world, it would be great if a person could select or flip between different personas and identities by hitting some macro key combination (say, Ctrl-I), and up would pop an identity persona menu that the user could easily choose between when starting to make their next connection/site/session/application.

Impersonation and Delegation

When we discuss digital identities and how they work, we often discuss them as if the user is actually doing all the physical steps involved in creating or using the identity. That's not always the case. In many instances of digital identity creation and use, it's really some piece of software, service, system, site, or service doing the actual work behind the scenes. Our authenticated digital identity has been transferred to the thing (usually software) actually authenticating on our behalf.

The process of software/processes/sites/services using a subject's authenticated identifier is known as *impersonation* or *delegation*. The software/process/site/service that does the impersonation is known as the *user agent*. For example, when the typical user browses the Internet, the user's Internet browser is often running in the context of the logged-on authenticated user. The browser is the user agent in that context. If the user is working with an email client, the email client is the user agent. When a user opens a word processing program and accesses their own previously stored document files, the word processor is considered the user agent, and the processes used to access the user's access-controlled documents are done by the word processor using impersonation of that user's subject identity.

It is common for a single computer system to run many different processes using different subject identities, some of which belong to the user and others that belong to the operating system or other previously installed applications. Figure 7-2 shows a sample image from my own computer system as I wrote this chapter, showing some of the programs running and what identities they were using at the time (i.e., roger, System, etc.).

Process	CPU	Private Bytes	Working Set	PID	User Name
ServiceShell.exe	< 0.01	107,696 K	80,028 K	22936	NT AUTHORITY\SYSTEM
wlanext.exe	< 0.01	7,556 K	12,020 K	5000	NT AUTHORITY\SYSTEM
WINWORD.EXE	< 0.01	778,332 K	526,088 K	23072	ROGERLAPTOP6\roger
StartMenuExperienceHost.exe		93,160 K	96,180 K	3792	ROGERLAPTOP6\roger
spoolsv.exe		18,668 K	34,052 K	4408	NT AUTHORITY\SYSTEM
splwow64.exe		6,604 K	21,612 K	17604	ROGERLAPTOP6\roger
SnippingTool.exe		194,772 K	182,892 K	27780	ROGERLAPTOP6\roger
SnagitEditor.exe	< 0.01	783,312 K	612,540 K	18584	ROGERLAPTOP6\roger
SnagitCapture.exe		306,048 K	137,088 K	10712	ROGERLAPTOP6\roger
svchost.exe		6,884 K	21,468 K	10868	NT AUTHORITY\SYSTEM
svchost.exe		2,648 K	8,604 K	9556	NT AUTHORITY\LOCAL SERVICE
svchost.exe		5,844 K	17,056 K	3816	NT AUTHORITY\LOCAL SERVICE
svchost.exe		2,160 K	10,428 K	7904	NT AUTHORITY\SYSTEM

Figure 7-2: Sample of the processes running on my computer and in which subject context.

Identity Binding

When a verified identity is involved in an event or transaction, the involved site/service/session/application should *bind* the involved subject's identity to the transaction. The site/service/session/application involved uses the subject's access control token as the subject's authenticated identity. Then, once the identity is involved in a transaction or event, it should be linked to that transaction or event until it ends. So, if I send a Facebook message, send an email, or attempt to upload a file to someone, the identity I am using should be recorded (i.e., bound) as being the subject involved in the transaction or event. This binding needs to be accurate and reliable. If anyone else connects to the same shared transaction or event, they can see what identity or identities are/were tied to it.

Federation

For a larger Internet high-trust identity ecosystem, we need to extend this idea of impersonation and delegation to computing pathways from beginning to end. The identity delegation and binding needs to be transparent and work reliably across sites/services/sessions/applications. For example, if I receive a message from someone on an intermediate service, say from email or social media, I need to be able to see what subject context (i.e., identity) was involved in it so I know who I am corresponding with.

Right now, when I read an email or social media message, I have no true way of knowing what originating identity sent that email or message. Sure, I can try to rely on what the site or service today is telling me, but we all know that it's far too easy today for an attacker to spoof the identity information for most systems. Our high-trust ecosystem needs to include a method that allows anyone using any site/service/session/application to reliably know who was involved in the shared transaction they are interfacing with. It needs not just to be a best guess but a reliable method of determining verified identity (if wanted).

The process that allows for the conveyance of authentication attributes and identity attributes across networked systems with different identity systems involved is known as *federation*. In a large high-trust ecosystem, we need a reliable federation. Strong federation involves starting with strong identities and then using strong protocols meant to be shared among very different types of relying parties. With federation enabled between relying parties, one relying party can go to another and say something akin to "Here's Roger A. Grimes. He's already authenticated. You can trust me that it's Roger A. Grimes." Then, the accepting party accepts the new Roger A. Grimes connection without asking Roger A. Grimes to re-authenticate.

One of the most popular forms of federation today is Open Authorization (OAuth). If you've ever gone to a website that gives you an option to log on with

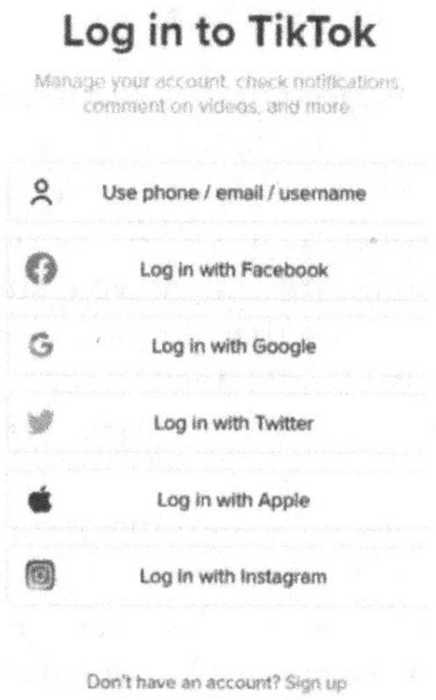

Log in to TikTok

Manage your account, check notifications,
comment on videos, and more

      👤   Use phone / email / username

      ⦿   Log in with Facebook

      G   Log in with Google

      🐦   Log in with Twitter

      🍎   Log in with Apple

      📷   Log in with Instagram

Don't have an account? Sign up

Figure 7-3: Example of OAuth-enabled federated login.

your Facebook, Google, Twitter, or Apple credentials instead, you have seen or used OAuth (see example in Figure 7-3).

A lot of people mistakenly think that OAuth stands for Open Authentication instead of the correct Open Authorization. This is because they are using OAuth to log on to something new and it looks and feels like authentication. But if you understand the difference between authentication and authorization, it will make more sense. Most of the time, when you click one of the available OAuth buttons (say Log In with Facebook), as long as you have already logged in to Facebook before clicking that button, you'll be immediately logged on to the new website. You won't be asked to log in again. Even if you are asked to log on and authenticate because your Facebook login is not previously cached, you'll be logging onto and authenticating with Facebook.com, not the new website. The new website simply gets your already authenticated federated identity because of federation, and you are now automatically logged on to the new website. You are not reauthenticating to the new website.

Here's a great NIST document on federation: `https://nvlpubs.nist.gov/nist` `pubs/SpecialPublications/NIST.SP.800-63c.pdf`.

We will need a great, strong, reliable federation across the Internet to have a high-trust identity ecosystem. OAuth is a great example of an example that is already working at a large scale. The only difference is that future services would need to work with different levels of trusted identity and indicate to the relying parties which levels of assurance are being presented and used. We are very close technology-wise to what we need.

Bounded vs. Roaming Authenticators

Authenticators can be bound to only one logon device/site/service/application (i.e., *bounded*) or can be used in multiple sites/services/sessions/applications and/or on multiple devices (i.e., *unbounded* or *roaming*). For a bounded example, most of the fingerprint scanners you find on laptops and phones work only on the laptop and phone where they were enrolled. So even though my wife and I both have cell phones that can be unlocked using our individual fingerprints, my wife's fingerprints don't unlock my phone, and vice versa, although they could be made to do so if we each registered again on each other's device.

The most common example of a roaming authenticator is your username and password used on a website. You can use that type of authenticator on any computer that can connect to the site. Another example of a roaming authenticator might be a Microsoft Windows Active Directory (AD) network logon. I can register my AD login credentials anywhere and readily use them on any device registered in the same AD domain/forest.

Some authenticators might be considered both bounded and roaming. For example, if I have a Fast IDentity Online (FIDO) device, FIDO requires a different authenticator for each website and service it uses. They can all be stored and used with the same physical FIDO device. In this sense, each individual FIDO ID is bound for each site and service. However, I can use the FIDO device on any FIDO-participating host device to log on to those sites and services. The individual IDs are bound to the same FIDO device, but I can roam with it. In general, the FIDO device is going to be considered bounded, because the authenticators are absolutely bounded to single FIDO device and each set of authenticators are bound to a single site/service/session/application. But they can be used from any computer that is FIDO-enabled to connect to the same sites/services/sessions/applications as the user bound to the same FIDO device.

Another similar term is channel binding. *Channel binding* refers to a unique authentication session being bound to a particular network channel. Without each authentication session being bound to a specific network channel, it is possible for an in-process authentication session to be maliciously redirected to another channel. In most cases, authentication involving channel binding is considered stronger than authentication not capable of channel binding.

In general, bounded authenticators are more secure than unbounded authenticators because they are harder for attackers to steal and reuse on other devices/sites/services/applications.

Previously Compromised Identities

In the real world, someone who commits crime is regarded as more likely to commit crime in the future. Same with digital identities. An identity previously reported as compromised or involved in rogue behavior is at higher risk for future compromises or rogue behavior. In traditional identity systems, an identity found to be involved in rogue behavior could be permanently disabled or blocked. However, in today's world, people's accounts and identities get stolen all the time, used in rogue behavior, and then their ownership recaptured by the original owner. The original owner is grateful to get their identity and account back and will usually not go on to commit rogue behavior. However, anytime your account gets compromised, usually because of social engineering, it does mean that the account is at higher risk for additional compromises than an account that has never been compromised before.

A global high-trust ecosystem needs to take into account that an otherwise trustworthy ID that was taken over by a malicious actor is back under the control of the original legitimate owner again. For example, suppose my computer is compromised by malware and used to send phishing emails using my email account, but I then remove the malware and change my email password. Identity systems need a way of notifying others when an ID is compromised, but also a way to notify others when the ID is back in the control of the original owner.

One way to do that is to adjust the account's trust assurance level rating over time. During the period of time when the account was compromised, its trust assurance level rating can be 0 (i.e., No Trust). But if the original owner regains control and the account isn't used maliciously anymore, perhaps the trust assurance level rating can be adjusted upward over time. How much trust a relying party gives to a previously compromised account when is up to the relying party.

For example, if six months have gone by, perhaps the relying party allows the previously compromised identity's trust assurance level to move up one level, and if 12 months goes by, it allows it to move up two levels. Another participant might remove the compromise as a factor to be considered at all in future ratings as if it never happened once 12 months have gone by. It all depends on the relying party's risk tolerance. But the fact that any identity was ever previously compromised should be recorded by the Trust Assurance Service and be something that is able to be queried by any relying party. The relying party can then decide how to treat.

note Alternatively, any compromised account could simply be marked as permanently untrusted.

Identity Management Lifecycle

Any identity management system needs to manage IDs over their lifetime from creation to destruction (known as *decommissioning/deprovisioning*).

Identity Creation

This is the process we discussed, covering how a subject enrolls and obtains an identity. Just like in this chapter and book, when discussing identity systems, this is where most of the discussion takes place. It's easy to get it wrong. It's easy for bad guys to abuse it. The largest Identity Service Providers (e.g., Microsoft, Google, etc.) spend tens of millions of dollars every year trying to stop attackers from obtaining fake accounts and they often fail. Although I'm not sure if there are any official statistics on this, my best guess would be that there are millions of fake accounts being used by attackers from each of the majority of identity providers every day. Because of this, most of the focus on identity must discuss this part of the identity lifecycle, creation, the most.

Identity Use

Users (and computers and services and groups, etc.) then use the identities they have when they want to use them. The security around identity use mostly focuses on the authentication process where the user confirms their ownership of the identity using one or more identity proofs. But identities can be stolen. Access control tokens can be stolen and reused. Any identity system must recognize and mitigate the unauthorized use of identities as best as it can.

Identity Management (Adds/Moves/Changes)

The information attached to any identity can change over time. People often change their names (e.g., marriages, divorces, etc.). Pictures have to be periodically updated. Betsy used to work in HR, and now she works in IT. Any identity management system must allow for safe, authorized changes to IDs.

Identity Decommissioning/Deprovisioning

When the ID is no longer used, it needs to be disabled and/or destroyed. It's this part of the identity system that is neglected the most. Identities are continually added over time and, with almost certainty, not deleted in a timely manner when no longer needed in most systems. Every active but unused account increases the security risk for the systems that accept those identities. Most identity systems are mostly, percentage-wise, full of unused, inactive accounts as compared to their actively used accounts. Every identity system must define and communicate rules that determine active and inactive accounts. Inactive accounts should be deactivated, archived, or deleted.

In a large, trusted identity system, this same sort of lifecycle must be applied to the Identity Service Providers. Identity Service Providers change over time, come into existence, get hacked, get decommissioned, and don't get appropriately decommissioned when they should. Everything I just said about identities should also be applied to Identity Service Providers.

Kim Cameron's Laws of Identity

A book largely based on identity such as this one would be remiss without mentioning Kim Cameron's March 2005 *Laws of Identity* (`https://docs.microsoft.com/en-us/previous-versions/dotnet/articles/ms996456(v=msdn.10)`). Cameron was an early identity brainiac and defined identity and the use of identity in huge global systems (which he called *identity metasystems*) better than most. I share his own one-sentence descriptions of each law here only so you'll know what those universal laws are or should be:

- Technical identity systems must only reveal information identifying a user with the user's consent.

- The solution that discloses the least amount of identifying information and best limits its use is the most stable long-term solution.

- Digital identity systems must be designed so the disclosure of identifying information is limited to parties having a necessary and justifiable place in a given identity relationship.

- A universal identity system must support both "omnidirectional" identifiers for use by public entities and "unidirectional" identifiers for use by private entities, thus facilitating discovery while preventing unnecessary release of correlation handles.

- A universal identity system must channel and enable the inter-working of multiple identity technologies run by multiple identity providers.

- The universal identity metasystem must define the human user to be a component of the distributed system integrated through unambiguous human-machine communication mechanisms offering protection against identity attacks.

- The unifying identity metasystem must guarantee its users a simple, consistent experience while enabling the separation of contexts through multiple operators and technologies.

That was great stuff to think and write about identity systems two decades ago.

This concludes our coverage of the basics of identities and identity systems in general. Now, we need to discuss the particulars of what we need for our high-trust Internet ecosystem.

Verified Identity in a High-Trust Ecosystem

As revealed in Chapter 6, our high-trust ecosystem system is based on three main types of IDs:

- Real ID
- Pseudo-identity
- Attempted anonymity

Real ID is the highest confidence in this pervasive identity system and means the online identity being claimed is tied to a single real-world human identity or a verified agent of an entity and is assured to be the person or entity claimed. A pseudo-identity is an identity much like we use on the Internet today for most sites and services, where we identify ourselves with some sort of chosen identity label (e.g., roger@banneretcs.com, rogerg/knowbe4, @rogeragrimes, frogman32, etc.). The pseudo-identity may or may not be strongly assured. It could be tied to a site or service we trust or self-supplied by the user/entity. Attempted anonymity identity is where the person communicating does not want to be identified in any way, to a real-world person or entity.

Identity Trust Assurance Levels

The Real IDs and pseudo-identities could have varying levels of assurance. Whatever the trust assurance levels are, they should be well-defined, clearly communicated, and enforced. Our identity system solution will evaluate the following criteria as they are allowed or required at various identity trust assurance levels.

- Assurance level required
- Is strong authentication (e.g., smartcard, CAC, phishing-resistant hardware-based MFA, etc.) required?
- Is MFA or equivalent required?
- Is phishing-resistant MFA or equivalent strength authenticator required?
- Is bounded authentication required?
- Is roaming authentication allowed?

- Is in-person identity proofing required?

- Is remote-only identity proofing allowed?

- Are strong, reliable identity documents required during identity proofing?

- Must the identity be precisely tied to a real person or entity (i.e., Real ID)?

- Is a pseudo-identity allowed?

- Are self-asserted attributes allowed?

- Is federation allowed?

- Has identity been reported as compromised or involved in rogue behavior in the recent past?

- Other requirements, as desired or needed

Table 7-1 shows some example assurance levels for our Internet solution.

Table 7-1: Assurance Levels

ASSURANCE RATING	DESCRIPTION	REQUIREMENTS
5	Highest trust	Issued by approved and active highest trust Identity Service Provider, requires strong authentication, requires phishing-resistant MFA or equivalent, bound authentication required, in-person identity proofing required, Real ID required, self-asserted attributes not allowed, federation allowed, multiple verified official government ID documents (e.g., U.S. government employee card, driver's license, birth certificate, passport, etc.), pseudo-identities not allowed, approval by top-level trust source, not reported as compromised or involved in rogue behavior in the recent past
4	Higher	Issued by active and approved higher to highest trust Identity Service Provider, requires strong authentication, requires phishing-resistant MFA or equivalent, requires bounded authentication, requires in-person proofing, requires strong identity documents, requires Real ID, Self-Asserted Attributes not allowed, federation allowed, not reported as compromised or involved in rogue behavior in the recent past

(continues)

Table 7-1: (*continued*)

ASSURANCE RATING	DESCRIPTION	REQUIREMENTS
3	High trust	Issued by active and approved high to highest trust Identity Service Provider, requires strong authentication, requires phishing-resistant MFA or equivalent, requires bounded authenticators, remote identity proofing allowed (but requires fraud mitigations), strong identity documents required, pseudo-identities allowed, not reported as compromised or involved in rogue behavior in the recent past
2	Medium trust	Issued by active and approved medium to highest trust Identity Service Provider, strong authentication not required, phishable MFA or equivalent allowed, bounded or roaming authentication allowed, remote-only identity proofing allowed, strong identity documents not required, pseudo-identities allowed, self-asserted attributes not allowed, federation allowed, medium security authenticators allowed, including passwords and other single factor authentication, may have been reported as compromised or involved in rogue behavior in the recent past
1	Low trust	Issued by active and approved low to highest trust Identity Service Provider, strong authentication not required, MFA not required, roaming authentication allowed, strong identity documents not required, pseudo-identities allowed, self-asserted attributes allowed, federation allowed, may have been reported as compromised or involved in rogue behavior in the recent past
0	No trust	No trusted Identity Service Provider required, strong authentication not required, MFA not required, roaming authenticators allowed, strong identity documents not required, pseudo-identities allowed, self-asserted attributes allowed, federation not allowed, no identification necessary, applies to attempted anonymity identities or identities who's attributes or assurance cannot be verified, reported as actively compromised or involved in rogue behavior, or not found

The key changes are that High trust and above require strong authentication, phishing-resistant MFA or equivalent, bounded authenticators, and strong identity documents. High trust allows remote-only identity proofing (with fraud mitigations) and pseudo-identities whereas higher and highest don't. Higher and highest assurance requires Real ID.

The highest assurance requires the Highest level of assurance and top nation-state approval. Higher and Highest are essentially the same technologies, but Higher doesn't require top nation-state or national military control and approval. This is to recognize that there is a class of assurance that exceeds all other classes and merits nation-state oversight for their nationalized purposes, much as Top-Secret security clearances do today. If you don't like the nation-state or national military being involved in your identity and those level relying party systems, but still want a very strong identity system, choose Higher. The Highest is for participants who want or need the nation-state or national military level trust.

Pseudo-identities can be used in low and medium trust assurance level, along with roaming authenticators, MFA or equivalent, and strong authentication documents are not required. Self-asserted attributes are not allowed at Medium-level, but are at low. Federation is allowed at all levels accept for no trust.

In the security solution that eventually fixes the Internet, we will likely see multiple levels of identity assurance. They may not match the ones in this chapter, but they will likely be something similar. Implementers can change the details as the design requires.

NIST Identity Assurance Levels

As a comparison, the example assurance levels given are loosely comparable to NIST's existing Digital Identity Guidelines identity assurance levels (IAL), which are:

- **IAL1**: There is no requirement to link the applicant to a specific real-life identity. Any attributes provided in conjunction with the subject's activities are self-asserted or should be treated as self-asserted.

- **IAL2:** Evidence supports the real-world existence of the claimed identity and verifies that the applicant is appropriately associated with this real-world identity. IAL2 introduces the need for either remote or physically-present identity proofing.

- **IAL3**: Physical presence is required for identity proofing. Identifying attributes must be verified by an authorized and trained CSP representative. As with IAL2, attributes could be asserted by CSPs to RPs in support of pseudonymous identity with verified attributes. A CSP that supports IAL3 can support IAL1 and IAL2 identity attributes if the user consents.

This is to say, NIST already has a pretty comprehensive set of guidelines and requirements that could be easily fitted to my Internet solution. I'm essentially extending NIST's three sets of assurance levels to five. We are not completely reinventing the wheel here, at least theory-wise.

A complete description of NIST assurance level requirements can be found at `https://nvlpubs.nist.gov/nistpubs/SpecialPublications/NIST.SP.800-63a.pdf`.

The list of needed requirements for a particular level of assurance is flexible according to the needs of the system so long as it is consistent, clearly communicated, and enforced across the entire system.

New Identity Technologies Needed for Internet Security Solution

The rest of this chapter discusses newer technologies, methods, and protocols, which would need to be designed, approved, and implemented to create the best secure Internet, only some of which are supported by existing technologies.

Trusted Identity Service Providers

Absolutely anyone can become an Identity Service Provider, including a malicious actor. We need well-intended Internet Service Providers to be tested and accredited to become Trusted Identity Service Providers. Identity Service Providers would apply for, be tested, and then accredited for various levels of assurance to become *Trusted Identity Service Providers*. The level of security controls and processes used by the Trusted Identity Service Provider gets increasingly stronger as they want to operate at higher levels of identity assurance. The top-level global Trust Assurance Service (discussed more in Chapter 11) would decide which Identity Service Providers get accredited as Trusted Identity Service Providers and at what levels of assurance.

There is historic precedence about accrediting involved identities and Identity Service Providers at a global level, including NIST and the Certificate Authority/Browser (CA/B) Forum. NIST has been setting U.S. standards that entities and products must be accredited at particular levels of accreditation to be accepted by the U.S. government and related agencies. Indeed, the NIST Digital Identity Guidelines (NIST SP 800-63) that underlies much of this chapter is the hand guide to how participating entities can meet particular criteria (in this case, EAL1, EAL2, and EAL3).

In the civilian world, the Certificate Authority/Browser (CA/B) Forum (`https://cabforum.org/`) has done similarly by trying to set the global standards for PKI digital certificates and the PKI certificate authorities that issue those certificates. It's made up of real-world practicing entities who create controls, standards, requirements, and enforcement. The members come up with the security requirements and then agree to abide by them. If a member violates rules or policies, they can be ostracized by the others and suffer significant reputational and operational harm. Neither NIST or the CA/B Forum has been perfect over the years, but in general, they have established clear controls and requirements, communicated them, and enforced them at national and global levels. The same needs to happen to create Trusted Identity Service Providers.

Trusted Identity Service Providers would be continually tested to ensure they are maintaining the required level of security controls and processes. The global Trust Assurance Service would have the sole discretion of who is or isn't included within a particular assurance level or whether an entity can participate as a Trusted Identity Service Provider at all. The global Trust Assurance Service is tasked with reviewing complaints against Trusted Identity Service Providers and lowering levels of allowed assurance or completely decommissioning a provider based on whether the Identity Service Provider violated clearly documented terms of service or was compromised.

Trusted Identity Creation

After meeting all the requirements for a particular type of identity and assurance level, a Trusted Identity Service Provider would create and issue the digital identity to the applicant, making them a subscriber. This process would be repeated for each needed identity and persona. Any identity can be disabled/revoked by the sole discretion of the Trusted Identity Service Provider, although an equitable and responsive appeals process should be implemented.

Each identity created by a Trusted Identity Service Provider would include the information, at a minimum, shown in Table 7-2.

Table 7-2: Information Provided by a Trusted ISP

Header Information Identifying Container as a Trusted Identity
Trusted Identity Unique Identifier
Trusted Identity Label
Trusted Assurance Level
Current Status (Active, Disabled, etc.)
Creation Timestamp (Unix time)
Last Update Timestamp (Unix Time)
Included Trusted Attribute Information
...
...
...
...
Trusted Identity Service Provider Identifier
Trusted Identity Service Provider URL
Trusted Identity Digital Signature

Each identity issued by a Trusted Identity Service Provider will contain a unique identifier that can be traced back to the Trusted Identity Service Provider and a specific issued unique identity label. The identifier should be globally unique and never repeated. The identity label should be unique to the Trusted Identity Service Provider.

The trusted identity label is the identity's recognized "name." It could be Roger A. Grimes, roger@banneretcs.com, rogerg/knowbe4, rogerg38, frogman32, etc. The trusted assurance level, 0–5, would be indicated. The identity's current status (e.g., active, temporarily disabled, permanently disabled, archived, decommissioned, etc.) must be indicated.

The identity could contain one or more previously verified trusted attributes related to the identity, if any, such as picture, group membership, physical location, age, date of birth, or company name. The maximum number of attributes that can be directly displayed in an identity is limited to 10; however, any of the attribute fields can be linked to more attribute fields stored at the Identity Service Provider.

Attributes can be inserted in the identity itself, as shown earlier, or linked to a unique identity attribute URL. If a user wants to make an attribute available to anyone that received the identity, they can include it directly in the identity. However, if the user wants to keep one or more attributes associated with the identity secret from all Relying Parties unless required, they should instead insert an Attribute URL in the identity. The identity can contain both permanent attributes and a single Attribute URL.

Attribute URL Lookups

We need a method for a single identity with one or more attributes to be able to provide one or more attributes upon request by a relying party to that rely party, if needed, to complete a connection. Here is a possible mechanism for accomplishing that.

Each identity attribute or set of attributes are stored at a different URL. You would need a separate URL for each attribute, set of attributes, or any combination thereof. For example, if a single identity has three attributes, they could be represented individually and as various sets by six different URLs.

- Attribute 1 – URL1
- Attribute 2 – URL2
- Attribute 3 – URL3
- Attribute 1&2 – URL4
- Attribute 1&3 – URL5
- Attribute 2&3 – URL 6

Table 7-3: URLs and Attributes

IDENTITY ATTRIBUTES INCLUDED IN URL LOOKUP	URL EXAMPLES
Picture	https://ispurl.com/q?id=23454352aeq312fa=147dadAfasdf
Location	https://ispurl.com/q?id=23454352aeq312fa=zx$%^47fbN
Date of Birth	https://ispurl.com/q?id=23454352aeq312fa=BBn(W^33n1
Picture, Location	https://ispurl.com/q?id=23454352aeq312fa=vZs399Des3
Picture, Date of Birth	https://ispurl.com/q?id=23454352aeq312fa=W#B&345N9
Location, Date of Birth	https://ispurl.com/q?id=23454352aeq312fa=$5udaquif&7
Picture, Location, Date of Birth	https://ispurl.com/q?id=23454352aeq312fa=%%Cc$kL*)o

If an attribute or set of attributes is needed to be submitted with an identity, the identity is sent to the relying party with the needed related attribute(s) URL. Table 7-3 shows another example.

The concept is that any identity/persona can be handed to a relying party with a particular attribute URL included that points to a single identity attribute or set of attributes. The user can send the identity with a particular URL that points to a single or set of attributes to one relying party and send another URL pointing to another attribute or set of attributes to another unrelated relying party without easily revealing unnecessary attributes. It should not be easy to determine the different URLs belonging to each attribute or set of attributes by obtaining a single attribute URL.

Other Identity Notes

The Trusted Identity Service Provider's unique identifier, URL and digital signature would be included at the end of the identity.

The following trusted identity fields cannot be updated: Header, Unique identifier, Assurance Level, and Creation Timestamp. And changes need to be verified, approved, tracked, and stored. Anyone relying upon the identity should be able to see changes over time.

Lastly, all included information, except for the Trusted Identity Digital Signature field, must be cryptographically hashed and signed by the Trusted Identity Service Provider's private digital signing key and then stored at the Trusted

Identity Service Provider's instance at the end of the identity itself, and with the global Trust Assurance Service (if requested).

Relying parties of a trusted digital identity can download the Identity Service Provider's public key using a DNS query tied to the Identity Service Provider's domain (much like what happens with Domain Key Identified Mail (DKIM) today) and use it to verify the digital signature of the trusted identity.

The Trusted Identity Service Provider will provide the trusted identity identifier and digital signature to the global Trust Assurance Service if and when requested.

Trust Assurance Service

There are two main types of Trust Assurance Services, one globally on the Internet and one locally on each participating user's device. The local Trust Assurance Service handles all the related Trust transactions for the user, device, sites, services, applications, and connections. It is a single service that interfaces with all the other participating applications and services on the local device. It handles many actions, including:

- Managing the users' trusted identities, personas, and attributes
- Helping the user to select the right identities, personas, and attributes for particular applications/sites/services, etc.
- Setting up new trusted connections
- Handling new requests from new and existing connections
- Interfacing with the user
- Interfacing with global Internet Trust Assurance Service

Different clients can handle how the local Trust Assurance Service works and interfaces with the users and other connections.

Trusted Identity Use in Practice

A user logs onto a device/site/service/session/application using a particular trusted identity. A user can use multiple identities or personas (with particular attributes, if desired) on the same device/operating system, but only one can be associated with each instance of a site/service/session/application. Figure 7-4 shows an example scenario of various different trusted identity levels for various applications on the same device.

Which identity/persona with particular attributes are used, and which application/session can be selected when the user starts the application/session?

There can be a single master login to the device that allows the user to select other identities/personas attributes for individual applications/sessions "on the fly." However, the master logon must equal or exceed the assurance

Example Identity Use Cases
Running Multiple Simultaneous Channels and Connections

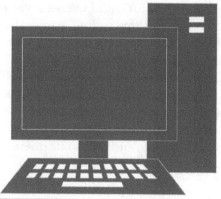

Identity Assurance Level 0	Identity Assurance Level 3	Identity Assurance Level 4	Identity Assurance Level 4
Connecting to Self-Help Group Using Anon Id	Connecting to Work	Connecting to Bank & Stock Accounts	Picking Up Secure Email and Using Secure Browser

Figure 7-4: Trusted identity use cases.

level of the identities being used. A person logged on with a master logon identity assurance level 3 can't automatically select and authenticate as an identity with identity assurance level 4 or 5, at least without re-authenticating to the higher assurance level with the master logon or separately for that involved session.

Which identity is used with which application can be saved and defaulted to in future sessions as long as the user is somehow visually aware of which level of identity assurance they are associating with the application or session (perhaps color-coded, as Qubes OS allows)?

At the higher levels of trust, it's very important that a trusted OS with hardware-enforced security domain isolation, like Qubes OS, be used so that if one identity or site/service/session/application is compromised, it cannot be as readily used to compromise other site/service/sessions/applications, even if they share the same identity (unless a shared environment is desired). This will be covered in more detail in Chapter 9.

When a user performs an action across a network to a remote site/service/session/application, their identity label, identity unique identifier, and digital signature are included as part of that connection and any associated transaction.

For example, if I write a message on Facebook, the Facebook service duly records the trusted identity label, the unique identifier associated, the assurance level, and the identity's digital signature, and makes it viewable and able to be queried by others involved in the same shared transaction.

If the involved identity is not associated with a known Trusted Identity Service Provider or is missing other required fields, the Trusted Identity Service Provider's unique identifier field should contain only four zeros. This would then indicate that the identity should be treated as untrusted and anonymous.

It is important that each participating site/service use its best controls to ensure that every content/transaction/event is associated with an identity and recorded in a way that is visible and able to be queried by others participating in the same shared content/event/transaction.

Trusted Identity Assurance Level Rating

Any participating user in the high-trust Internet ecosystem receiving a connection request or participating in a shared content/event/transaction with a trusted identity should be able to quickly query the global Trust Assurance Service, which then queries involved Trusted Identity Service Provider using the identity's unique identifier to find out/verify identities:

- Current status
- Identity label
- Trusted Identity Assurance Level
- Creation timestamp
- History of attribute changes
- Digital signature
- Find out if the identity has been reported as currently abused or compromised at the Trust Assurance Service

Any trusted identity can be queried at the global Trust Assurance Service using its Unique Identifier to obtain the identity's identity label, trust assurance level, and current status. If the global Trust Assurance Service does not have a particular trusted identity in their database, the global Trust Assurance Service can query the related Trusted Identity Provider Service to get the needed information.

For example, if I receive a request to communicate from a new identity, my device's local Trust Assurance Service can send a network packet query (similar to DNS) to the global Trust Assurance Service, essentially sending the trusted identity's unique identifier along with asking "What's the status of this identity?"

Here's what an Identity Status lookup packet might look like coming from a client request:

Date/Time of Request
Device ID (of requesting client)
Query Flag (0=standard query, 1=server status check, etc.)
Trusted Identity Unique Identifier (of requested ID)
Trusted Identity Digital Signature (of requested ID)
Type of Assurance Level Check (e.g., 0=All, 3=Trusted Identity)
Trusted Identity Service Provider Unique Identifier (of requested ID)
Trust Assurance Service URL (of requested ID)

The global Trust Assurance Service would receive the query; send a request to the related Trusted Identity Service Provider, if needed (if the information wasn't already cached, was missing, or expired); and receive the following information:

- Trusted Identity Unique Identifier
- Trusted Identity Label
- Trusted Identity Assurance Level
- Current Status (Active, Disabled, etc.)
- Trusted Identity Service Provider Identifier
- Trusted Identity Digital Signature

The global Trust Assurance Service would then query its own database to see if the Current Status needs to be modified based upon reported information to the service, such as abuse or exploitation, and send back the same identity information as it received or had, along with a Trusted Identity Assurance Level rating from 0 to 5.

Here's an example of the logical makeup of what an Identity Status lookup packet might look like coming back to a client in response:

Date/Time of Response
Device ID (of requested ID)
Query Flag (0=standard response, 1=client status check, etc.)
Error Codes, if any
Trusted Identity Service Provider Unique Identifier (of requested Trusted Identity)
Trusted Identity Digital Signature (of requested Trusted Identity)
Trusted Identity Assurance Level (of requested Trusted Identity)
Current Status of Trusted Identity requested

| Trust Assurance Service Identifier |
| Trust Assurance Service Digital Signature |
| Digital Signature of Reply from global Trust Assurance Service |

Identity Attribute Querying Service

Identity attributes, previous or current, should be something that can be queried by participating relying parties using their local Trust Assurance Service to the global Trust Assurance Service, which then proxies them to the Trusted Identity Service Provider (if needed). Each Trusted Identity Service Provider should run a service to expect said queries and respond to them in a timely manner. Anyone with a trusted identity's attribute URL can submit it in a query and get back a list of attributes and values to which the URL pointed. The URLs are bearer tokens and, if known, should be able to request the related identity attributes successfully.

Thus, a user can use a single identity with various attached attributes and send one or more different attributes to different relying parties. Relying parties can request particular attributes and, depending on the success or failure of an identity attribute retrieval, decide how to proceed. Attribute URLs should be protected between sender and receiver so that they cannot be eavesdropped on.

Bonus: The Identity Attribute Querying Service may be expanded to handle other types of privacy issues. For example, in one of the early identity attribute examples covering how many people have to reveal their date of birth (and perhaps everything on a driver's license) to a store clerk to purchase alcohol or cigarettes, an online Trusted Identity Service Provider with an Identity Attribute Querying Service could potentially calculate an answer from the identity's date of birth to respond to a Relying Party's query of "Is Identity holder 21 years or older?" It would minimize the attributes being revealed, protect privacy, and decrease risk for both the identity holder and the relying party (who could never be accused of using someone else's personal attribute information).

Identity Attribute Request

Either side of an attempted connection or shared content/event/transaction can request one or more identity attributes from the other in order to complete the shared content/event/transaction. If the necessary identity attributes were not submitted along with an identity in the original connection request, the participant can send a request to the global Trust Assurance Service, which then connects to the remote identity's local Trust Assurance Service to ask for those missing identity attributes. Depending on the participant's policy, the attributes can automatically be sent to the relying party or the involved user can be

Figure 7-5: Mockup of an identity attributes visual request.

visibly queried for approval. Figure 7-5 shows a representative example of a visible approval request sent to a user.

If the user responds with OK, the device's local Trust Assurance Service can query the global Trust Assurance Service, which then queries the identity's Trusted Service Identity Provider (if needed) for the necessary related attribute URL and then send it in response to the other side's request. If the user chooses Cancel, the request is ended, and the requestor can determine how to handle it.

This sort of process is very similar to how additional permission requests are currently handled in OAuth. This level and functionality technology already exists.

Summary of Trusted Identity Overview

A user enrolls for one or more trusted identities at one or more Trusted Identity Service Providers. Those Trusted Identity Service Providers have been tested and accredited by the global Trust Assurance Service. Upon meeting the enrollment requirements, the user is issued a trusted identity with a particular assurance level and other attributes, which can now be used and submitted to other sites and services.

When the user logs into their device, using a master login, they can choose a particular identity/persona to use and can associate different sites/services/ sessions/applications with the same or different Trusted Identities (or an anonymous account). When they connect to use other sites/services/sessions/applications, the involved sites/services/sessions/applications use impersonation/

delegation to present the user's selected trusted identity to the site/service/session/application.

Both sides of any connection get to choose which minimum level of assurance is needed with the provided trusted identity before the connection gets past its initial setup (cover more in Chapter 11). Any shared content/event/transaction the user is involved in is recorded and identified as attached to the trusted identity's unique identifier, identity label, and assurance level by the involved site/service/session/application.

If site/service/session/application tries to connect to a user's computer, the same happens in reverse. The user's site/service/session/application is defined with a trusted identity and trust assurance level that must be met to connect to particular sites/services/sessions/applications. The user agent must approve (or previously approved by policy) the remote identity and trusted assurance level and any required attributes before a connection is approved.

The user of either side can request one or more identity attributes related to a particular trusted identity using their local Trust Assurance Service, and query and receive the results from the global Trust Assurance Service. After completing any anticipated connection, either side can quickly request a status update on the involved trusted identity from the global Trust Assurance Service to see if the currently involved trusted identity has been reported as exploited or abused. This results in a trusted identity assurance Level returned by the global Trust Assurance Service related to the trusted identity.

The participating relying party can look at the trusted identity's assurance level to determine if they want to allow the anticipated connection to continue. Depending on the results, they can do whatever the user/site/service/session/application wants to do, including complete the connection, disconnect the connection, or subject the connection to additional inspections due to trust issues. The involved user or device can also decide not to participate in these trusted identity checks at all, and the only negative outcome would be if the other side of the connection did not also agree and decided not to continue.

Each side (i.e., relying party participant) has the ability to request that the other side have a trusted identity of a particular trust assurance level before an anticipated connection continues. Either party can also run an identity check of the involved trusted identity to see if the global Trust Assurance Service has reported current or past exploitation or abuse of the identity. And then, each side can choose how to proceed based on the information learned.

This sort of trust check can be performed on the device, OS, application, action, and network-levels as well (as covered in later chapters). The selection of identities and requirements can also be determined by security policies enabled at the device/application/site/service level or remembered from prior selections without additional or new input from the user. The less decisions the user has to make to use their system and applications the better, as long as the security policies are reasonable for the involved scenario.

Chapter Summary

This chapter started by discussing identity basics, covering basic terminology and operations. It then discussed the high-trust identity ecosystem as needed to better secure the Internet. The second part covered identity systems, many of which are new and needed for a far more secure Internet. Many of the involved technologies are just extensions of existing technologies (such as NIST's IALs and phishing-resistant MFA authenticators). Other mechanisms, such as both the local and global versions of the Trust Assurance Service, are new and have to be created. However, if implemented, it could result in a significantly more secure Internet.

Key concepts are:

- High-trust ecosystem
- Trusted identity providers
- Trusted identities
- Assurance levels
- Identity attributes
- Real ID
- Personas
- Identity binding
- Identity management lifecycle
- Enrolling
- Subscribing
- Claimant
- Decommissioning/deprovisioning
- Bound versus unbounded authenticators
- Access control
- Access control tokens
- Authorization
- Delegation/impersonation
- Federation
- Trust assurance service
- Trust assurance levels

Chapter 8 covers safe and trusted devices.

Safe and Trusted Devices

When you're trying to create a pervasive trusted ecosystem with trusted identities, trusted devices, trusted OS, trusted applications, trusted actions, and trusted networks, it begins with having a trusted hardware foundation. Having trust in devices comes down to ensuring the device is not maliciously modified and isn't known to participate in maliciousness.

This chapter covers how to create and obtain reliable, safe, and trusted devices with reliable device identities and why that is important. It begins by covering trusted devices and device identity in general and then finishes with the specific device identity technologies needed for our Internet security solution.

Trust Anchors

When you're in the business of determining trust, when you see something, you ask, "What is that thing's trust based on? Is it trustworthy, and can I rely on it?" And when you find what that thing's trust is based on, you ask the same question again . . . until you can't find anything lower . . . until you come to the original base upon which everything else is based. We call these *trust anchors*, *trust roots*, or *roots of trust*. Everything in the same trust path is part of the *chain of trust*. Trust anchors are important because if the trust anchor is suspect, everything based on it is suspect.

Trust anchors are applicable to computers and computing. The best and most trusted computers have trusted devices, trusted boot processes, a trusted operating system, trusted applications, trusted actions, and trusted networks. It's important to get every layer correct, but more so for the lower layers. If a low layer, like the hardware, can be compromised, then nothing above, no matter how trustworthy it was designed to be, can be trusted as much. Systems with trusted devices, trusted boot sequences, trusted operating systems, trusted applications, trusted actions, and trusted networks are going to have high assurance, and vice versa.

Trusted Devices

Even when a device is being used by a legitimate person for legitimate purposes, we must ensure that the hardware and firmware aren't maliciously modified. We need to make sure its BIOS/UEFI boot code isn't maliciously modified. We need to make sure that everything hardware-wise and firmware-wise is legitimate and not maliciously modified before handing off control to the operating system and applications.

Protected Memory

Memory is either volatile (e.g., RAM, SRAM, DRAM, etc.) or non-volatile (e.g., ROM, BROM, SSD, etc.) storage. Many of the technical mechanisms working to keep hardware and software safe and secure necessitate dividing memory involved in different critical tasks into separate, protected, isolated memory areas. Many attacks involve violating those isolated memory boundaries. Memory protection happens at many levels on a device. As computing devices and OSs have matured, vendors and defenders have realized the importance of trying extremely hard to prevent hackers from crossing memory boundaries. Do it well, and entire classes of attacks do not work, and vice versa.

Relevant to this chapter, most of today's CPUs and other hardware components have dedicated memory areas that are protected. You may hear CPU memory protection referred to as a trusted execution environment (TEE) (https://en.wikipedia.org/wiki/Trusted_execution_environment). Every CPU has different memory areas, and CPU vendors try hard to prevent attackers from crossing memory boundaries inside of the CPU. The entire hardware boot process, beyond just the CPU, often has its own memory protections. Devices, components, and hardware with built-in memory protections are going to be more trusted than those without.

Boot Process

When you turn on any computing device, the electricity or battery power surges through the system, and every mechanical and electrical circuit and chip becomes energized and active. Immediately after that, instructions, usually in the form of firmware code, instruct the device what to do from there.

Firmware is programming instructions that provide low-level control of hardware. Firmware is usually located on non-volatile memory chips. Non-volatile memory doesn't immediately go away when power is lost. Most firmware can be updated, modified, deleted, or overwritten. That process is known as *flashing*. Usually, flashing is done using software, but if the firmware is brand new or is corrupted badly enough, it could take a specialized physical flashing device to do it. Almost all hardware has firmware. Firmware can have security vulnerabilities that attackers can take advantage of, just like software.

Mentally, I think of firmware as "harder to update software." But that's not really true. In most cases, firmware is as easy to update as software, but in practice, it just isn't. Many firmware programs don't auto-update, so it never gets done. Others auto-update, but the checks are not performed daily (like software usually is). Other times, the auto-update is accomplished, but the involved system requires a reboot to apply the update, and the user is never notified. Most users almost never think about updating firmware.

Conversely, most of the time, firmware is as easy to attack as software. It just isn't as attacked as much because most attackers just aren't as familiar with attacking firmware. Over the last three decades or so, there have been only a handful of widespread attacks against firmware. That's recently started to change. Over the last year or two, firmware attacks have happened a half-dozen or more times a year, and the pace is accelerating.

For many computing devices, the initial firmware instructions take control immediately after the hardware power-up and come from firmware areas known as Boot Read-Only Memory chips (BROMs). The Boot ROM could be a separate chip or be part of the CPU. The Boot ROM instructions are located in the same place in memory on every new startup, and the computing device's central processing unit (CPU) knows to load that memory area first and start executing.

The Boot ROM will do a hardware test known as the Power On Self Test (POST). If the hardware has any issues, the Boot ROM will make one or more beeps (assuming the speakers are functioning), halt processing, and display an error on the screen (assuming the display is working). If the hardware is physically good and passes all self-checks, then the Boot ROM will continue the hardware boot-up routine.

On today's computing devices, Boot ROMs come in two main flavors: Basic Input/Output System (BIOS) or the newer Unified Extensible Firmware Interface (EUFI). You can't have both, you either have a BIOS or UEFI. They can do self-checks on the hardware itself and serve as an instruction bridge to the operating system.

UEFI is a newer open standard specification intended to replace BIOS. Every BIOS is completely proprietary for the vendor who created it. For that reason and a few others, the computing industry rallied around UEFI about the time Microsoft Windows Vista was coming out (around 2006), although it took another decade before it was more widely accepted. Apple computers also adopted UEFI, as have many other computer manufacturers. Many computing devices allow the manufacturer, installer, or user to choose between the legacy BIOS or

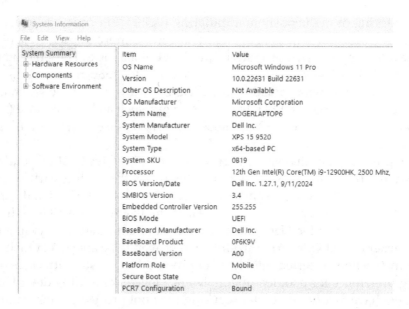

Figure 8-1: Windows system information showing UEFI, secure boot, and PRC options.

newer UEFI before or as they install the operating system. If the user wants to change from BIOS to UEFI or vice versa later on, they typically have to reinstall the whole operating system.

If you have a Windows computer and want to check if you are using a BIOS or UEFI, at a command prompt, type in *msinfo32.exe* or type in "system information" in a prompt box and hit Enter. Then, look for the BIOS Mode field. If you have a BIOS, the value will say Legacy. If you have UEFI, it will say UEFI. Figure 8-1 shows an example MSInfo32.exe result.

When the Boot ROM (BIOS/UEFI) is finished, execution is handed off to the operating system's boot process.

Boot Malware

As mentioned earlier, firmware really is similar to software and can be maliciously exploited like any piece of software. If an attacker can compromise your BIOS/UEFI instructions, you can't trust the device at all, no matter how many security systems you install. Many BIOS/UEFI firmware interfaces are protected by passwords and can only be officially updated by digitally signed code from the manufacturer. However, hackers have learned how to maliciously modify BIOS/UEFI settings outside of the official GUI and outside the standard update pathways. And for sure, any attacker can easily wipe out or erase a BIOS/UEFI setting by using crude malware.

Corrupting or maliciously manipulating BIOS/UEFI code has never been hugely popular, but it does happen and is getting more popular. There have been a few computer viruses that specifically targeted BIOS. The CIH computer virus in 1998 (`https://en.wikipedia.org/wiki/CIH_(computer_virus)`) was probably the most widespread of any BIOS malware. Today, we see malware that specifically targets UEFI a few times a year, such as MoonBounce (`https://www.tomshardware.com/news/moonbounce-malware-hides-in-your-bios-chip-persists-after-drive-formats`).

A popular type of malware program that manipulates boot-up routines is known as a *bootkit* (or *rootkit*). Bootkits often insert themselves early on in the boot process so that when an antivirus scanner is run, the bootkit malware can better hide itself from prying eyes. The earlier malware can insert itself into the boot process, the better. "He who loads first can manipulate everything else." Any hacker or malware writer would be in heaven to be able to get their malicious instructions inserted into the boot process. Nation-state attackers have a strong preference for boot-loading malware. Hence, computing device manufacturers have focused on better securing the boot process against malicious manipulation since the arrival of UEFI.

Device Secure Boot

Computers that protect their boot process against unauthorized modifications use a set of processes and mechanisms collectively known as *secure boot*. Many manufacturers and operating system vendors call the process exactly that . . . secure boot. And the earlier the boot process is protected against malicious manipulation, the better.

Most secure boot processes run something like this: The device powers on and boots up. Sometimes, various pieces of hardware will have their own firmware code (from the boot ROMs) to load and check just before the main firmware code located in the BIOS/UEFI is launched. The BIOS/UEFI checks its own integrity after loading into memory but before executing. On a secure boot device, the BIOS/UEFI is protected against unauthorized malicious modifications, usually allowing updates only from official sources with the right digital signatures.

The BIOS/UEFI code has usually been digitally signed or has some sort of integrity check, and that signature or integrity check value is stored (or protected) by the firmware. The BIOS/UEFI code will do an integrity check by checking its current self against the previously stored integrity value. Any differences will cause a critical stop.

> **note** You may see the term *secure boot* used by various vendors in different ways, but they all basically mean there is some trust anchor that then allows reliable integrity checking by the higher layers. All secure boot options give users and relying parties more trust.

After the BIOS/UEFI code is loaded and executed, the firmware, instructed by values set in its configuration, finds the first storage disk or memory disk to load (if the device has multiple drives). The firmware finds the first storage disk and looks for the *master partition table* (known as *GUID partition table* (or *GPT*) in UEFI). The partition table tells the firmware where the first priority disk volume is and how to access it. A single storage disk could have multiple volumes, so the partition table tells it which one to load first. Then, at this point, the OS boot code on the first volume is located and executed. The rest of the OS boot process will be covered in Chapter 9.

Secure boot in the BIOS/UEFI "binds" the OS and OS boot process to the device where it is enabled. The secure boot process will be bound to a particular OS vendor's digital certificate so that only that OS can be installed and boot, at least without disabling secure boot. When you go into the BIOS/UEFI of a device that supports secure boot, you will see an option called Secure Boot, and usually, the installed OS vendor's digital certificate option will be visible right next to the Secure Boot option. Installing another OS will usually require a brand new BIOS/UEFI firmware image from the involved device vendor and another digital certificate from the involved OS vendor or from an open source project like coreboot (https://www.coreboot.org).

When secure boot is enabled in the device's BIOS/UEFI, you can't install a different OS vendor's image over the existing secure boot-protected OS currently installed on your device. The secure boot mechanism prevents overwriting or updating the OS on the protected device. An attacker will have a hard time even physically attacking the device if the attack involves modifying or replacing the existing OS. Secure boot can even be frustrating to legitimate users who want to replace or upgrade their existing OS with another one their device did not originally come with. For example, I bought a Dell laptop, which came preinstalled with Microsoft Windows. I had to go into the BIOS/UEFI and disable secure boot so I could install Qubes OS on the laptop as the booting OS.

Device Identity in General

Whether you know it or not, the device you are using on the Internet is regularly checked out as part of the authentication process by all sorts of sites and services you use on a daily basis. Not every site and service you visit, but many of them. Certainly, the largest and most popular sites and services are doing this.

Vendors have learned that returning legitimate users using the same device and other session characteristics are less likely to be malicious. Vendors are aware that legitimate user login credentials are stolen by the millions every day, and if a user logs on from a brand new device and/or location, that may be a sign that the user's credentials have been compromised and are now under the control of a malicious hacker.

Vendors also want to identify devices that have been previously and consistently associated with maliciousness because that increases the odds that the device will be involved in maliciousness again. So, often, when you visit or attempt to log on to a site or service, the vendor attempts to determine what device you're using and if you're coming back with the same device as you usually do.

To do that, they need to enumerate the *device's identity* (or *device ID*). Sometimes, that's done by querying the device and essentially asking "What's your device ID?" and trusting the answer, and/or other times, it's collecting enough information about the device to determine whether it is or isn't the same device the user used before. If the vendor collects enough reliable information about the device the user is using, they can calculate the odds that the device is or isn't the same as before. This is generally known as *device fingerprinting*. The better the vendor can answer whether the same user is using the same device, the better it can rule in or out potential maliciousness.

Device ID Assurance

When trying to determine a device's ID, reliability is key. A good device ID is:

- Globally unique for every device
- Not modifiable once created
- Is always sent as the device ID consistently
- Can be queried remotely without end-user interaction
- Can be securely transmitted
- Cannot be easily faked

Device IDs that do this well would be considered to have high assurance. Device IDs that do this poorly would be considered low assurance. Many times, our devices are assigned device IDs by professionals, such as at work, and have computer/device accounts that log on and log off to the network. Those types of device IDs might be considered medium assurance. Early types of device IDs were often low assurance.

Low Assurance Device IDs

Most of the common types of device IDs used by today's devices are low assurance. Here are some examples.

Hostname

Many computing devices have names that the users give them when setting them up. One of those is known in the computing world as the (Unix) *hostname*. Back in the early days of computers, especially in the days when Unix was the most popular operating system, the definitive way to name a computer was to give it a hostname, which populates the hostname variable in memory.

If you are on a Microsoft Windows, Apple, Google Chrome, or Linux computer and get to a "command prompt," you can type in hostname and hit Enter to find out what your device's hostname currently is. Mine, as I type this chapter, is RogerLaptop14. The problem is that the hostname can be almost anything, isn't guaranteed to be globally unique and is easy to change and fake.

IP Address

In the early days of the Internet, it might have been good enough to ask what the IP address of the device was. In the early days of the Internet, every device had its unique public IP address that rarely changed. Today, only a small percentage of devices attached to the Internet have unique, unchanging public IP addresses. Most devices get their (private) IP addresses from their local network, and their local network is assigned a public IP address that may change.

But when trying to identify a device, vendors will often query its IP address. What they get back is usually the device's public network IP address, but that will often give the vendor a clue about where that device is physically located, because public IP addresses will often be affiliated with particular geographic regions. If the vendor is lucky, the public IP address might even be tied to a particular mailing address.

But today, most devices end up with many different private and public IP addresses over time, and many different devices may be seen as having the same IP address. A device's IP address isn't seen as particularly trustworthy (i.e., low assurance) in telling the vendor if they are dealing with the same device or a different one. Today, hackers often use virtual private networks (VPNs) to change their public IP address to appear as if they are originating from anywhere in the world. A vendor may track a device's IP address, but it provides only one low-assurance data point to consider when identifying a device. The IP address isn't reliable enough to be trusted alone.

MAC Address

Every networked device has a number "burned" into the hardware called a Media Access Control (MAC) address, which is unique to the device or network interface of the device. MAC addresses are typically six groups of two hexadecimal digits separated by a dash or colon. For example, my current MAC address as I write this chapter is 14-75-5B-DC-B6-3F. The first three sets of digits are assigned to a particular vendor of the device or network interface (e.g., Intel, Broadcom, etc.), and that is something anyone can look up.

You can usually look up your device's MAC address in its administrative interface or run a command. For example, on Microsoft Windows computers, you type *ipconfig /all* into a command prompt, and it will return a lot of networking information. In the results will be one or more "physical address," which is your device's MAC address(es). Apple and Linux devices can try *ifconfig* instead.

However, there are a few problems with MAC addresses. First, they can be fairly easily forged. Even if they are "burned" into the hardware, they can be changed using software and presented to device ID queries as something else. Second, they are really tied to network interfaces and not devices. My laptop has two network cards, wired and wireless, and thus has two MAC addresses. I have VMware installed for virtual machine operations, and that creates another handful of MAC addresses as each VM has its own virtual MAC address. And I can tell VMware what to make the MAC address of each virtual instance. Lastly, they are not guaranteed to be globally unique.

When you visit a site or service, it may query and collect these very low assurance device IDs from you, but they aren't reliable enough to be relied upon for identification and security purposes.

User Agents

User agents are one of the most popular ways devices are enumerated and identified. In Chapter 5, I introduced the site `https://www.deviceinfo.me` as a good example of what information can be learned about your computer simply from visiting a website, but there are hundreds of other websites that do the same thing (e.g., `https://whatmyuseragent.com`). Enumerating your user agent values happens every time you visit most websites, whether you know it or not. The website just isn't throwing the information on the screen so that you can see it.

Most device enumeration is really browser enumeration, which is "What can I learn about your browser and the stuff your browser knows about?" But learning about your browser values can tell me what type of OS you are using. For example, if you are using Safari, you're on an Apple device. If you're using Microsoft Edge, you're probably on a Microsoft Windows device, and so on.

> **note** Many devices run multiple browsers, which means they will look different when enumerated by a site or service depending on which browser the user is using during the visit.

Browser enumeration was started decades ago as a way for websites you are visiting to figure out the basics about your browser session so they can best correctly display their site or service on your browser and device. So, the powers that be built in a method for HTTP-enabled sites and services to quickly learn what type of browser, along with other desired details, you (really your device) are using. How you and your device appears (or wants to appear) to sites and services is known as a *user agent* in the browser world.

Note: If you want to learn all about user agents, see `https://accreditly`
`.io/articles/the-ultimate-guide-to-user-agents`.

When your browser connects to a site or service, the browser will send user agent information in the header of the HTTP Request server connections. The server will take that information and decide if it needs to display something differently based on your hardware or software configuration. A great example is that many websites will display content differently based on whether you are using a small form-factor mobile device screen versus a bigger-screen computer.

For example, if you've ever visited a website on your mobile phone by typing in the site's general URL only to see the URL updated to have "m." before the URL, that means the website detected you coming from a mobile device and then sent you to the web pages built to render their content better on your mobile device.

What a site can learn about your system from the user agent post is pretty wild at times, including your default language, browser add-ins, do you have a mouse or a speaker, do you use ad blockers, and so on. It's not uncommon for a site or service to learn more than 100 pieces of information about your browser and device from a browser user agent. Sites and services can add to the information they learn from the browser user agent to other information they can detect, such as your IP address, from which they can learn who you use for your Internet access, whether you are using a VPN, etc.

Together, any site or service you visit can get a ton of information about you. Even though they can collect more than 100 pieces of information on you, it's been said many times that it takes only about 5–8 pieces of that information to be able to detect you and your unique session as distinct from anyone else. These sites and services can "fingerprint" you even without you ever putting in a logon name or password. It is also the way that many sites and services track you across unrelated sites and services. Your user agent fingerprint is very valuable to marketers. They share your unique device fingerprint that basically says "This is a Roger A. Grimes device visiting us today." This is in addition to how you are tracked by the various browser add-ins, cookies, and most websites. Your identity can be tracked when you're visiting a website without you manually providing any information.

Again, they also know that if it is you logging on as coming from your same regular device, browser type, and IP address as you usually do, it's less likely to be a fraudulent connection simply using your login credentials. So, vendors will "register" your device(s) and other user agent values in a database and compare those values when you try to log on next time.

Many sites and services, when you are connecting with what it thinks is a new device or user agent, perform extra security checks on our login session and monitor you more closely. For example, the site or service might send you an SMS login code to your phone number to enter in addition to your normal login name and password credentials. Attackers don't like the extra scrutiny.

> **note** Going to a site or service with a browser different from the one you normally use is enough to make that site or service think you are using a new or different device.

User Agent and Device Spoofing

Hackers, if they want to hack a site or service you visit using your credentials, will often pretend to be using your device, well, at least your user agent values. They will often use various methods to learn what your legitimate device and user agent values are (usually through phishing) and then spoof those as their own user agent characteristics when connecting to sites and services you visit. So, even though the hackers might be using, say, Linux OS and Firefox, but know that you use Windows 11 and Microsoft Edge, they will spoof their user agent to pretend to be you and your device. That way, the site doesn't hit them up for extra authentication or do extra monitoring.

Conversely, sometimes hackers want to pretend to be anyone other than who they really are. If I'm a hacker hacking lots of other people, sites, and services, pretty soon my own device and user agent characteristics are going to start to be used by the involved vendor to block the device. So, hackers will use user agent and VPN spoofing tricks to appear to be other devices than the one they are really originating from.

When trying to come up with a secure and reliable device ID, there are really two things we are trying to do. First, ensure that if someone (really their device and user agent values) says they are a particular device, they really are that device. Second, if they are a particular device but are trying to hide it, we can reliably detect which device they are really using. Preventing both types of fraud is crucial to better securing the Internet.

The challenge is that hostnames, IP addresses, MAC addresses, and user agents are things the client submits on its own behalf with low reliability (i.e., assurance), and if the user is intentionally malicious or the device is compromised, the device can claim to be any device. Remember, as covered in the previous chapter, we give low to no trust to self-asserted claims.

Medium Assurance Device IDs

There are some other common intermediate forms of device ID that are marginally better than self-attested user agents. With these forms of device ID, there is some device attestation involved, but it isn't the strongest and isn't hardware-enforced. For example, when users connect to Microsoft Active Directory (Microsoft's on-premise version) or Microsoft Entra (Microsoft's cloud-based identity management system), it is often required that the device the user is using to log on has its own computer account and log on. The device actually presents its own authenticators and logs onto Active Directory, before the user is able to log on. Users never see this device login and never have to update the device's password, so to the average user, it just isn't something they think or know about. But device logins with device passwords are happening "behind the scenes."

Another type of medium assurance device ID might be some sort of software that is installed on the device that works hard to accurately identify the device. I've seen some software programs that collect, store, and compare more than 100 different types of information about a device. Some device ID programs store custom values that they can enumerate when needed. The more information they collect about a device, the more likely that two devices reporting the same values are the same device. For example, if the software program collects IP address, MAC address, hostname, location, user agent information, patching information, and same custom stored value, and that is the same between two sessions, then it's more likely to be the same device.

Medium assurance device IDs are better than self-asserted values, like user agents, but really suffer most of the same issues, mainly self-assertion, with no easy way to prevent malicious submissions. To have strong device identity assurance, we need something beyond simple device self-assertion claims. We need something hardware-enforced and hard to maliciously manipulate even if the user or the exploited device tries.

High Assurance Device IDs

Any self-attested value without any underlying supporting evidence can't be trusted, especially when self-reported by a device. It's too easy for hackers to fake. It's too easy for hackers to fake being someone else using device emulation. We can't trust simple self-attested user agent information. It's too easy for criminals to use VPNs and device emulation to appear to be devices in other locations and with other IP addresses.

So, what can we do?

Luckily, a good solution already exists.

Trusted Computing Group

Any discussion about device identity and trusted hardware would be remiss without discussing the Trusted Computing Group (https://trustedcomputing group.org/), which was formed in 2003 to create and improve open, vendor-neutral, trusted computing standards, starting with the hardware. Much of what is in my overall Internet security fix solution started from what I learned from reading TCG materials and standards more than two decades ago. The biggest success of the Trusted Computing Group is the Trusted Platform Module (TPM) specification, which plays an important part in many components of my solution.

Trusted Platform Module

One of the first things the Trusted Computing Group created was the Trusted Platform Module (TPM) chip and specification. It's a specialized cryptographic chip that can be placed on devices to help secure and store digital keys, digital certificates, and passwords. It can also help store or protect those measurements of integrity used in secure boot environments.

After it boots up, the TPM checks its own integrity and health. It contains an Attestation Identity Key, which hashes different sections of the firmware and software before they are executed. The TPM contains a master Endorsement Key, which can be used be used to secure other keys and information.

The TPM has a master Storage Root Key, which can be used to encrypt other keys used by other parts of the same system and software. For example, Microsoft utilizes it with Microsoft BitLocker to protect its hard drive volume encryption keys. When a BitLocker Full Volume Encryption Key is created and used to encrypt a BitLocker volume, it is then encrypted by the BitLocker Volume Master Key. The BitLocker volume master key can then be encrypted by the TPM's Storage Root Key (a process known as *wrapping* or *binding*) and is stored locally on the disk (not within the encrypted area of the related volume). Upon booting an encrypted volume, the Storage Root Key is used to decrypt the BitLocker Full Volume Master Key, which decrypts the Full Volume Encryption Key, which decrypts the encrypted volume. Lots of applications and processes use the TPM chip for hardware-based authentication, integrity, and key wrapping.

> **note** A lot of encryption on a computer device is similar to how Microsoft BitLocker works, with one key encrypting another key that encrypts another key, and so on. It's how computer encryption works usually.

Although TPM chips (and other chips like them) have been around since 2006 and most experts believe they allow for increased trust, not all devices or systems have them. For a long time, only business or "professional" versions of Windows devices had them. Starting with Windows 11, all Microsoft Windows computers require a TPM chip. But outside of the business world, right now, there are probably more computers without TPM chips than with.

Learn more about the TPM chip here: https://trustedcomputinggroup.org/work-groups/trusted-platform-module/ and here: https://www.pcmag.com/explainers/what-is-a-tpm-and-why-do-i-need-one-for-windows-11.

Apple Secure Enclave

Other vendors may have similar types of chips. For example, Apple has a *Secure Enclave* chip that has many of the same functions (https://support.apple.com/guide/security/secure-enclave-sec59b0b31ff/web). Not as much is known about it because it isn't an open standard, but it is believed to have functionalities and capabilities very similar to the TPM. Secure Enclave is available on many Apple devices, including iPhones, iPads, Macs, Apple TVs, Apple Watches, and HomePods.

Any device with a dedicated cryptographic chip that allows a hardware-enforced device ID will be more trusted than one that does not.

Secure Device IDs

One way to get a high-assurance device ID is to use TPM-chip-like devices to attest to the identity of a device. The Trusted Computing Group calls this *secure device identity*. You can read more about it here: https://trustedcomputinggroup. org/wp-content/uploads/TCG_IWG_DevID_v1r2_02dec2020.pdf.

TPM Endorsement Keys are "hardware-burned" into a TPM chip. It can't be changed for the life of the TPM chip. Endorsement Keys are asymmetric encryption keys with both private and public keys. The private portion never leaves the TPM chip. The public key can be sent anywhere.

If using the TPM and you want a hardware-enforced secure device ID, two other permanent, non-changeable keys are created and placed into the TPM chip at the time of the device's manufacture: a Device Attestation Key and a device ID certificate. Both certificates have a subject name equal to the same device ID. The device ID is unique to the device and vendor and very likely globally unique. The device ID certificate is signed by the Device Attestation Key and looks like any other digital certificate. The device ID certificate is stored on the TPM chip and can be queried through the TPM's API. Figure 8-2 shows a simulated device ID certificate.

The part that follows is an example of how the TPM's device ID certificate could be used in a high-trust Internet ecosystem, but it does not reflect how it is used today.

The device ID certificate subject must be a globally unique identifier that is trackable back to the manufacturer and brand. A public copy of the device's device ID certificate can be sent (i.e., "registered") to the global Trust Assurance Service upon successful manufacturing or the first time a user turns on the device and connects to the Internet.

The device ID certificate attributes can contain any information that seems necessary to a future high-trust Internet ecosystem, but common attributes might be manufacturer, brand, manufacture date, device description, device platform (i.e., PC, laptop, mobile phone, etc.), cryptography used in a digital certificate, TPM flag, and version of TPM chip. Perhaps it also includes a unique identifier of the CPU chip or motherboard of the device. These details can be fleshed out later. A device ID certificate is identical to any other digital certificate, except it is created and stored on a hardware chip and identifies the device when it was created.

For any remote connection wanting to confirm the device's ID, before they begin subsequent connections, it can connect to the device's local Trust Assurance

Figure 8-2: Simulated device ID certificate.

Service and ask for the device's secure ID. The local Trust Assurance Service would then establish a secure connection to the device's TPM chip using a TPM API and request the device's device ID certificate. The device's local Trust Assurance Service would then securely transport the device ID certificate to the requestor. This is done using cryptographically sound mechanisms to prevent fraud and tampering.

The requestor could then note the device's ID and decide on how to handle or work further with the Trust Assurance Service (covered in a moment). The requestor could "register" the device ID with their own local and global Trust Assurance Service to quicken up future sessions. Requestors receiving secure and validated device IDs could, alternatively, store them with their local Trust Assurance Service for future sessions.

What's to Stop a Device ID Thief from Stealing Someone Else's Device ID?

If all participating devices have a unique device ID, what's to stop a criminal from connecting to that device, enumerating its device ID, and then reusing it whenever it wants? Good question. It's handled cryptographically. This sort of dilemma and challenge is very common in the cryptographic world, and many solutions have evolved to handle it.

One example solution could be that the device ID is part of a digital certificate with a private and public key. The service checking the ID also has a digital certificate with a private and public key. What the private key encrypts only the related public key can decrypt, and vice versa. The private key is really what is ultimately seen as the device's ID (in the cryptographic world) and not the plaintext device ID that we all see and more readily read. The private key never leaves the device, and in instances where the device has a TPM-like chip, it would never leave the chip. Attackers could not see or get to the private key.

The service requesting the device ID (in our scenario, the global Trust Assurance Service) could send a randomly generated string of characters (known as the *nonce*) to the device (known as the *challenge*) using the device's public key and also store the nonce in the global Trust Assurance Service's database along with the device's device ID. Only the device with the correct corresponding private key can decrypt something sent with its public key.

The device would use the decrypted nonce, its device ID, and a predefined mathematical algorithm to generate what is known as the *response*, which is then encrypted (i.e., signed) by the device's private key. The service's public key would be used by the device to send the response to the service. The service would use the device's public key to decrypt the response. The service would then do the same calculation as the device did, using the nonce, the device ID, and the algorithm. If both what the device sent back and what the service calculates agree, then only the device with the correct device ID and private could have created it. Subsequent connections from the same device with the same private key and device ID would create similar verified responses.

I'm not a cryptographic expert and if have this example wrong, we'll just let the cryptographic experts handle this portion of the device ID check. Just know that cryptographically checking and verifying values without sharing the actual value with anyone is pretty routine in the cryptographic world.

Location

The trustworthiness of a device (and the associated user identity) can also be partially determined by its physical location. If I get an email from my aunt, who physically lives in Virginia in the United States and isn't much of a traveler, but her device appears to be currently located in Russia or China, it probably isn't her. There are several ways to reliably track a device's location, including GPS (the most reliable), Bluetooth, Wi-Fi, and cellular. Even if a hacker is using a VPN to spoof their device's origination location, I've seen services, such as Google, figure out what the device's real location is. Using a VPN to spoof your origination location is not foolproof.

GPS

Nearly all of today's substantial computing devices contain a chip on the motherboard that can determine the device's Global Positioning Service (GPS) coordination locations. GPS works because the Earth is surrounded by 18 or more GPS satellites funded by the U.S. government. Any terrestrial or flying device that has a GPS chip and "line-of-sight" to at least four of the satellites can generate its exact location accurately to a few feet or less. The GPS client doesn't send any information; it simply receives radio signals from 4 or more GPS satellites and can determine its own location.

Bluetooth Tracking

Bluetooth can also be used to track devices with varying levels of accuracy. Most of today's devices contain both Bluetooth chips. Bluetooth is a short-range communication technology and standard primarily meant to connect devices to other devices over distances of 33 feet or less. Many of us use Bluetooth to connect our wireless earbuds to our mobile phone, our mobile phone to our car's entertainment system, or our wireless speakers to play our music.

Bluetooth can also be used to track devices as those devices walk past other Bluetooth-enabled tracking devices. Most of the time, this is done for marketing purposes; see this example: `https://gizmodo.com/digital-kiosks-snatch-your-phones-data-when-you-walk-by-1851368948`. However, it can also be used to track devices for surveillance or identity purposes.

Wi-Fi Tracking

Everyone knows Wi-Fi is a very commonly used wireless technology that allows wireless Wi-Fi-enabled devices to connect to Wi-Fi wireless networks. Most of us have a Wi-Fi network in our house, at work, and likely in our cars (if you've bought a car in the last 10 years). But most people don't know that many vendors use Wi-Fi tracking, like GPS tracking, to track your device as it moves around the world. As you walk past various Wi-Fi networks, even if you don't connect to use them, your device is enumerating them and connecting to them (in case you decide to connect). This initial connection information can be collected and tracked by vendors and used to locate your device.

The first vendor I was aware of doing this was Google in the late 1990s, as they did Google GPS "street survey" mapping for their popular Google Earth service. An investigation revealed that Google was also, for reasons unknown at the time, recording every Wi-Fi network they came across. This allowed Google (and now others doing similar Wi-Fi network mapping, like Apple) to track where your device is or was as it moved past various Wi-Fi networks in the world around us because our devices are constantly doing "hello handshakes" as we move past Wi-Fi networks in our travel. Today, more people are aware of this due to "Find My Device" apps and small tracker devices we can throw in our luggage. Wi-Fi tracking can also be used as a way to identify your device.

Cellular

Many devices also contain cellular network chips, and when subscribed to a cellular service provider, they can be tracked as the device moves past various cell phone towers and networks. Cellular tracking is usually done to cellular phone numbers, which can be fairly easily moved device-to-device for legitimate means or by rogue attacks. If you are interested in learning more about attacks that steal other people's phone numbers look for "SIM swap attack" on the Internet.

note Most of these wireless tracking technologies do not work underwater, in caves, or in building structures that block radio waves (although Bluetooth and Wi-Fi tracking will still work anywhere those involved transmitters are).

Geo-Tracking

Technologies and services that track our device's location are generally known as *geo-tracking*. Any of the technologies listed earlier can be used to locate, identify, and even block your device. For example, if my device is shown as only working in North America all the time and it suddenly appears as if it is in Russia, there's a good chance that there might be malicious device emulation involved.

Geo-Blocking

Many online services routinely track and compare our current location to our past locations. If reported locations between sessions vary too much or are physically impossible to travel to in the involved time (e.g., my email system says I logged in from Texas, United States, at 12:10 a.m. and then from China at 2:30 a.m.), we might be sent a warning or have to change our account password. Some services refuse to work with particular countries.

Similarly, I could potentially have an identity that works only when I'm at a particular location, such as being a research assistant at a university or working as a government employee within a particular building. If I try to use it in another location, I could be prevented from logging on. These types of blocks are known as *geo-blocking* or *geo-fencing*.

Really Offline?

Surprising to most people, even when our devices are powered off or if we have intentionally disabled one or more tracking technologies, that technology is often still tracking us. Most of the literature says all this tracking is mostly for marketing or operational purposes, but it can be used for other purposes, such as device tracking and device identities.

Location Privacy Concerns

Location tracking can be great for determining the validity of a device, identity, event, or transaction. Unfortunately, many devices we own readily share our location data with lots of vendors. If you are not aware of this, there is a multi-billion-dollar consumer surveillance industry that strives on tracking every single person every single day every single second. If you've got a device that connects to the Internet, it's probably tracking your location (and more information about you). Your devices (and installed applications) often send your (supposedly anonymized) location and actions to multiple data aggregators, who then sell that information to others. If you're not aware of consumer surveillance, I encourage you to watch my one-hour webinar on it: `https://blog.knowbe4.com/you-really-are-being-surveilled-all-the-time`.

The device and application vendors constantly tell everyone that their location data is only being collected for marketing, is anonymized, and cannot be used to track a particular individual. This is not true much of the time. The vendor collecting the data may have intended this when they proactively collected your location, but many ancillary services exist to track you exactly (well, you through devices and applications tied to your identity) and sell that information to others. Here's one example: `https://www.404media.co/email/f459caa7-1a58-4f31-a9ba-3cb53a5046a4/`.

Because of privacy concerns, many location-enabled devices and applications will ask for your permission to share your location first before doing so. Many devices and applications collect your location information and share it with others without asking or simply informing you as part of a long "end-user license agreement" that everyone ignores while clicking OK.

But it is also common for a user to be asked by a device or application "Can we share your location information?" or something like that. Some applications will tell you they cannot function or function as accurately without location-sharing services being turned on and allowed. Most people have dozens to hundreds of devices and applications tracking their every move. Most of that data is collected and sold.

You have to be an extreme privacy advocate who intentionally searches for and disables all location-tracking technology in order for this not to happen. Removing the ability for your devices and applications from being geo-tracked can be among the most technology-difficult things any individual can try to do when so motivated. And if you are successful, it means you can't use many popular applications and are, in general, adding much more inconvenience to your life.

Location as a Part of Device Identity

While the privacy intrusion aspects of geo-tracking are terrible, location sharing can be a legitimate part of any device's identity and can ensure stronger computer security for those who want it. Location sharing is likely to be an integral part of any significantly improved Internet security solution. Your device can simply offer up where it is physically located as a part of its identity, "Here is where I am physically located." Or the vendor can use every technique and trick to learn where you are physically located, even if you try to lie to it. Contacts on the other side of a shared content/event/transaction could require a device to share its location to be allowed to participate.

Location Assurance

If location sharing is used as part of determining a device's identity, it should be based on one of the more reliable technologies. GPS is considered the most reliable technology and more difficult to fake. Bluetooth and Wi-Fi are often based on IP addresses and MAC addresses and aren't considered nearly as secure, but Wi-Fi tracking is commonly used. Cellular technology is considered fairly weak and too easy to spoof. We might perhaps consider them medium assurance. Devices can very easily fake what location they are in using weaker technologies, such as User Agents, VPNS, etc. These types of "location services" should be considered No or Low Trust assurance.

Globally Unique and Registered

Device IDs for the upper levels of device trust assurance levels should be globally unique and reported to the global Trust Assurance Service when created or first turned on. In general, there is no guarantee today that most device IDs are globally unique. They often have to be unique to the manufacturer (so they can manage and service it over its lifetime), can be unique to a particular vendor network (e.g., Microsoft Active Directory), and many vendors attempt to assign globally unique IDs (but it isn't guaranteed). There are some early attempts to have some types of devices have globally unique IDs and registered in global databases. For example, the U.S. Food and Drug Administration (FDA) is requiring globally unique IDs that are registered for every medical device (https://circle.cloudsecurityalliance.org/HigherLogic/System/DownloadD ocumentFile.ashx?DocumentFileKey=b664b449-3a9f-4734-80ac-0193f341ff1a). So, the requirement and needed technology is already there for some applications. It just needs to be expanded.

Previously Compromised Devices

Historically, a device previously reported as compromised or involved in rogue behavior is at higher risk for future compromises or rogue behavior, and this should be a part of its current trust assurance level rating. Devices currently *not* reported as exploited or involved in rogue behavior but previously reported as compromised or rogue behavior may be more trusted as time goes on if they don't incur additional compromises or get involved in new rogue behavior. Each participant can determine the period of time needed without an additional compromise or rogue behavior for the trust assurance level of a previously compromised device connecting to them to rise. For example, if six months have gone by, perhaps a participant allows the other device's trust assurance level to move up one level, and if 12 months go by, it allows it to move up two levels. Another participant might remove the compromise as a factor to be considered at all in future ratings as if it never happened once 12 months have gone by. It all depends on the participant's risk tolerance and the policies followed by their devices and applications.

Trusted Device Assurance Levels

Trusted device trust assurance levels would be decided using the following factors:

- Does the device have a hardware-enforced secure boot?
- What is the rating of the device's trust assurance network (covered in Chapter 10)?
- Is the device currently reported as actively compromised or involved in rogue behavior?
- Has the device been reported as compromised or involved in rogue behavior in the recent past?

Trusted device trust assurance levels would look something like Table 8-1.

Table 8-1: Trusted Device Trust Assurance Levels

TRUSTED DEVICE TRUST ASSURANCE LEVELS	DESCRIPTION
5 – Highest trust	The device has a hardware-enforced secure boot, not currently reported as compromised or involved in rogue behavior in the recent past, part of the highest trust assurance level network.
4 – Higher trust	The device has a hardware-enforced secure boot, not currently reported as compromised or involved in rogue behavior in the recent past, part of a higher trust assurance level network.
3 – High trust	The device has a hardware-enforced secure boot, not currently reported as compromised or involved in rogue behavior in the recent past.
2 – Medium trust	Not ever reported as compromised or involved in rogue behavior in the recent past.

TRUSTED DEVICE TRUST ASSURANCE LEVELS	DESCRIPTION
1 – Low trust	Not currently reported as compromised or exploited, but was previously reported as compromised or involved in rogue behavior in the past.
0 – No trust or compromised	Reported as currently compromised or associated with rogue behavior regardless of other attributes, or not found.

Local Trust Assurance Service would determine the device's trusted device assurance level, store it in its local Trust Assurance Service database, and optionally report it to the global Trust Assurance Service.

Once we have a trusted device, we can more likely rely on any device ID it claims.

Device Identity Assurance Levels

Device identity trust assurance levels would be decided using the following factors:

- Does the device use hardware-based secure boot (i.e., Trusted Device)?
- Is the device ID hardware-enforced?
- Was the device ID previously registered with the global Trust Assurance Service?
- Is the device ID currently reported as compromised or involved in rogue behavior?
- Was the device ID reported in the recent past as compromised or involved in rogue behavior?
- Is the device's reliable physical location reported?

Device identity trust levels would look something like Table 8-2 below.

The local Trust Assurance Service would determine the device's device ID assurance level, store it in its local Trust Assurance Service database, and optionally report it to the global Trust Assurance Service.

Device Identity Trust Assurance Service

Every participating device, level 3 or higher, should report its device ID and device assurance level to the global Trust Assurance Service using the local Trust Assurance Service upon boot up. The local Trust Assurance Service is

Table 8-2: Device Identity Trust Levels

DEVICE IDENTITY TRUST ASSURANCE LEVELS	DESCRIPTION
5 – Highest trust	Hardware-enforced device secure boot, hardware-enforced device IDs, registered with global Trust Assurance Service, reliable location determined, the device is not currently reported as compromised or associated with rogue behavior in the recent past.
4 – Higher trust	Hardware-enforced device secure boot, hardware-enforced device IDs, registered with global Trust Assurance Service, reliable location determined, the device is not currently reported as compromised or associated with rogue behavior in the recent past.
3 – High trust	Device ID attested to by non-hardware, business service like Microsoft Active Directory/Intune, reliable location determined, registered with global Trust Assurance Service, the device is not currently reported as compromised or associated with rogue behavior in the recent past.
2 – Medium trust	Device ID attested to by non-hardware, like Microsoft Active Directory/Intune, not registered with global Trust Assurance Service, medium assurance location determined, the device is not currently reported as compromised or associated with rogue behavior; could have been reported as compromised in the recent past.
1 – Low trust	Device ID is self-attested, like user agent, low assurance location reported, the device could have been reported as compromised or associated with rogue behavior in the recent past.
0 – No trust or compromised	No device ID reported, no location reported, or device reported as currently compromised or associated with rogue behavior regardless of other attributes.

responsible for accurately obtaining those values and reporting them and the device's current location to the global Trust Assurance Service.

Good, legitimate devices are compromised all the time. Devices are compromised by malware by the millions each year. There needs to be a way for a particular trusted device and/or device ID to be reported as potentially malicious. That's where the global Trust Assurance Service comes into play again, as it did in the previous chapter.

Any participating device in the high-trust Internet ecosystem receiving a connection request or participating in a shared transaction with another device ID should be able to quickly query the global Trust Assurance Service using the device's ID to find out/verify the device's:

- Current status
- Trusted device trust assurance level

- Device ID trust assurance level

- Device physical location (if required)

- Manufacturer creation timestamp

- Digital signature of the requested device

- Find out if the device ID has been reported as currently compromised or involved in rogue behavior (or in the past) at the global trust assurance service

Any trusted device and/or device ID can be queried at the global Trust Assurance Service using a valid device ID to obtain further information, including current status. The current status can contain one of these values:

- Disabled

- Currently reported as actively compromised or used in rogue behavior

- Not currently reported as actively compromised or used in rogue behavior, but has been reported as compromised or involved in rogue behavior in the past

- Not found

For example, if I receive a request to communicate from a new device on the Internet, my device's local Trust Assurance Service can send a network packet query (similar to DNS) to the global Trust Assurance Service, essentially sending the connecting device's device ID along with asking "What's the current status of this connecting device?"

Table 8-3 is an example of the logical makeup of what a device status lookup packet might look like coming from a client request.

The global Trust Assurance Service would receive the query, look up the current status in its service, and send back the following:

- Device ID

- Trusted device trust assurance level

Table 8-3: Device Status Lookup Packet

Date/time of request
Device ID (of requesting client)
Device ID (of client requested)
Query Flag (0=standard query, 1=server status check, etc.)
Type of Assurance Level Check (e.g., 0=All, 1=Trusted Device, 2=Device Identity)
Device ID
Device ID Digital Signature

Table 8-4: Device ID Status Lookup Response

Date/time of response
Query Flag (0=standard response, 1=client status check, etc.)
Error Codes, if any
Device ID (of the requested device)
Trusted Device Identity Assurance Level (of the requested device)
Current Status of Device ID (of the requested device)
Device Physical Location (if required) of the requested device
Trust Assurance Service Identifier
Trust Assurance Service Digital Signature

- Device ID trust assurance level
- Device physical location (if requested or required)
- Current status (Disabled, Active compromise, Past compromised, Not found, etc.)
- Trust Assurance Service identifier
- Trust Assurance Service digital signature

Table 8-4 is an example of the logical makeup of what a device ID status lookup response packet might look like coming back to a client in response.

Many of the technologies discussed in this chapter are already available, such as secure hardware-based IDs and reliable location services. We just need to make sure all future devices contain some sort of TPM-like chip that is capable of identifying and reporting reliable device identities, ensure more devices use secure booting, and ensure reliable location services. The new technology portion of this chapter will be using local and global Trust Assurance Services to provide participants with the current rating of the device based on its trusted device and/or device ID assurance level, physical location, and whether the device was currently reported as compromised.

Chapter Summary

This chapter covered trusted devices and trusted device identity, including low, medium, and high assurance forms. Hardware-enforced trusted devices and trusted device IDs will help us get to a significantly more secure Internet. Trusted device IDs created and stored on cryptographic hardware, like the TPM chip, and reliable location services provide the best chance of a reliable and secure device ID.

Key concepts are:

- Trusted Platform Module, secure enclave, etc.
- Device secure boot
- Trusted device ID
- Trusted devices
- Location services

Chapter 9 will cover Trusted OSs and applications.

Trusted OSs and Apps

A high-trust Internet ecosystem must have trusted devices that are far less likely to be critically compromised and include trusted operating systems and applications. This chapter covers OS secure booting, trusted operating systems, trusted applications, and trusted actions.

OS Secure Boot

Every computing device has a "boot" process, where the hardware is initialized and the OS is loaded in pieces, starting with the critical core sections followed by the "upper layer" OS code and applications. Figure 9-1 below summarizes the common logical boot process around most computing devices and OSs today (it could vary based on the device).

The more secure and reliable devices and OS have protection and integrity checks along the entire boot process. We covered hardware and firmware booting and safety checks in the previous chapter.

After the hardware and firmware is checked and verified, operations are handed off to the OS. The best OSs have their own checks and verification, starting from the booting of the operating system and beyond. These days most OS boot code has some sort of integrity check that is securely stored and protected by the BIOS/UEFI (or other chip will be covered soon). After the OS boots, the early critical drivers and services/daemons of the OS will load, and all will be integrity checked along the way. If trusted applications are involved, they will be loaded as called, each time integrity checking themselves along the way.

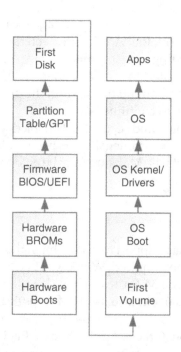

Figure 9-1: Logical boot process.

This gives involved applications the best chance of being allowed to work in a trusted way without malicious modification. It doesn't mean the app isn't maliciously modified or can't be maliciously directed to do something harmful, but it does mean those applications have the best chance of functioning as intended, at least until they start handling data or being controlled by the user.

Any device with a dedicated cryptographic chip that allows trust root measurements and hardware-based key protection is going to be a more trusted device than one that doesn't. Systems with TPM and Secure Enclave chips meet that definition.

As mentioned in the previous chapter, the Trusted Computing Group's TPM chip is perfect for this. It is a specialized cryptographic chip that not only can perform cryptographic actions but can securely store values and measure existing values. So, as an example, the device can cryptographically hash firmware code and store that hash result in the TPM. The TPM can be used to help measure (i.e., re-hash) the firmware code as it's placed into memory before it is executed. Then, the existing hash result can be compared to the storage hash result, and if the two hashes are not identical, the firmware code is stopped from executing.

The TPM has multiple secure memory storage locations known as Platform Configuration Registers (PCRs). A TPM-protected device can have separate PCRs dedicated to recording measurements of the BIOS/UEFI, boot ROM on add-in cards, a PCR dedicated to the OS loader, etc. If the PCR value is different than measured during boot up or missing, the device can display a critical error message and refuse to continue booting.

With a TPM chip activated and secure boot enabled, you can get a fairly strong validation that the boot process integrity has been maintained, each part being checked before the next starts. Malware may be able to get into the process, but it's going to be a lot harder to do.

Windows Secure Boot

Microsoft Windows has had support for TPM chips since Windows Vista (released in 2006), although it was not required. Windows 11 is the first Windows operating system version to require TPM. So, if you have Windows 11 or above, you have a TPM chip. Google Chromebooks also use TPM chips (`https://chrome.googleblog.com/2011/07/chromebook-security-browsing-more.html`), as do other server brands, such as those from Oracle. Apple's Secure Enclave chip has similar boot protections (`https://support.apple.com/guide/security/secure-enclave-sec59b0b31ff/web`), although since it's not an open standard, it's less clear how it operates and what parts of the boot process it protects.

You can read more about the TPM chip here: `https://trustedcomputinggroup.org/resource/tpm-library-specification/`.

Hardware with cryptographic protection is going to be more secure and trusted than hardware without.

Fully Patched OS

Operating systems missing critical patches or other offsetting mitigations are at higher risk for exploitation. A trusted OS should have all critical patches applied in a timely manner or have other offsetting mitigations. The patch status of the OS needs to be assessed locally and reported to the local Trust Assurance Service.

Trusted Operating Systems

After the hardware has started, the firmware code finds the first disk, the first partition, and launches the installed operating system. Operating systems can have similar types of secure boot protection and hardware-enforced security isolation (i.e., OS Secure Boot) as devices can (i.e., Device Secure Boot).

Many operating systems and applications already do self-integrity checks, including Microsoft Windows and Microsoft applications. For example, Microsoft Windows has Secure Boot and Trusted Boot (https://learn.microsoft.com/en-us/windows/security/operating-system-security/system-security/trusted-boot) to protect the OS during and after the boot process. Here are some of the TPM PCRs that Windows uses when it boots:

- PCR 0: Core root-of-trust for measurement, UEFI boot and run-time services, UEFI drivers embedded in system ROM, ACPI static tables, embedded SMM code, and BIOS code.
- PCR 1: Platform and motherboard configuration and data. It also hands off tables and UEFI variables that affect system configuration.
- PCR 2: Option ROM code.
- PCR 3: Option ROM data and configuration.
- PCR 4: Master boot record (MBR) code or code from other boot devices.
- PCR 5: Master boot record (MBR) partition table. Various UEFI variables and the GUID partition table (GPT).
- PCR 6: State transition and wake events.
- PCR 7: Computer manufacturer-specific (i.e., Microsoft will use this).
- PCR 8: NTFS boot sector.
- PCR 9: NTFS boot block.
- PCR 10: Boot manager.
- PCR 11: BitLocker access control.

When Windows starts, it loads the Windows OS bootloader into memory. If OS Secure Boot is enabled, the firmware is checked to see if it is digitally signed (mitigating malicious modifications). In TPM systems, this value is stored in one of the PCR registers of the TPM chip. Then, it will check to see if the OS bootloader itself is digitally signed and check against a value stored in the TPM chip. More checks are performed the same way, including against the OS kernel (called *Trusted Boot* by Microsoft by this point) and low-level boot drivers, anti-malware drivers, and startup files, checking all code involved in the OS booting process before the OS is launched. Only if all prior checks are passed is the complete Windows OS loaded.

If you have a Windows computer, you can check to see if you have a TPM-protected boot process by using System Information (Msinfo32.exe) and looking for the Secure Boot State value (as shown in Figure 9-2 below). It will say "On" if OS Secure Boot is enabled and operating.

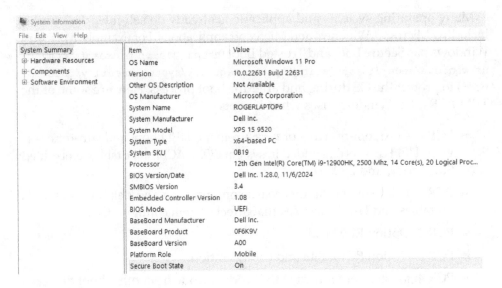

Figure 9-2: Example Msinfo32 report showing a Secure Boot State of On.

Whether the operating system itself is further protected against malicious modification depends on the operating system, the version, and whether the involved feature is enabled. Microsoft has had some sort of hypervisor-enforced OS protection since Windows 10. The underlying technologies and their names have changed (e.g., Device Guard, Code Integrity, Windows Defender Exploit Guard, Virtualization-based Security, etc.). In Windows 11, it's called Microsoft Hypervisor enforced Code Integrity. Essentially, Microsoft runs its OS kernel code in a virtualized container protected by a hardware hypervisor.

Hypervisors

Since I've mentioned it a few times, now is a good time to discuss hypervisors, which many OSs, such as Microsoft Windows, Qubes OS, and VMware, use. A *hypervisor* is a physically isolated memory area on a computer that is protected against encroachment by other processes and connections on the same computer. Hypervisors can create one isolated memory area or create many different isolated memory areas. It's significantly harder for something in one isolated memory area to infer or exploit another memory area. Anytime something you use is using a hypervisor, that's good for your security.

The security isolation imposed by the hypervisor can be software- or hardware-enforced. Hardware-enforced hypervisors are considered more secure than software-enforced hypervisors. The hardware hypervisor enforcement on today's personal computers (collectively known as the x86 platform) is often provided by the main CPU or by dedicated cryptographic chips. Intel has had embedded hypervisor functionality since 2005, known as Intel virtualization (VT-x). AMD made their version available in 2006, called AMD virtualization (AMD-V). There other chips from other manufacturers that support hardware-enforced hypervisors.

There are other related hardware-enforced virtualization technologies such as an Input–Output Memory Management Unit (IOMMU), Second Level Address Translation (SLAT), Extended Page Tables (EPT), Interrupt virtualization, Input/Output virtualization, graphics virtualization, and network virtualization, which can also play a role. Dedicated cryptographic chips, such as the TPM and Apple's Secure Enclave, can also play a part in hypervisors. When these various hardware virtualization technologies are available, you may need to still go into your BIOS/UEFI configuration setup program to enable them.

Virtual machine (VM) functionality and software often take advantage of hypervisors. Virtual machines allow operating systems and applications to be run in their dedicated memory environments. VMware is probably the biggest producer of VM software and products. Microsoft's VM software is known as Hyper-V. Apple has its own built-in virtualization framework, although many Mac users run a third-party product known as Parallels. Even Google Chrome has built-in VM capabilities. The world's most popular free VM software is Oracle's Virtual Box. You can download and use Linux-based Gnome Boxes as well. We have VM software everywhere.

If the VM functionality uses hardware-enforced hypervisors, it is known as a Hardware Virtual Machine (HVM). OSs and software running in an HVM is considered pretty good security isolation. HVMs are gaining in popularity. Over time, Microsoft, Apple, and Linux-based distributions have been adding more and more HVM functionality to their OSs. There is a decent chance that every single computing device in the future will basically be an OS running a bunch of HVMs. That's what Qubes OS is already doing today better than all the others (more on this later).

On a Windows system, you can use System Information (Msinfo32.exe) to show if you have these types of hypervisor memory protections enabled. Figure 9-3 shows an example.

Figure 9-3: Example Msinfo32.exe showing various hypervisor-enabled memory protection technologies on a Microsoft Windows system.

Virtualization-based security means a hypervisor is being used to provide protection to the OS. Apple and other operating systems have similar protections.

Qubes—OS Security Domain Isolation

Some operating systems go even further and allow a user to isolate, using a hardware hypervisor, one or more applications (and network stack) into different virtualized machines.

Qubes OS (https://www.qubes-os.org) is even more of the type of operating system needed to pull off a comprehensive high-trust ecosystem. It is a free and open-source OS that provides OS and application protection using a hardware-based hypervisor (called Xen) to provide virtual machine isolation between different security boundary isolations (known as *qubes*). It essentially allows different parts of the OS and different applications to work alongside each other in what looks like the same operating system and desktop but are really different hardware-protected virtual machines with hardware-enforced security separation. Some of the technical complexity is hidden from the user, but the user can choose among templates, qubes, and other types of objects when setting up their environment.

You can run different operating systems, including different Linux distros, Microsoft Windows, in a qube. You can run multiple operating systems on the same desktop. The information stored in a qube can be intended to be persistant which Qubes calls *vault*, or temporary, which are known as *disposable* qubes. Each qube can be configured to have different trust levels from complete to non existent and different identities. The default "application qubes" are labeled as personal, work, untrusted, and vault, although you can create and name them whatever you want.

Different "sub systems" of your normal OS can have their own isolated qubes and can be shared between and within qubes. For example, the network stack that allows an OS or application to communicate off the local machine to the local network and Internet is in its own isolated, disposable qube known as net-sys by default. The USB subsystem that allows you to interface USB devices with an OS or application has its own isolated subsystem known as usb-sys. Similarly, the shared firewall is in a qube called sys-firewall. They can be shared between different qubes or isolated to only be used with a single qube. You can also create isolated individual qubes for each of those functions. It's up to you and the security you desire.

Qubes OS comes with several default Linux-based OSs to install and choose from. They are installed as "templates" that you can create and copy from. The default OSs are Debian, Fedora, and Whonix. Whonix (https://www.whonix.org/) is a hardened free and open-source Debian desktop fully integrated by default into the privacy-advocating Tor network. In general, Qubes makes it fairly easy to use secure, hardware-enforced, isolated security domains running different

OSs and applications specifically designed for security and privacy. Its core principle is that if one of the qubes is compromised by hacker or malware, the hacker or malware can't as easily get to other qubes. It's a pretty awesome concept, especially when you consider that each qube is its own hardware-enforced hypervisor, easily accessible on a single desktop.

The different qubes with varying levels of trust can be visually indicated by colors, so you can easily see which qube has which trust level just by looking. The different VMs are handled by the Qube Manager and can be pre configured using templates to simplify the setup of each VM. The desktop runs in its own qube. Figure 9-4 shows an example Qubes OS desktop view with three sample qubes running.

Each color represents a different isolated qube running its own application and OS instance, although we could instead be running multiple applications from the same qube or the same application from two qubes of the same or different levels of isolation.

In our perfect world, for our Internet security solution, a user could create or use a trusted identity and logon and tie it to one or more qubes, thus better guaranteeing strong identity assurance starting at the OS and application level, which then carries through to the other side of the connection, if there is one. A trusted OS and trust apps would have both self-integrity checking and hardware-enforced security isolation. Qubes OS can already do this today.

note In a Qubes OS-like environment, the local Trust Assurance Service would run in its own shared vaulted qube with the highest level of assurance.

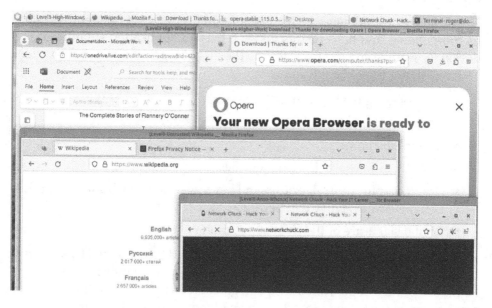

Figure 9-4: Example Qubes OS desktop with three qubes running.

Trusted Applications

Once the hardware and OS are secure and trusted, it's time to try to secure the applications. This section covers many of the most popular ways to secure applications.

Globally Unique Application Identifier

Each trusted application would need a globally unique application identifier, which would be registered with the global Trust Assurance Service by its developer upon publication. Each globally unique application identifier would tie the application to its vendor, its publication date, and version. Each developer would need to register a globally unique developer identifier with the global trust assurance Service before submitting trusted applications.

Trusted application identifiers could be made up as cryptographic hash from a combination of the following factors:

- Developer's globally unique identifier
- Application/service/module official name
- Date of publication
- Version

A globally unique application identifier might look something like this:

f93f4a5067fbd8e4063ab92cda23f5603e33578d8c6bd4251624fae1cb44c7f6

The developer would generate the globally unique application identifier, store its components, and hash results for each trusted application submitted. The developer would send the following to the global Trust Assurance Service for each registered trusted application:

- Developer's globally unique developer ID
- Developer name
- Application name
- Globally unique application identifier
- Cryptographic hash algorithm and key size used to hash trusted application registration entry (i.e., SHA-256, etc.)
- Digital signature of the trust application

Something like this has been previously done and incorporated by some different operating systems (like Microsoft Windows) and platform services (e.g., Apple Store and Google Store), although global registration to an Internet-wide service and a guaranteed globally unique identifier was not required.

Applications without a registered globally unique developer ID and globally unique application identifier would be treated as untrusted.

Securely Coded Applications

The more securely designed and coded an application is, the less likely it is to be exploited and abused. Securely coding applications is generally known as *secure coding* or *security development lifecycle*. Secure coding involves things like preventing buffer overflows, preventing memory-type mismatches, and preventing developers from coding in hard-coded login credentials. All trusted applications should be threat modeled during design and its threat model released to the public for review and feedback. This will be the focus of Chapter 15, "Secure Coding."

Self-Checking Applications

Every application has a chance to do a self-integrity check before it continues its execution. Optimally, you would want another mechanism to verify the integrity of the application before it is executed rather than the application itself. Even better would be if the integrity check value was stored in some hardware-protected location like a TPM PCR. But anything an application does to protect itself from malicious modification helps. To be thorough, the application would need to check the integrity of any other programs and files upon which it depends (i.e., *dependencies*).

Another alternative type of check is to place the entire application and any dependencies into a container or some sort of compressed image. When the application is launched, it checks the integrity value of the container or image before "exploding" the individual application components and executing. Probably the masters of self-checking applications are the antivirus vendors who have to defend their products from malicious modification. Other vendors should follow what they are doing to protect their own applications.

Application Memory Protections

The memory areas that applications run in often have additional memory protections provided by the hosting operating system to keep one application from exploiting another or to keep application data of the application from negatively impacting the execution of the application. Some of the memory protections are innately provided by the OS by default. Some can be turned off, others can't. Some memory protections must be enabled when developing the program in the programming languages and tools used to make the program. Some are hardware-enforced, and others are only enforced by software. Applications with memory protections are going to be more trusted than applications without.

For some software protection examples, in Microsoft Windows, an application's memory areas are protected by many software-enabled memory protection mechanisms, including Control Flow Guard, Stack Guard, Data Execution Protection, Address Space Layout Randomization, and Structured Exception Handling Overwrite Protection. Depending on the Windows OS version and underlying hardware, some application memory protections can be hardware enforced. Hardware-enforced application memory protections are even better.

> **note**   On Microsoft Windows computers, you can download and run Process Explorer (`https://learn.microsoft.com/en-us/sysinternals/downloads/process-explorer`) and enable the columns DEP Status, Control Flow Guard, ASLR Enabled, and Stack Protection to see which of your processes and applications have what memory protections.

Application Security Domain Isolation

It is common for attackers to compromise one service or application on a user's computer and then use that first exploitation to move on to other applications and services and eventually take complete control of the compromised device. Many times, the compromised device is then used to compromise more devices on the network (if any), and in a short period of time, an attacker can usually move from a single exploited application/service on a single device to take over the entire network and environment of the target. This is the normal way hacking is done in most environments today when the hacker is not just targeting a single device.

For example, a user gets socially engineered into clicking a malicious link in an email. That link compromises the user's email client, which installs a backdoor malware program. The backdoor malware program elevates its security access from the security context of the email application to become an elevated administrator or local system account. That account is used to enumerate service account passwords, some of which are shared across the user's entire work network on every device. The attacker uses the service account logins to compromise the network servers, which store all user passwords. The attacker now has the ability to log on as any user or administrative account across the network. The network is "pwnd."

Applications running in their own secure memory areas, especially if hardware-enforced, like on Qubes OS, are going to be more resilient against attack and more easily prevent broader exploitation beyond the application than applications that don't have this type of protection. In a scenario involving apps running in hardware-enforced security domains, the attacker in the previous scenario would be able to control the email app but nothing beyond it. They don't get to the user's login credentials (beyond the email client) as easily. They don't get to the local Administrator account as easily. They don't get the local device's service/daemon accounts as easily. This prevents the hackers from then more easily moving across the network to even more targets. This is the primary reason why Qubes OS was invented.

The application security domain isolation can be software-enforced (fairly common) or hardware-enforced, like in Qubes OS. Hardware-enforced application security boundary isolation is significantly more resilient to attack.

Secure Configuration

Even secure applications can become exploited and compromised if insecurely configured or left unpatched. Devices in trust assurance levels 4 and 5 (Higher and Highest) require an assessment and attestation of secure configurations. Secure configurations include:

- Strong password policy
- Strong authentication used
- Users performing end-user actions not logged in as root or administrator
- Secure OS configuration settings
- Secure application configuration settings
- Least privilege permissions and group memberships
- Host-based firewall with a good default ruleset
- All critical patches applied in a timely manner
- Running up-to-date antimalware software
- Running aggressive security event logging

This means there needs to be a secure configuration assessment service running on the computer, assessing the OS and various applications and their settings. The service can be open-source, commercial, provided for by a trusted group, or provided by the nation-state (for level 5). The assessment service analyzes the computer on startup and periodically after that (no less than once a day), gives a pass/fail rating, and reports the assessment results to the local Trust Assurance Service. The vast majority of users would probably love to offload this task (i.e., security assessments, confirming safe configurations, etc.) to someone else.

Application Control

Administrators can also run *application control* programs like built-in Microsoft's Windows Defender Application Control (named Software Restriction Policies and AppLocker in previous Windows versions), which controls which programs or scripts can execute. If you're not a program or script on the application control program's allowed list, you can't execute. Application control programs aren't considered official security boundaries, but if implemented by more device users, they would result in significantly less malware execution. Application control programs are one of the most underutilized security defenses.

Security-Bounded Cookies

As discussed in Chapter 2, "How We Are Attacked," access control token (cookie) theft is one of the most common types of attacks in the world today. This is because these tokens are bearer tokens, meaning whoever has them can use them to appear to be the rightful logged-on user. Attackers often steal them from browsers on compromised computers or use adversary-in-middle attacks to copy them as they are in transit to the user. Millions of tokens are stolen and abused each month.

There are some recently developing technologies that are trying to tie tokens to the devices they were originally placed on. Google has been on the forefront of the fight to better secure access control token cookies: `https://security.googleblog.com/2024/07/improving-security-of-chrome-cookies-on.html`. One technology is Device Session Credentials (`https://blog.chromium.org/2024/04/fighting-cookie-theft-using-device.html`), which allows servers to generate and place public keys on involved client computers in addition to normal cookies. If that key can be securely stored, it may be harder for attackers and their malware to move it to another computer, and the stolen cookie alone becomes worthless to the attacker.

Another Google anti-cookie theft technology is known as Application-Bound Encrypted Primitives (`https://security.googleblog.com/2024/07/improving-security-of-chrome-cookies-on.html`). In this instance, all the application's data, including the related access control token (cookie), is locked to the current application session. It's a lot harder to steal and reuse an encrypted token. It is hoped that these secure cookie technologies, or something like it, take off to help prevent access control token (cookie) theft, although currently they seem more focused on preventing local cookie theft than adversary-in-the-middle attacks.

Trusted Actions

There is also the concept that we need to monitor and watch user actions within applications, sites, and services, looking for unusual or risky actions and perhaps asking for additional authentication before allowing the risk action to be performed. For example, if a cloud storage client is suddenly encrypting all their data files, is that the legitimate client doing that or the client being taken advantage of by ransomware? If a substantial part of a user's U.S. bank account balance is being moved to a strange, never-seen-before North Korean–based bank, is that a U.S. person deciding to violate U.S. laws or North Korean hackers stealing money?

note Trusted actions are a core component of many zero-trust architectures.

There are some actions that are riskier than others. This would need to be coded into the particular service or application, but to complete the entire trust stack of a high-trust ecosystem, looking at individual user actions, transactions, and events of each involved site/service/application would need to be part of the system.

A *trusted action* is defined by the developer based on a user's requested action against a particular protected resource. The requested action could be a requested action like READ, WRITE, or UPDATE. The developer would look at the requested action involving protected resources and threat model various risks. For example, if a user wants to delete one file, that action might be considered usual and low-risk. If the user wants to delete all files at once, that might be considered a high-risk event.

For trusted actions to work, each developer would have to define them for their own site/service/session/application and create a methodology for assessing and tracking requested actions before they are performed.

Globally Unique Trusted Actions

It would be up to the developer to define trusted actions along with their risk-rating. Trusted action risk ratings would typically be binary, Low, or High, or they could be along a more granular scale if desired. Each trusted action and associated risk would have to be defined by the vendor, associated with a globally unique trusted action identifier, created, and sent to the global Trust Assurance Service.

Trusted action identifiers could be made up as cryptographic hash from a combination of the following factors:

- Developer's globally unique identifier
- Trusted application name
- Trusted application identifier
- Trusted action name
- Trusted action identifier
- Trusted action risk score
- Date of publication

A globally unique action identifier might look something like this:

f93f4a5067fbd8e4063ab92cda23f5603e33578d8c6bd4251624fae1cb44c7f6-
b4a592759328fa27a5ac85ecfff5c2d525e4840c3298355a902daaacd759eec6

The first part is the hash of the globally unique identifier of the trusted application and the second part, after the dash, is the hash trusted action.

The developer would generate the globally unique action identifier and store its components and hash results for each trusted action submitted. The developer would send the following to the global Trust Assurance Service for each registered trusted action:

- Developer's globally unique developer ID
- Developer name
- Application name
- Globally unique application identifier
- Trusted action name
- Trusted action identifier
- Cryptographic hash algorithm and key size used to hash trust action registration entry (i.e., SHA-256, etc.)
- Digital signature of the trusted action

Currently, trusted actions, as they are defined here, are not implemented by any developer I'm aware of. However, many current vendors have already defined high-risk actions that can be performed on their site/service/session/application, look for these being performed, and then ask the user for additional authentication and/or enable more secure monitoring. For example, if I buy something on Amazon.com and go to ship it to a new shipping address I've never used before, I'm asked to do additional verification beyond what it takes for a purchase being sent to one of my previously registered shipping addresses.

So, many individual sites/services/sessions/applications are already defining and using trusted actions in some way. Additionally, some zero-trust architectures essentially require that all critical applications define and analyze trusted actions (albeit not currently called trusted actions in zero-trust architectures documents). Over time, however, it is expected that user behavior and trusted actions will become pervasive across the Internet.

The needed step for a high-trust ecosystem is for trusted actions to be far more pervasive and for them to be registered at the global Trust Assurance Service.

My dream scenario for the items covered in this chapter would be Qubes-like OS with the hardware-enforced pre-boot protections, hardware-enforced OS Secure Boot, secure configurations, all critical patches applied in a timely manner, hardware-enforced security domain protections, application control manager to prevent malware executions, trusted applications, security-bound cookies, and trusted actions.

Trust Assurance Service

The local Trust Assurance Service will evaluate the OS, applications, and actions separately.

Trusted OS Assurance Levels

Trusted OS assurance levels would be decided using the following factors:

- Does the OS have hardware-enforced OS Secure Boot?
- Does the OS have software-enforced OS Secure Boot?
- Are all publicly known critical OS vulnerabilities patched or mitigated?
- Is the OS securely configured?
- Is the device currently reported as compromised or associated with rogue behavior or in recent past?

Trusted OS assurance levels would look something like what is shown in Table 9-1 below.

Trusted OS Trust Assurance Service

Any device with a secure boot is going to be a more secure and trusted device, especially if that secure boot process is protected by a TPM-like chip. Each participating device could be verified by its local Trust Assurance Service for its secure boot status, and optionally, that status could be reported to the global Trust Assurance Service. Devices with secure boots, hardware to OS, and hardware-enforced would be given the Higher/Highest assurance. Devices with software-enforced secure boots or t cover only part of the boot process would be given medium assurance. Low assurance would be given to systems without secure boot processes.

Any participating node in the high-trust Internet ecosystem receiving a connection request or participating in a shared transaction should be able to quickly query the global Trust Assurance Service using the connecting device's ID to find out/verify the following:

- Device's trusted OS assurance level
- Digital signature
- Whether the device has been reported as currently abused or compromised at the global Trust Assurance Service

For example, if I receive a request to communicate from a new device on the Internet, my device's local Trust Assurance Service can send a one network packet query (similar to DNS) to the global local Trust Assurance Service,

Table 9-1: Trusted OS Assurance Levels

TRUSTED OS ASSURANCE LEVELS	DESCRIPTION
5 – Highest trust	Thorough, hardware-enforced OS Secure Boot, registered with global Trust Alliance Service, all critical OS patches applied, the device is not currently reported as compromised or associated with rogue behavior or the recent past.
4 – Higher trust	Thorough, hardware-enforced OS Secure Boot, registered with global Trust Assurance Service, all critical OS patches applied, the device is not currently reported as compromised or associated with rogue behavior or the recent past.
3 – High trust	Partial OS Secure Boot process (software- or hardware-enforced), registered with global Trust Assurance Service, all critical OS patches applied, the device is not currently reported as compromised or associated with rogue behavior or in the recent past.
2 – Medium trust	Partial OS Secure Boot process (software- or hardware-enforced), not proactively registered with global Trust Assurance Service, OS critical patches status not known, the device is not currently reported as compromised or associated with rogue behavior; could have been reported as compromised in the recent past.
1 – Low trust	No secure boot process, OS critical patches status not known, the device is not currently reported as compromised or associated with rogue behavior in the recent past.
0 – No trust or compromised	Reported as currently compromised or associated with rogue behavior regardless of other attributes; or not found.

essentially sending the device ID along with asking "What's the current trusted OS assurance level of this device?"

Table 9-2 is an example logical makeup of what a trusted OS status lookup packet might look like coming from a client request.

The global Trusted Assurance Service would receive the query, look up the current status in its service, and send back the following:

- Device ID
- Trusted OS assurance level

Table 9-2: A Trusted OS Status Lookup Packet

Date/time of request
Device ID (of requesting device)
Query Flag (0=standard query, 1=server status check, etc.)
Type of Assurance Level Check (e.g., 0=All, 4=Trusted OS)
Device ID (of the requested device)

Table 9-3: A Trusted OS Status Lookup Packet

Date/time of request
Device ID (of requested device)
Query Flag (0=standard response, 1=client status check, etc.)
Error Codes, if any
Trusted OS Assurance Level (of requested device and OS)
Current Status (of requested device)
Trust Assurance Service Identifier
Digital Signature of Reply from Trust Assurance Service

- Current status (Active, Disabled, Active compromise, Past compromised, Not found, etc.)
- Trust Assurance Service identifier
- Trust Assurance Service digital signature

Table 9-3 an example of the logical makeup of what a Trusted OS Status lookup packet might look like coming back to a client in response.

Trusted App Assurance Levels

Trusted app assurance levels would be decided using the following factors:

- Does app have a registered globally unique application identifier?
- Is app securely coded?
- Does app do self-integrity checking?
- Does app run in its own isolated security domain?
- If so, does app run in hardware-enforced isolated security domain?
- Is app securely configured?

- Is app controlled by an application control program?
- If app uses access control token cookies, does it have security-bounded cookies?
- Has the application been reported and confirmed as compromised or associated with rogue behavior?

Trusted application levels would look something like Table 9-4.

A trust assurance value would be reported to the requesting client. Communications would happen between the client's local Trust Assurance Service and global Trust Assurance Service. The client would receive results back from the global Trust Assurance Service and handle them according to its own defined handling rules.

Once an application has been confirmed as exploited or engaged in rogue behavior, it will be marked with level 0 application trust assurance (No trust or Compromised). Either it contains a vulnerability that will need to be patched, creating a new version and application identifier, or it was intended to be used maliciously and will be permanently banned. The latter does not apply to legitimate applications used by rogue users for nefarious purposes.

Table 9-4: Trusted Application Levels

TRUSTED APP ASSURANCE LEVELS	DESCRIPTION
5 – Highest trust	App has globally unique trusted application identifier, is securely coded, does self-integrity checking, runs in its own hardware-enforced isolated security domain, securely configured and attested by nation-state accepted assessment program, controlled by application control program, has security-bound access control token cookies, the application has not been reported as compromised or engaged in rogue behavior, involved in the highest trust ecosystem.
4 – Higher trust	App has globally unique trusted application identifier, is securely coded, does self-integrity checking, runs in its own hardware-enforced isolated security domain, securely configured and attested by higher trust accepted assessment program, controlled by application control program, has security-bound access control token cookies, the application has not been reported as compromised or engaged in rogue behavior, involved in the Higher Trust ecosystem.

TRUSTED APP ASSURANCE LEVELS	DESCRIPTION
3 – High trust	App has globally unique trusted application identifier, is securely coded, does self-integrity checking, runs in its own software-enforced isolated security domain, securely configured and attested by high trust accepted assessment program, controlled by application control program, has security-bound access control token cookies, the application has not been reported as compromised or engaged in rogue behavior, involved in the high trust ecosystem.
2 – Medium trust	The application has not been reported as compromised or engaged in rogue behavior, involved in the medium trust ecosystem.
1 – Low trust	The application has not been reported as compromised or engaged in rogue behavior, involved in the low trust ecosystem.
0 – No trust or compromised	The application has been confirmed as compromised or engaged with rogue behavior; or not found.

Trusted App Trust Assurance Service

Any device with trusted applications is going to be more secure and trusted than a device not running trusted applications. Each participating application could be verified by the local Trust Assurance Service for its trusted application status, and optionally, that status could be reported to the global Trust Assurance Service. Applications with secure coding, self-checking, hardware-enforced application security domain isolation, secure configuration, application control, and trusted actions would be given the highest trust.

Any participating node in the high-trust Internet ecosystem receiving a connection request or participating in a shared transaction should be able to quickly query the global Trust Assurance Service using the connecting device's ID to find out/verify the following:

- Device's trusted app assurance level
- Digital signature
- Whether the device or involved app has been reported as currently abused or compromised at the global Trust Assurance Service

For example, if I receive a request to communicate from a new device on the Internet, my device's local Trust Assurance Service can send a one network packet query (similar to DNS) to the global local Trust Assurance Service, essentially sending the device ID along with asking "What's the current trusted application assurance level of this app."

Table 9-5 is an example logical makeup of what a trusted app status lookup packet might look like coming from a client request to the global Trust Assurance Service.

A separate request would need to be made for each trusted application to be queried.

The global Trust Assurance Service would receive the query, look up the current status in its service, and send back the following:

- Device ID
- Trusted app assurance level
- Current status (Active, Disabled, Active compromise, Past compromised, Not found, etc.)
- Trust Assurance Service identifier
- Trust Assurance Service digital signature

Table 9-6 is an example of the logical makeup of what a trusted app status lookup packet might look like coming back to a client from the global Trust Assurance Service in response.

Table 9-5: A Trusted App Status

Date/time of request
Device ID (of requesting device)
Query Flag (0=standard query, 1=server status check, etc.)
Device ID (of the requested device)
Type of Assurance Level Check (e.g., 0=All, 5=Trust App)
Application Unique Identifier

Table 9-6: A Trusted App Status Lookup Packet

Date/Time of Request
Device ID (of requested device)
Query Flag (0=standard response, 1=client status check, etc.)
Error Codes, if any
Trusted App Assurance Level (of requested device and app)
Current Status (of requested device)
Trust Assurance Service Identifier
Digital Signature of Reply from Trust Assurance Service

Trusted Action Assurance Levels

Trusted actions assurance levels would be decided using the following factors:

- Does action occur in a trusted application?
- Is action/event/scenario defined as a trusted action?
- If so, is trusted action defined as high-risk?
- If trusted action is defined as high-risk, was additional authentication and monitoring performed before action was allowed?
- Has the application been reported as compromised or associated with rogue behavior?

Trusted action levels would look something like Table 9-7.

Table 9-7: Trusted Action Levels

TRUSTED ACTION ASSURANCE LEVELS	DESCRIPTION
5 – Highest Trust	Involves a trusted application, defined as a trusted action, defined either as low-risk or as high-risk and additional authentication and monitoring is performed before allowing the action to proceed, involved application has not been reported as compromised or engaged with rogue behavior, involved in the highest trust ecosystem.
4 – Higher trust	Involves a trusted application, defined as a trusted action, defined either as low-risk or as high-risk and additional authentication and monitoring is performed before allowing the action to proceed, involved application has not been reported as compromised or engaged with rogue behavior, involved in the higher trust ecosystem.
3 – High trust	Involves a trusted application, defined as a trusted action, defined either as low-risk or as high-risk and additional authentication and monitoring is performed before allowing the action to proceed, involved application has not been reported as compromised or engaged with rogue behavior, involved in the high trust ecosystem.
2 – Medium trust	The involved application is not registered as a trusted application and has not been reported as compromised or engaged in rogue behavior, involved in the medium trust ecosystem.

(continues)

Table 9-7: (continued)

TRUSTED ACTION ASSURANCE LEVELS	DESCRIPTION
1 – Low trust	The involved application is not registered as a trusted application and has not been reported as compromised or engaged in rogue behavior, involved in the low trust ecosystem.
0 – No trust or compromised	The involved application is not registered as a trusted application and *has* been confirmed as compromised or engaged with rogue behavior; or not found.

> **note** Until trusted actions become more pervasive, it's likely that requesting clients will have to give more leeway to evaluating if trusted actions can even be evaluated as part of a high-trust ecosystem. If there are zero or very few trusted actions, it might not make sense to use them in trust enforcement decisions, at least until they become more pervasive.

Trusted Action Trust Assurance Service

Any device with trusted applications and actions is going to be more secure and trusted than a device not running trusted applications and actions. Each participating application and its trusted actions could be verified by the local Trust Assurance Service for its trusted application status, trust actions status, and optionally, that status could be reported to the global Trust Assurance Service. Trusted applications with trusted actions that are additionally confirmed before allowing them to proceed would be given the Higher/Highest trust.

Any participating node in the high-trust Internet ecosystem receiving a connection request or participating in a shared transaction should be able to quickly query the global Trust Assurance Service using the connecting device's ID to find out/verify the following:

- Trusted action assurance level
- Digital signature
- Whether the device or involved app has been reported as currently abused or compromised at the global Trust Assurance Service

For example, if I receive a request to communicate from a new device on the Internet, my device's local Trust Assurance Service can send a network packet query (similar to DNS) to the global local Trust Assurance Service, essentially sending the device ID along with asking "What's the current trusted action assurance level of this site/service/application/session?"

Table 9-8 is an example logical makeup of what a trusted action status lookup packet might look like coming from a client request to the global Trust Assurance Service.

A separate request would need to be made for each trusted application to be queried.

The global Trust Assurance Service would receive the query, look up the current status in its service, and send back the following:

- Device ID
- Trusted app assurance level
- Current status (Active, Disabled, Active Compromise, Past compromised, Not found, etc.)
- Trust Assurance Service identifier
- Trust Assurance Service digital signature

Table 9-9 an example of the logical makeup of what a trusted app status lookup packet might look like coming back to a client from the global Trust Assurance Service in response.

Table 9-8: A Trusted Action Status Lookup Packet

Date/time of request
Device ID (of requesting device)
Query Flag (0=standard query, 1=server status check, etc.)
Device ID (of the requested device)
Type of Assurance Level Check (e.g., 0=All, 6=Trust Action)
Action Unique Identifier

Table 9-9: A Trusted App Status Lookup Packet

Date/time of request
Device ID (of requested device)
Query Flag (0=standard response, 1=client status check, etc.)
Error Codes, if any
Trusted App Assurance Level (of requested device)
Current Status (of requested device)
Trust Assurance Service Identifier
Digital Signature of Reply from Trust Assurance Service

Chapter Summary

This chapter covered trusted OS, trusted applications, and trusted actions. Any OS with a secure boot process is going to be considered more secure and more trusted than a system without it. Any application securely coded, with self-integrity checking, security domain isolation, secure configuration, application control, and security-bound cookies is going to be more trusted than one that is not. Actions verified as trusted and lower-risk are going to be seen as more trusted than unverified or higher-risk actions.

Key concepts are:

- OS Secure Boot
- Trusted OS
- OS security domain isolation
- Globally unique developer IDs
- Globally unique application IDs
- Secure coding
- Self-checking applications
- Secure configuration
- Trusted applications
- Application control programs
- Security-bound cookies
- Trusted actions

Chapter 10 covers trusted networks.

Trusted Networks

Trusted networks should work end-to-end no matter what other rogue entity is in between the source and destination. This chapter covers different types of trusted networks and how they will be evaluated and used in a high-trust Internet ecosystem.

What Does Trusted Network Mean?

You could have all the trusted devices, OS, applications, and verified identities to create and communicate with others, but if the network channel you are communicating over is compromised, it can lead to malicious manipulation of the communicated data.

The simplest traditional example is two users, Alice and Bob, communicating with each other, sending data back and forth. But suppose Eve, the eavesdropper, is able to insert herself between Alice and Bob (i.e., an adversary-in-the-middle [AitM] attack). Alice thinks she is communicating with Bob, but she is really communicating with Eve. Bob thinks he's communicating directly with Alice, but he's really communicating with Eve. Eve is able to see everything that Alice and Bob are sending each other, and Eve can simply review the data and re-transmit it to the other side or maliciously manipulate the data.

For example, suppose Alice asks Bob, "Should we bomb the target tonight?" Bob gets this question and replies, "No, we have important assets visiting the target tonight." But Eve intercepts Bob's response and changes it to, "Yes." Eve's manipulation could have big negative consequences.

note Network devices are sometimes generally known as *network nodes* or just *nodes.*

Data Integrity and Security

When most people are talking about network security and trusted networks they are talking about identity integrity (device and person), data integrity, and data privacy (usually achieved through encryption). But trusted networking can mean more than just protecting communications against eavesdropping and manipulation. A good network works to keep malicious users and devices from interacting with it.

Node Validity

Node validity is the concept that only authorized network devices should be communicating using this network. On a wireless network, access may be controlled through the use of a Wi-Fi password. On wired networks, it may be allowed or prevented using some sort of logical or physical network-blocking technology. The general term for this is *network access protection*.

Node Identity

This is essentially the same as device identity. Every node on a network should have a unique, reliable identity so everything else about it can be tracked.

Node Compliance

This is the concept that any node wanting to join or stay on a network must meet policy requirements set by the network. This can be things like patching status, installed and up-to-date anti-malware software, and minimum OS versions. Compliance may be checked and enforced before the node can connect to the network and again to rejoin it for continuing operations. The compliance checking and remediation can be automated. When it is automated, it is often called *orchestration*.

You can make an easy argument that a network that allows very easy-to-hack computers on it puts the rest of the network nodes more at risk than not. There are places on the Internet that are known to be full of hackers, such as 4Chan or many Internet Relay Chat (IRC) channels. If you decide to participate with them, you know that you are at increased risk of attack.

Conversely, a network that requires that involved network nodes be strongly secured to join or remain on the network is at lower risk to the participating network nodes. A strongly secured network node means many things, including:

- Secure OS with secure boot enabled
- Strong authentication required
- Verified identities needed
- Secure configuration settings

- Host-based firewall with a good default ruleset
- All critical patches applied in a timely manner
- Running up-to-date antimalware software
- Running aggressive security event logging
- Required software

There are other requirements some resilient networks add, but the concept is that the strongest, trusted networks require strongly secured nodes. Over my career, I have belonged to several networks that did all of this, and if your computer was not in compliance, you could not join the network to communicate. If you were not in compliance, you could be forced off the network. Some networks gave you time (say two days) to fix the out-of-compliance condition; others forced you off immediately, and you would have to resolve the issue to get back on.

Compliance was often assessed by software or a service running on the network or network node. It could be done by some network software that was supplied by the network device vendor, a company-provided custom piece of software, an open-source project, or a commercial vendor. The compliance assessment needs to be verified by a trusted, knowledgeable source, however that is defined and accomplished. In most instances, the assessment is automated. A client node wanting to be on a network has to allow a centralized assessment service or local client service to run on their node, doing the assessment and compliance work.

At the Highest level of assurance (level 5), it would be an assessor approved by the nation-state. Level 4 (Higher) would require an assessment by a commercial vendor or a level 4 trusted open-source project. At the High assurance (level 3), we could have some sort of corporate assessment, a trusted level 3 open-source project, or a commercial vendor. Level 2 assurance (Medium) would be self-asserted. Level 1 would be no assessment, and level 0 would be an unknown or compromised node. To re-summarize, node compliance can be:

- Verified or unverified as to meeting network compliance
- Forced to comply to join and/or remain on a network
- Assessed using a locally installed client or centralized source
- Assessed by a commercial vendor, trusted group, nation-state, or trusted open-source project
- Low assurance if compliance assessment is self-asserted

Network Availability

We want our networks to be available and run at the highest possible throughput. A resilient network should have anti-DoS/anti-DDoS mechanisms built-in or involved. A resilient network should prevent others from interfering with my communications and prevent others from forcing me prematurely off the network. On the average network, it is possible for one misbehaving node to intentionally force all other nodes off the network (called *bumping* or *knocking*).

Safety

We want our networks to be safe and not be bins of maliciousness and constant hacking. There are many networks on the Internet that are exactly that, and most participants know this and prepare accordingly. Resilient networks have content filtering, anti-malware detection, anti-DDoS defenses, and network intrusion detection abilities.

Not only do the originating nodes want these types of assurances, but the communicating nodes on the other side do as well. No one wants a node communicating with them to originate from a hostile network or be worried about continuous connection issues.

Different Types of Network Trust

Different types of networks deliver trust in different ways. Most networks try to deliver a relatively safe and reliable network that is fairly free of maliciousness but leave it up to the individual nodes for most other protections.

HTTPS

The most common type of network protection is Hypertext Transfer Protocol Secure (HTTPS), which is the world's most common online security protocol. Data encryption and server node identity are provided by a protocol known as Transport Layer Security (TLS), although you'll often hear it referred to by its older, now insecure, outdated version, Secure Sockets Layer (SSL).

With HTTPS, the participating servers/nodes on the Internet have a TLS digital certificate, which, if digitally signed by a Certification Authority (CA), attests to the server's identity/name using DNS nomenclature (e.g., www.microsoft.com). So, if my browser connects to https://www.microsoft.com and the resulting digital certificate says I'm connected to www.microsoft.com or microsoft.com, I can be relatively assured that my browser is connected to a server on or authorized for microsoft.com and not somewhere else (assuming I didn't get tricked into accepting a fraudulent certificate on another site). In most instances of HTTPS networks, only the server's identity is authenticated. The client's identity is not required to be authenticated to the server simply to connect.

When HTTPS is enabled, all data sent between the client and server and vice versa is encrypted using a session-negotiated symmetric encryption key. The session encryption key is generated and communicated using TLS asymmetric encryption between the client and the server. This is called a *public key exchange* or a *key encapsulation mechanism*. The actual shared symmetric encryption key that the client and server use and share to encrypt the data is never directly communicated between the client and the server, but enough information is shared so that the correct shared session key can be identically generated on each side.

It used to be that HTTPS was very sparingly used on the Internet, used only when server integrity and data encryption were required. Perhaps only a few percent of websites used or required HTTPS for the first few decades of the Internet. Today, however, because of a Google browser security requirement announced in 2017, HTTPS is used on a much higher percentage of all websites. While just over 50% of all of today's websites by pure numbers alone have HTTPS enabled, all the most popular websites do, with enablement rates of more than 90%. Today, most websites that most people connect to on a daily basis have HTTPS enabled.

Unfortunately, because of Google's HTTPS requirement and a change in the cost structure of getting a TLS certificate, most malicious websites now also use HTTPS. This is because some CAs, like Let's Encrypt (`https://lets encrypt.org/`), allow anyone to request and get a free TLS digital certificate without having to prove legitimacy of any type. Prior to the creation of Let's Encrypt in 2015, the cost of a web server TLS digital certificate ($35–$5000), along with the CA doing at least some minor legitimacy checks, prevented most malicious hackers from getting TLS certificates. But now Let's Encrypt allows anyone, maliciously intended or not, to quickly request and get a free TLS digital certificate.

Let's Encrypt has a good argument (`https://letsencrypt.org/2015/10/29/ph ishing-and-malware/`) for why they do so, but it still hurts to see so many malicious websites with valid TLS digital certificates after years of browsers showing a "lock icon" whenever someone connected to a site with a TLS digital certificate. Even today, a large percentage of the world thinks that any website with a valid HTTPS/TLS certificate is a "legitimate" website. Unfortunately, the lock icon means safety to most users. For that reason, Google Chrome just recently stopped displaying the locked icon when Chrome connects to an HTTPS-enabled site. Today, Chrome displays an icon that shows two connection bars instead.

HTTPS AitM Attacks

HTTPS was specifically created to prevent our proverbial Eve from inserting herself in between Alice and Bob, at least without them knowing about it. When HTTPS is desired, either Alice or Bob, or both, can get and use a TLS-enabled digital certificate, which identifies them to the other. When they connect to each other, the TLS-certificate they get from the other confirms that they are connecting to each other and no one else.

In theory, Eve would not have a digital certificate or would not have Alice or Bob's address on her digital certificate (or she would, but it would not be digitally signed by a trusted public CA attesting to the address). So, theoretically, if either Alice or Bob got tricked into connecting to Eve, not seeing the other's valid TLS certificate when using HTTPS, they would know that Eve is there in between them performing an AitM attack.

This works if Alice and Bob notice that their HTTPS connections are not connected to the right places. However, in the real world, a large percentage of Alice and Bob nodes connect to Eve, and even though their browser displays Eve's digital certificate (or no certificate), they don't notice or understand enough about what is going on to react correctly. And because they don't notice or react correctly, they continue communicating as if they are really directly connected to each other when they aren't. So, despite HTTPS and TLS certificates working the way they were intended, there are still tens of thousands to millions of successful AitM attacks involving HTTPS and TLS each day.

The most common real-world attack example happens when Eve sends Alice a fraudulent email pretending to be from Bob, inducing Alice to click on the link in the email to supposedly connect to Bob. If Alice looked at the link she was sent by Eve, she would see that it isn't taking her to Bob, but Alice doesn't notice, so she clicks it and is taken to Eve instead. Then, Eve connects to Bob, completing the AitM attack. Everything that Alice and Bob send each other is now viewable and modifiable by Eve. Here's a great demo of a simulated real-world attack: `https://www.youtube.com/watch?v=xaOX8DS-Cto`.

This is to say, as mentioned in Chapter 4, "Challenges," sometimes people simply don't understand the technology even when the technology works. My Internet security fix would have additional methods, including the global Trust Assurance Service, to let website visitors know what the assurance level of the site they are visiting is and whether it has been reported as involved in maliciousness. It turns out HTTPS and TLS were never intended to attest to legitimacy or maliciousness. It only indicates that there is an encrypted data stream between the client and server, and the server is located at the DNS location stated on the TLS certificate.

HTTPS has some other security issues, such as only the data being encrypted and not the full network packet involved. This is to say that other people can see where or to whom you are sending the encrypted data, just not the data itself. It's also possible for an attacker to modify the data stream and remove the TLS portion (essentially changing HTTPS to HTTP) and a large percentage of the participating users would not notice. There are also concerns of side channel attacks, a lack of client authentication, and a few other attacks that users of HTTPS need to worry about. My Internet security solution would address many of these.

Encrypted End-to-End

Many communication applications, like Signal and WhatsApp, are enabled with *End-to-End Encryption* (*E2EE*). E2EE means the data (and sometimes header information) of communications is encrypted from source to destination, and any involved vendor that is helping to facilitate the app cannot decrypt the data. For example, even though Meta owns WhatsApp, the data of a WhatsApp communication stream is encrypted end-to-end, and no one else besides the source and destination, including Meta, has the decryption key and sees the data of the communication. The idea is that no one else besides the originally intended recipients should be able to see the data.

This is distinct and different from non-E2EE encryption streams where the vendor or involved middlemen may be able to access the data in cleartext. There is a big push for all popular communication apps to have E2EE enabled by default. In general, any network stream with E2EE enabled is better for privacy and security than one without.

There are some potential issues, including if all aspects of the involved application enable E2EE by default. There is a history of some applications only using E2EE on some parts of their application while failing to clearly tell users when it is not being used. Also, E2EE does not always have to have strong node authentication, meaning that AitM scenarios are possible with some of the apps, although in practice, E2EE apps are abused far less than HTTPS-enabled applications. Also, E2EE encryption is enabled on a per-application basis, meaning that it is easy for users to use non-E2EE apps, such as SMS. When you use an E2EE app, the user(s) you are corresponding to must usually use the same application. If I'm using WhatsApp, anyone I want to communicate with must use WhatsApp. If I use the Signal app, all the other people I want to communicate with must also use Signal, and so on. I have seven different E2EE communication apps on my phone to communicate with people who use various E2EE apps. It's a big pain.

VPNs

A *virtual private network* (*VPN*) is a logically separated and protected network intended to work across other network architectures, whether they are trustworthy or not. A good VPN should be able to keep your data private and with good integrity, even if the network(s) you are transmitting are hostile. An example would be visiting your local coffee shop and using its Wi-Fi while some malicious hacker is also using it and trying to hack other nodes. A good VPN would keep the hacker from being able to compromise or exploit other nodes and their data.

VPN clients can automatically start and log on to the VPN without any user interaction when the user starts their device or require a secondary logon exclusive to the VPN itself (and it may require multifactor authentication (MFA). VPNs are often required to allow remote users to connect to corporate networks. The idea is that it's less likely for a hacker trying to attack a particular network to also have the necessary VPN software and credentials installed, meaning they can't even access the network. However, in practice, this theory doesn't seem as strong, as most corporate networks that get compromised also run required VPNs. Hackers just seem to get around them or use them.

Hundreds of vendors (e.g., https://nordvpn.com) offer VPN solutions where the personal or corporate user subscribes and is then able to use the VPN. Some of the VPN providers often provide additional protective services such as anti-malware scanning, blocking trackers, blocking malicious websites, E2EE, and so on. Many VPN vendors promise absolute security so that even if law enforcement comes to them asking for data on a particular user, they won't have it or provide it.

The VPN allows the data connection the user is using to be even more secret than if they were only using HTTPS connections. With HTTPS, the user's originating Internet Service Provider could see the user's header information and at least figure out what sites and services the user was visiting. With a VPN, the Internet Service Provider only sees the user's connection to the VPN service, usually over HTTPS, and everything else, including all other connections made using the VPN, is obscured from the Internet Service Provider (and other unauthorized parties).

Unfortunately, hackers use VPNs to obscure their origination point and to intentionally appear as originating from other physical locations where they are really not located. There is also a history of some VPN vendors, even though they were claiming they were private and trustworthy, not turning out to be. Some VPN vendors who claimed they would never work with law enforcement when contacted by law enforcement, did turn over client information, making impacted customers mad. There are even "free" VPN services, which are just really malware programs that turn users into unwilling bots on a botnet. If you use a VPN, make sure it is a safe and trusted.

Tunneling

Another way to avoid unnecessary traffic inspection is to connect to a remote computer, using HTTPS or a VPN, and then use that host to do all your computing and network communications. As long as that host computer isn't monitored or logged, anything you do from it won't be visible to anyone eavesdropping on your originating network traffic.

In the early days, hackers would set up a proxy tunnel between their originating node and the remote computer using tunneling software. In practice, the originating client first sets up client tunneling software on their end. They have to configure their browser to send all traffic to the local tunneling client. This is usually as easy as inputting the "local IP address" (i.e., 127.0.0.1) and a TCP port used by the tunneling software on the local computer (e.g., 127.0.0.1:

8001). This will route all browser traffic to the tunneling client. The tunneling client is configured to connect to the remote computer, and everything sent over the tunnel will be invisible to eavesdroppers except for the HTTPS traffic to a single remote destination.

At the remote node, a tunnel client or server piece of software receives the connection and then uses the local computer to send out traffic. It can be configured to send to particular ports as indicated by the originating client or to send everything to the remote computer's browser. So, if the originating computer user types in www.microsoft.com in their browser, that command is sent to the local tunnel software and then sent to the remote computer's tunnel software, where it is executed on the remote computer's browser, and the result is then returned to the originating user. Today, tunneling is considered a legacy technology and not used that much.

Virtual Machine Nodes

The growing common type of tunnel today is for a user to connect to a remote VM out on the Internet somewhere, where they can then do all their computing and networking. VMs can be subscribed to and made permanent or disposable, where all new data and settings are erased every time the user ends the session. A good example of that type of service is https://browser.networkchuck.com.

Trusted Network Communications

In 2005, the Trusted Computing Group (makers of the Trusted Platform Module standard) created the Trusted Network Communications standard (https://trustedcomputinggroup.org/work-groups/trusted-network-communications). It covers the whole gambit of trusted networking, including access, compliance, safety, and security orchestration. With that said, the Trusted Network Communications standard never became super popular like the Trusted Platform Module did. Still, the Trusted Network Communications standard is a great model for anyone wishing to create a trusted network.

All other things considered equal, a client node belonging to a verified trusted network is going to be more trusted than one that is not located on a trusted network.

Zero-Trust Architecture

Conversely, there is a growing system of belief, called *zero-trust architecture*, that no nodes and no networks should be trusted and granted extra trust simply because they are in what we would otherwise consider to be trusted networks.

There is a lot of validity to this idea because attackers constantly make it onto our most trusted networks. The U.S. government is requiring that regulated agencies move to zero-trust architectures, and a sizable percentage of corporate networks are doing the same. For a few years, it seemed every new computer security product released or marketed had the term *"zero trust"* somewhere in the description (much like the term AI today).

A big part of zero trust is the idea that no node and no user is automatically trusted, and if the heavily monitored environment sees you doing something risky (i.e., not a trusted action), then additional computer defenses jump into action and either stop the action or ask for additional authentication (known as *dynamic authentication*). This is a great idea and one I supported in the previous chapter when discussing trusted actions.

The problem is that very few people really understand what zero-trust architecture means or how to obtain it, and every vendor seems to claim that it is part of any zero-trust architecture solution, obscuring which ones really are. If I could boil zero-trust architecture down to three main points, it would be: 1) Never trust any node or user; 2) essentially make every client-to-server connection its own little, isolated, granular network security domain; and 3) ask for additional authentication when a risky action is being performed.

NIST has a great document on zero-trust architecture: `https://csrc.nist.gov/pubs/sp/800/207/final`.

The end result of a zero-trust network architecture is creating and using the very best mechanisms to perform user and device identity using strong authentication, access control, and auditing. Pretty much most of the same things as preached in this book, with the primary difference being that my solution involves levels of assurance, and zero trust would state that all traffic and nodes be treated as a single no-trust level of assurance.

Some critics may even rightly say that my Internet security solution is the opposite of zero trust, which may be true. But even as I love many of the ideas and benefits of a zero-trust architecture, I don't see zero trust ever really becoming a pervasive reality any time soon. I mean, no one is a stronger proponent for zero trust than the U.S. government, and it's still full of differentiating security clearances (e.g., Secret, Top Secret, etc.) that, when a user obtains, gives them access to particular types of information and networks. I don't see the U.S. government getting rid of their security clearances (which are really levels of assurance) any time soon. I don't see the U.S. government getting rid of users needing high-assurance Common Access Cards (CACs) to access government systems.

My ultimate takeaway from zero-trust architectures, and what I think most security defenders really get from it, is the idea that any network node can be compromised or contain bad people. Your network and systems have to be designed as if you are, today, already compromised or could easily be compromised. And your security defenses need to be designed to contain a bad nodes and minimize malicious actions if they get inside of your networks or servers.

Stephen Northcutt, an early cofounder of SANS and an early mentor of mine, used to say to me, "Eat the watermelon and spit out the seeds!"

Read and understand zero-trust concepts and see which ones might make sense to apply in your environment as part of your computer security defenses.

Trusted Network Determination

A trusted network is a sum of its components, including:

- Node identity
- Node validity
- Data integrity
- Data security
- Node compliance
- Network availability
- Network safety

A network that has highly assured secure components is going to be more trusted than one that does not.

Trusted Network Assurance Levels

A trusted network policy would clearly define specific requirements to meet various levels of assurance. It would involve the components listed earlier, along with whether the network has been reported as compromised or not in the recent past.

Table 10-1 below shows some examples of trusted network assurance ratings.

Previously Compromised Networks

Historically, a network previously reported as compromised or involved in rogue behavior is at higher risk for future compromises or rogue behavior, and this should be a part of its current trust assurance level rating. Networks currently not reported as exploited or involved in rogue behavior but previously reported as compromised or rogue behavior may be more trusted as time goes on if they don't incur additional compromises or get involved in new rogue behavior. Each participant can determine the period of time needed without an additional compromise or rogue behavior for the trust assurance level of a previously compromised network connecting to them to rise. For example, if 6 months have gone by, perhaps a participant allows the other device's trusted network assurance level to move up one level, and if 12 months goes by, it allows

Table 10-1: Trusted Network Assurance Ratings

ASSURANCE RATING	DESCRIPTION	REQUIREMENTS
5	Highest trust	All trusted network components required: Node identity, node validity, data integrity, data security, verified centralized enforced node compliance, network availability, network safety; verified compliance required, network not currently reported as being compromised or involved in rogue behavior, now or in the recent past, part of the Highest Trust ecosystem.
4	Higher	All trusted network components required: Node identity, node validity, data integrity, data security, verified centralized enforced node compliance, network availability, network safety; verified compliance required, network not currently reported as being compromised or involved in rogue behavior, now or in the recent past, part of the Higher Trust ecosystem.
3	High trust	More than half of trusted network components: Node identity, node validity, data integrity, data security, verified enforced node compliance can be self-reported or centralized, network availability, network safety; compliance required, network not currently reported as being compromised or involved in rogue behavior, now or in the recent past, part of the High Trust ecosystem.
2	Medium trust	More than half of these trusted network components: Node identity, node validity, data integrity, data security, node compliance, network availability, network safety, no enforced compliance, network not currently reported as being compromised or involved in rogue behavior, now or in the recent past, part of the Medium Trust ecosystem.
1	Low trust	A few of these components, but not all: Node identity, node validity, data integrity, data security, node compliance, network availability, network safety, no enforced compliance, no network status reporting.
0	No trust	No trusted network components or reported as actively compromised; or not found.

it to move up two levels. Another participant might remove the compromise as a factor to be considered at all in future ratings as if it never happened once 12 months have gone by. It all depends on the participant's risk tolerance and the policies followed by their devices and applications.

Network Trust Assurance Service

Any node communicating with any other node should be able to check the trusted network assurance level of the other node by querying the global Trust Assurance Service using the other node's device identity to learn or verify the following information:

■ Current status of device ID

■ Device ID's trusted network assurance level

■ Device ID's digital signature

■ Whether the involved network has been reported as currently abused or involved in rogue behavior now or in the recent past at the global Trust Assurance Service

If the global Trust Assurance Service does not have a particular device ID in its database, is missing information, or the information has expired, the global Trust Assurance Service can query the requested device's local trust assurance level to get the needed information.

For example, if I receive a request to communicate from a new identity/device, my device's local Trust Assurance Service can send a network packet query (similar to DNS) to the global Trust Assurance Service, essentially sending the trusted device identity along with asking "What's the trusted network assurance level and current status of this device?"

Table 10-2 is an example logical makeup of what a Trusted Network Status lookup packet might look like coming from a client request.

The global Trust Assurance Service would receive the query and check its own database to see if the requested device's trusted network assurance level and current status was already registered (and not expired). If so, it would send that result (i.e., trusted network assurance level and current status) to the requesting client. If the global Trust Alliance Service did not have the requested information in its database (or it was expired), it would initiate a query to the local Trust Assurance Service of the involved requested node. If it obtained the requested information, it would update its database, set a new expiration date and time, and send the result to the requesting node.

Table 10-2: Logical Makeup of a Trusted Network Status Lookup Packet

Date/time of request
Device ID of requesting device
Query Flag (0=standard query, 1=server status check, etc.)
Type of Assurance Level Check (e.g., 0=All, 7=Trusted Network)
Device ID (of the requested device)

Table 10-3: The Potential Logical Makeup of a Trusted Network Status Response Packet

Device ID (of requested device)
Query Flag (0=standard response, 1=client status check, etc.)
Error Codes, if any
Trusted Network Assurance Level of requested device
Current status of the device ID of requested device
Trust Assurance Service Identifier
Trust Assurance Service Digital Signature
Digital Signature of Reply from global Trust Assurance Service

The result would include the following information:

- Device ID (of requested device)
- Trusted network assurance level (of requested device)
- Current status of device ID (Active, Disabled, Compromised, etc.)
- Trust Assurance Service identifier
- Trust Assurance Service signature

Table 10-3 above is an example of the logical makeup of what a trusted network status response packet might look like coming back from the global Trust Assurance Service to a client in response.

The requesting client would receive the requested information to its local Trust Assurance Service and distribute the results to required agents and make the appropriate security risk decisions.

Chapter Summary

This chapter covered the components of a trusted network, different types of network trust, along with some of their strengths and weaknesses. It ended by covering how the Trust Assurance Service would help participating devices determine what level of trust assurance to assign.

Key concepts are:

- Node compliance
- Network trusts
- Zero-trust architecture
- Trusted network

Chapter 11 covers the Trust Assurance Service.

Trust Assurance Service

Trust plays a significant role in whether people want to use the Internet or not. Part of that trust is in identifying who is who when communicating across a network. Identity is base and essential to network communications. Most computers have multiple "identifiers" to communicate over a network.

Nearly every computer has an Address Resolution Protocol (ARP) service (to resolve local IP addresses to physical addresses), a Dynamic Host Configuration Protocol (DHCP) client (to get assigned an IP Address), a Domain Naming Service (DNS) client (to convert domain names to IP addresses), Remote Procedure Call (RPC) service, and NetBIOS resolution client. These are all the clients and protocols needed to make the average computer device connect over a network and work by default. Even if you tell your local firewall to block all connections by default, it will usually still allow these services to send and answer essential network requests. If it didn't, your computer would not work over the network, leaving the average user very confused about what is going on.

But we don't have a default Internet security service to ask and determine "Can I trust this connection or content I'm about to interact with?" Nope, all our computers will just as readily connect to a rogue site and interact with malicious content just as readily as it will interact with legitimate sites and content. The computer has no way of knowing if what it is connecting to or displaying is malicious or not. And any software you can install or buy to inspect sites or content only works on a very small part of the problem. Perhaps, then, it shouldn't be shocking that we have rampant Internet crime.

This chapter covers the new security service that every device needs. Nothing like it exists yet. We would have to create it from scratch and populate it across every participating device that wants protection. We will start off by covering trust stack, cover the local and global versions of the service, and end by discussing the related challenges, which are sure to be many.

Trust Assurance Levels Review

Just as a quick review, Figure 11-1 shows the various trust assurance levels introduced in the previous chapters.

Levels 0–3 are essentially what we have with today's Internet. Level 3 begins to add in some of the new trust assurance components, but they aren't super resilient until we get to levels 4 and 5. Levels 4 and 5 are basically identical to each other, only separated by whether the trust stack is controlled by a nation-state entity or not.

Trust Stack

In prior chapters, we have discussed the following types of trust checks that would benefit a high-trust Internet ecosystem:

- Verified user identities (Chapter 7)
- Safe and trusted devices (Chapter 8)
- Trusted OSs (Chapter 9)
- Trusted applications (Chapter 9)
- Trusted actions (Chapter 9)
- Trusted networks (Chapter 10)

In each of the individual chapters, any user or device interfacing with another remote user or device (i.e., new incoming connection attempt or shared transaction/event) could send a request to the global Trust Assurance Service and ask about the trust assurance level, 0–5, that each of these trust components has. In practice, your local Trust Assurance Service would usually be enumerating

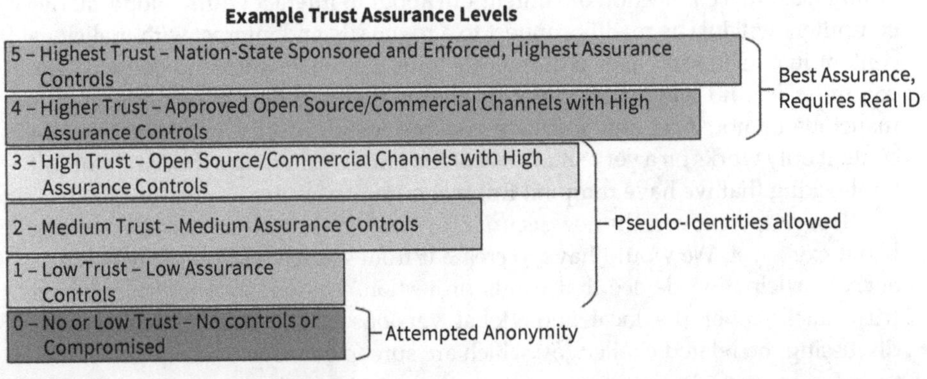

Example Trust Assurance Levels

5 – Highest Trust – Nation-State Sponsored and Enforced, Highest Assurance Controls

4 – Higher Trust – Approved Open Source/Commercial Channels with High Assurance Controls

} Best Assurance, Requires Real ID

3 – High Trust – Open Source/Commercial Channels with High Assurance Controls

2 – Medium Trust – Medium Assurance Controls

1 – Low Trust – Low Assurance Controls

} Pseudo-Identities allowed

0 – No or Low Trust – No controls or Compromised

} Attempted Anonymity

Figure 11-1: Trust assurance levels.

Assurance Levels	0	1	2	3	4	5
Assurance Levels	No	Low	Medium	High	Higher	Highest
Trusted Device	-	-	UEFI	UEFI	UEFI	UEFI
Device Identity	-	Legacy	Legacy Attested	User Agent+ Location	UEFI device ID	UEFI device ID
Trusted OS Boot	-	-	Software Secure Boot	Software Secure Boot	UEFI Secure Boot	UEFI Secure Boot
User Identity	-	Legacy	Any MFA	High+	Real ID	Real ID
Trusted Apps	-	-	-	Trusted App App Control	Trusted App App Control H/W	Trusted App App Control H/W
Trusted Actions	-	-	-	If possible	If possible	If possible
Trusted Network	-	-	-	High+	Higher+	Highest
Trust Assurance Service	-	-	Yes	Yes	Yes	Yes

Figure 11-2: Example component trust stack level requirements.

the other node across the entire list of individual components in the *trust stack*. Figure 11-2 gives an example of a possible trust stack.

In the previous chapters, a client requesting information on the other side was presented as if the client was interested only in one component of trust (e.g., device, user, OS, application, etc.). And, yes, a client can ask about only one trust component of the trust stack if they like. But in most cases, the client would be querying the other side's entire trust stack. In most Trust Assurance Service queries, one side of the connection would be asking about all the trust components of the other side, to be able to make a better trust decision.

From a theoretical perspective, a participant query would look something like this: "What is the trust stack of such-and-such a client?" It would be a single, DNS-like query packet originating from the participant's local Trust Assurance Service going to the global Trust Assurance Service. The global Trust Assurance Service would respond with a single network packet containing all the answers across the trust stack for that requested client back to the original requestor.

The answer could be something like all components meet or exceed a certain trust assurance level (say a 4) or could be a mix and match of different trust assurance levels. No matter what the answer is, the requesting client will get the answer and then determine how to proceed. For all of this to happen, we need to have a service to make the trust query and one to answer.

Trust Assurance Service

The Trust Assurance Service is made up of two different services: one global and one local.

Global Trust Assurance Service

At the center of a more trusted Internet is a brand-new hierarchical service dedicated to trying to make the Internet more secure. It would be located on the Internet, much like our existing DNS services, and function as closely to our existing hierarchical DNS services as is practically possible. At the same time, I recognize that a global Trust Assurance Service would be the most complex Internet service to date and would require broad automation at scale along with a sizable contingent of human staffers. Like DNS, it would be made up of multiple, distributed instances.

Global Components

Each global Trust Assurance Service instance would have the following components: server service, database, public allow lists, public block lists, automation, human staff, investigation, appeals process, international liaison, and accreditation services.

Server Service

The primary reason for the service is to receive DNS-like one-packet trust queries from local Trust Assurance Services. Like DNS, it would use HTTPS and digital certificates and be capable of taking many billions of requests a day very quickly.

Database

The global Trust Assurance Service database would contain the following:

- Device identities
- User identities
- Trust assurance levels across the trust stack for every participating node
- List of accredited local Trust Assurance Services
- List of accredited trusted identity providers
- List of trusted applications
- List of trusted actions
- Block list entries

It would be capable of taking billions of requests a day and answering most within a second or two. Answers placed in the global Trust Assurance Service database would be cached and have short expiration periods (say 5 minutes). Requests not found in the database for a particular participant, not cached, or expired, would initiate an information request by the global service to that involved participant's local Trust Assurance Service. Any information learned from a query would be placed into the database and then sent to the requestor.

Public Allow Lists

This would be a list of known good URLs, email addresses, domain names, phone numbers, and other items. Thus, if participants submit URLs for review that are known to be good, such as www.microsoft.com or facebook.com, they can be quickly approved and given high assurance. A participant can also submit an item that is on the public allow list for additional investigation; however, too many false-positive reports from the same identity in a quick period of time could result in their submissions being discarded, delayed handling, or the identity being blocked. This sort of response is needed for people with malicious intent trying to slow the investigation component down. Any item on the public block list takes precedence over the public allow list.

Public Block Lists

The global Trust Assurance Service would be responsible for maintaining several block lists, including:

■ Items Currently Reported as Malicious or Compromised (e.g., devices, user identities, email addresses, URLs, phone numbers, networks, trusted applications, etc.)

■ Items previously listed on a Currently Reported as Malicious or Compromised block list

■ Permanently blocked devices, sites, services, identities, and other items

Many cybersecurity vendors, law enforcement, government agencies, and group entities have their own block lists. A large percentage of the overall badness on the Internet is known as to where it originates by particular vendors today. I think that information should be publicly shared and free available for query. I would respectfully request that accredited entities report their own block list data to the global Trust Assurance Service in a timely manner so that everyone can take advantage of it.

Automation

As stated in Chapter 1, there are more than 1.1 billion legitimate and malicious websites. Google has stated that around 10% are intentionally malicious or legitimate websites maliciously modified or abused for some period of time. There are billions of identities. Hundreds of thousands to millions of them a day are newly compromised. Many stolen accounts may never be gained by their rightful owners. Malicious groups create tens to hundreds of thousands of accounts that are then used to send malicious content. There are billions and billions of new connections a day.

Every new connection between any two computers could/would result in a query to the global Trust Assurance Service. The global Trust Assurance Service would have to be designed and implemented to work at hyperscale. As much of the required tasks would be handled with automation as possible.

Human Staff

As much of the responses from the global Trust Assurance Service would be automated. But in the world of cybersecurity, no matter how great your automation is, humans can when needed review the same requests/sites/services and make more accurate, albeit much slower, decisions. Any global Trust Alliance Service would have to be staffed with the appropriate amount of humans to help make the service as accurate, responsive, and resilient as possible. We would want the human staff to be full of full-time, well-paid, subject matter experts.

Investigation

One of the primary tasks of the global Trust Assurance Service would be to report sites/services/sessions/applications/identities that have been submitted as malicious by the local Trust Assurance Services. If someone gets a malicious email, visits a malicious website, or sees a malicious message on a social media website, they should be able to report it to the global Trust Assurance Service as malicious/potentially malicious, have the submission investigated (using the appropriate combination of automation and humans), and a decision made (within a guaranteed service level, say 24 hours). The results of the investigation should be reported to the submitter, recorded in the database, and available for query for future connections involving the same items.

Large cybersecurity events should always be investigated by the subject matter experts of the global Trust Assurance Service in cooperation with the Internet Global Security Alliance (covered in Chapter 12), victims, and other relevant groups (e.g., CISA, SEC, FDA, etc.) as needed. After every aircraft crash, the National Transportation Safety Board (NTSB) thoroughly investigates the crash, learns all the pertinent details, determines the causes of the accident, and if appropriate, makes new federal aircraft laws. We want the global Trust Assurance Service and the Internet Global Security Alliance to do the same thing for big cybersecurity events.

Appeals Process

Mistakes will be made during the investigation process. Wrong outcomes will be determined. There should be a way for any submitter to appeal the first decision to obtain a second decision. The appeals process should be easy to locate and initiate and result in a timely investigation and decision. A second appeal could be made of the second decision, and it would always involve human review and be a slower review process.

It is expected that malicious individuals will make false reports at scale to devalue and slow down the global Trust Assurance Service and its investigatory methods. The system will have to be designed to expect mass false reports and include a method to aggressively block identities and systems involved with multiple false reports. An inability to prevent this sort of maliciousness would likely doom the system.

International Liaison

Each global Trust Assurance Service hierarchy will be topped by its own nation-state-level hierarchy. There will be times when international cooperation is needed. For that reason, each global Trust Assurance Service hierarchy should include a liaison team to correspond and coordinate with other global Trust Assurance Services of other countries and alliances.

Accreditation Services

Lastly, global Trust Assurance Services can offer accreditation services to other entities wanting to be local Trust Assurance Services, Trusted Identity Service Providers, Trusted Applications, node compliance software, and so on.

Global Trust Assurance Service Authority

The very top of the global Trust Assurance Service would be the central hub of a hierarchical set of services managed by each involved nation-state. Each nation-state would have its own global Trust Assurance Service or a single functional shared one administrated by shared allies (similar to the existing "Five Eyes" model of cybertrust currently serving the joint interests of the United States, United Kingdom, Australia, Canada, and New Zealand).

The decision to top the hierarchy with a nation-state administrative service was not an easy one. Many people (rightfully) distrust their government.

Certainly, fewer citizens trust the governments of other countries. However, the top legal jurisdiction of what can be defined, administrated, managed, and enforced always ends at the nation-state level. The involved laws that apply to each citizen stop at the nation-state level. Even with a multilateral agreement between nations, it's still up to the nation-state to decide whether they will allow pursuing something across national borders. And no nation is going to trust the other nation's global Trust Assurance Service to make the right decisions on their behalf. Different countries are likely to disagree on what constitutes each trust assurance level. Some countries are going to want more control and others less. Some are going to want to guarantee more privacy for its citizens and others less.

Participants who are adamant about not relying on their government for trust decisions can choose a lower level in the hierarchy. Perhaps one participant decides they want to rely on a trusted open source, community-sourced version of the global Trust Assurance Service. Another participant decides that they only trusted Microsoft to make the right trust decisions. Another participant only trusts Google. Some of these Trust Assurance Services might be free, and some might cost to join. It's up to each individual participant and who they trust. Each individual is allowed to choose which global Trust Assurance Service you want to participate with or none at all. This is something you decide to voluntarily join (or not). Most devices would come preconfigured with what the global Trust Assurance Service location the vendor picked for their customers to use by default, but any user can update their currently selected global Trust Assurance Service at any time.

The various global Trust Assurance Services lower in the global hierarchy can choose to be at the top of their own hierarchies, point to other higher-level global Trust Assurance Services, or point to the very top, the nation-state-level global Trust Assurance Service. Figure 11-3 below shows an example global Trust Assurance Service hierarchy logical diagram.

Each participating global Trust Alliance Service would have to undergo application, accreditation, and constant review to ensure they are meeting the standards of their trust assurance levels.

The global Trust Assurance Services would work hand-in-hand with the client's local Trust Assurance Service.

Local Trust Assurance Service

Each participating device should be running a local Trust Assurance Service, either pre-installed by the device or OS vendor or installed by the user. The local Trust Assurance Service client can be created by any developer or vendor, free or commercial, as long as it is reviewed and approved by the global Trust Assurance Service. The local Trust Assurance Service should be among the best-secured services/applications running on the client. If it is running on an OS similar to

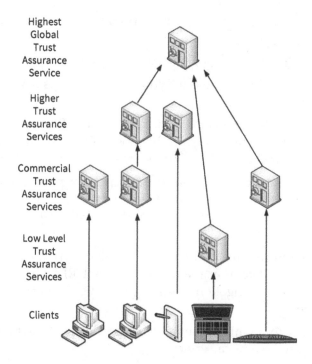

Figure 11-3: Example global Trust Assurance Service hierarchy.

Qubes OS, it should be running in its own isolated, hypervisor-enforced security container. It must be remotely contactable over HTTPS by the global Trust Assurance Service it is registered with. Its primary purposes include:

- Interfaces with the user
- Manages the user's own trusted identities, personas, and attributes
- Allows the user to select the identities, personas, and attributes for particular applications/sites/services, etc.
- Helps set up new connections
- Handles new remote requests from new and existing connections
- Interfaces with global Internet Trust Assurance Service
- Determines verified identity trust assurance level for all identities, both used by the originating user and used by the other side of any connection
- Locally queries and obtain the needed values to establish a device's and identity's trust assurance levels across the trust stack (i.e., trusted device, device ID, user ID, trusted OS, trusted applications, trusted action, and trusted network)

- Reports the device's and identity's current trust stack values to the global trust alliance service

- Takes queries from the global trust alliance service

- Send queries for newly detected connection requests that are not already cached or are expired

- Automatically submits email addresses and URLs (and other content items, like phone numbers) to the global Trust Assurance Service for trustworthiness when a user views them

- Allows the user of the local service to report suspected compromises of the current system or any involved sites/services/sessions/applications/ content the user is interacting with to the global trust alliance service for investigating

- Identifies and submits for review to the global Trust Assurance Service any new content items (e.g., email addresses, URLs, phone numbers, etc.) for review or investigation to see if they have been previously reported as malicious

- Allows user to submit any suspected suspicious content for review to the global Trust Assurance Service

Trust Assurance Service Identity Selection

When a user logs on or initiates a new connection to a site/service or executes a local Trusted Application for the first time after logging in, the local Trust Assurance Service can automatically associate a particular pre-selected user identity/persona with that newly started site/service/session/application instance (based on policy or defaults) or optionally, visually/verbally query the user to select which ID to use for the new connection. Figure 11-4 below shows an example mockup local Trust Assurance Service prompt that a user might see when starting a new application.

Ideally, most users would not see this dialog box when connecting to most sites and services or starting an application, as the selections would already be chosen by policy, defaults, or previous selections. However, it should be presented when needed or when the user requests it. The user should be able to hit a "hot key" (e.g., Ctrl-I) to bring up the local Trust Assurance Service identity selection dialog box and choose which identity to associate with a particular site/service/application.

Trust Connection Queries

Each local Trust Assurance Service sends queries to the global Trust Assurance Service for every new connection it initiates or is initiated to it (for which it does not have a current cached non expired entry). It then receives a response

Figure 11-4: Example mockup Trust Assurance Service identity selection.

from the global Trust Assurance Service with the remote connection's trust stack data. The data is available to any local service or application and can be treated according to the user or existing policy. But essentially, once the data has been obtained and stored by the local Trust Assurance Service, the local Trust Assurance Service ends its participation (for that current connection or until some preset renewal time period).

Verifying Items

Any URL shown to/or item accessible to user interaction (e.g., email address, website, phone number, etc.) should automatically be transmitted to the global Trust Assurance Service as a query. The global Trust Assurance Service should report whether the submitted item has been previously submitted as malicious.

New Inbound Connections Attempts

Whenever a new connection attempt comes into a device, it can be handled according to predefined policy or visually displayed to the user for review and approval. The local graphical user interface (GUI) displayed to the user can be different according to how the developer creates, according to a predefined policy, or when the sites/services/sessions/applications involved want to take advantage of the local Trust Assurance Service. In some/most cases, all the obtained information and trust decisions can be completely hidden from the user and handled completely within the confines of the participating services and applications with predefined policies or defaults. The fewer decisions and distractions shown to the user the better.

Alternatively, if needed, the incoming query can be displayed to the user for them to view and react to. Figure 11-5 shows an example of a local Trust Assurance Service screen that could be displayed to the user for evaluation and a decision.

Note: The default response option should always be Deny, so that if the user ignores or just hits Enter, the default response will be to deny the connection.

The type of trust confirmation prompt described might be far too much information for many low-tech users and confuse them. That's why, if possible, the decision should not be visibly shown to the user, but be an automated decision based on policy or defaults. User interface experts can design a more understandable end-user interface prompt that would be more readily understood by more people, but the mockup in Figure 11-5 demonstrates some of the information needed to make a decision.

It's possible that any user can be socially engineered into making the wrong trust decision. Social engineers do that all the time today with other scams and technologies. Scammers successfully get victims to bypass multiple warnings and run malicious programs and scripts all the time. Scammers get victims to allow overly permissive OAuth permissions. Scammers get victims to allow their malicious programs to exploit other programs and services. The ability of scammers to fool people into making the wrong trust decision will always be present. However, a high-trust ecosystem will at least present the user with the correct verified identity trying to the scam the user before they make a particular trust decision. The new high-trust ecosystem has that going for it.

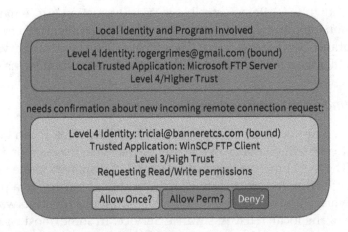

Figure 11-5: Example of local Trust Assurance Service prompt.

Automatically Checking Identities, Content, and Links

When viewing new potentially dangerous items and content (e.g., URLs, email addresses, phone numbers, etc.), it would seem pretty natural that a local Trust Assurance Service GUI would automatically identify the item to be investigated, automatically submit it to the global Trust Assurance Service for review, get the answer, and then identify the item according to its trust assurance level.

One of the best resulting treatments could be a visible colored "wrap" around verified items. High-trusted, confirmed, non malicious devices, identities, URLs, etc., could be wrapped in green, indicating that the queried item was investigated and determined to be ranked level 4 or 5 trust assurance level and not to be currently reported as malicious or exploited. Items detected as malicious or currently exploited would be wrapped in red. Items not found or previously reported as exploited (but not currently known to be) can be wrapped in yellow. The individual trust assurance level components reported by the global Trust Assurance Service could be displayed as part of the wrapper. The idea is to make it easy for most people to see if a connection or item they are considering interacting with has been reported as malicious, along with the trust assurance levels across the trust stack. Figure 11-6 shows some simulated wrapping outcomes.

Each time the user reviews the item, it should be re-submitted for inspection to the global Trust Assurance Service, if not previously cached or expired. That way, if something previously trusted becomes compromised at a later date, the item isn't still wrapped as trusted. Trust is something that is checked every time the user is relying on it.

The wrapping should be performed in such a way that it would be hard for malicious coding to fake. You wouldn't want a malicious site/service/session/ application able to easily fake a local Trust Assurance Service confirmation message or content wrapper. Security solution vendors face this sort of threat and try to offer various mitigations. Microsoft has long done this with their User Account Control feature prompting, and most browser manufacturers

rogeragrimes66@gmail.com

TAL scores: Dev-3, DevID-3 (bound) UID-3, OS-4, App-3, Act-0, Net-0

www.badsite.com/badlink/badsession.html

TAL scores: Dev-0, DevID-1 UID-0, OS-0, App-0, Act-1, Net-0

www.goodsite.com/goodlink/session.html

TAL scores: Dev-4, DevID-4 UID-4, OS-3, App-3, Act-1, Net-3

Figure 11-6: Simulated wrapping outcomes.

try to prevent fake security prompts as well, to varying degrees of success. We need the same sort of thoughtful protection done for the local Trust Assurance Service and its responses.

Who Makes the Local Trust Assurance Service?

The local Trust Assurance Services can be made and distributed by any trusted developer or entity, including open-source projects and commercial vendors. Each local Trust Assurance Service would be digitally signed and approved by one or more of the global Trust Assurance Services. The global Trust Assurance Service would not allow registration and participation unless previously registered, accredited, and allowed. A single client could run one or more local Trust Assurance Services. They all should run at the device level. A device could be a computer, a piece of network equipment, a TV, a vehicle, an IoT device, etc.

Issues and Challenges

A service dedicated to trying to solve the world's Internet security problems is going to be a huge, huge hacker target. It will not only be under constant assault by bad people intentionally trying to undermine it but also be bypassed or ignored by otherwise well-meaning participants. Both local and global Trust Assurance Services must be designed with integrity and security foremost in mind.

Securely Designed

Each Trust Assurance Service must be designed and coded securely from the beginning. Involved developers must be trained in the security development lifecycle (SDL) and use programming languages and tools that work to support SDL. The programming languages should be memory-type safe. The services should be threat modeled (more on this in Chapter 13) at the beginning of design, code reviewed, and continuously penetration tested during development and after release. Services should be enrolled in bug bounties, and appropriate rewards should be paid for any security bugs found. All code should be self-checking, to see if it has been maliciously modified prior to execution and while running. If running on an OS, like Qubes OS, that provides isolated security domains, the local Trust Assurance Service should run in its own isolated domain.

The current status of a requesting client querying a global Trust Assurance Service should be checked by the Global Trust Assurance service before responding. Clients currently reported as malicious should not be responded to. Both local and global services should be designed to minimize the impact of DoS and DDoS attacks as best as can be done. The service should be self-patching without requiring user input in a timely manner.

Securely designing both the local and global Trust Assurance Services should be among the highest priorities. Success or failure of the Internet's new high-trust ecosystem rides on how well these services can be protected against constant maliciousness.

How to Fund?

Local Trust Assurance Services can be funded by users who buy it or as open-source projects. The global Trust Assurance Service will require significant resources, including cloud resources, network resources, programmers, subject matter experts, and investigators, and so will take significant funding, on a higher order of magnitude than we have previously experienced with other Internet services. Funding will likely take political approval in each participating country. But it is time for all citizens to have a significantly safer Internet and so we must seek and approve the necessary funding.

How would this funding be done? Here are some potential options:

- Included in part of nation-state's normal budgeting
- Included as a small fee on everyone's Internet service provider's bill
- Paid as part of the local Trust Assurance Service subscriptions

The funding will likely be harder to accomplish than the technical components.

Why Fund?

There are hundreds of vendors who already have their own individual internal review and reputational checking services, which are maintained for the benefit of their products and customers. All the anti-malware companies do. All the major vendors, like Microsoft and Google, do. Even smaller vendors, like KnowBe4, Inc., do. There are many hundreds of individual reputation services and block lists, all with their own teams of people. So, why do we need to fund the global Trust Assurance Service?

First and foremost, none of the vendor's individual teams does anything close to what is being proposed for the global Trust Assurance Service. It's reputational-checking on steroids. But the bigger reality is that even the largest vendor reputational service teams have fewer than a dozen people on them. Most teams are just a handful of people. Many teams are just one or two people. Most customers see some multibillion-dollar company and assume that its malware-checking and reputational-checking teams must be huge, hundreds of workers. But most are run by just a handful of people. They just seem large because of marketing and branding. That's not a bad thing. That's what all companies do.

But these small teams can't begin to handle the sheer volume of the whole Internet like that needed for the global Trust Assurance Service. We need a service that is global in scale, very accurate, and able to respond in real time. To be all of that, it needs to be well-funded. The global Trust Assurance Service will easily be the largest global Internet group and service of its kind, and it needs to be adequately funded.

Much of our lives are spent online. We are well past when this should have already happened. Every country has a well-funded Department of Defense that focuses on kinetic battles and digital defenses as a side job. We need a dedicated entity full of subject matter experts and technology, focusing only on all our digital threats to identify and prevent them in real-time. The global Trust Assurance Service could be queried by anyone or anything (within reasonable limits) and can be used to supplement any vendor's own individual efforts, if they want.

Proof of Concepts First

It goes without saying that any project of this complexity and scale needs to be tried in several smaller proof-of-concept projects first. I can envision the first small-scale proof-of-concept project involving just a few medium-sized companies, followed by additional proofs of concept at some very large companies (e.g., Google, Microsoft, Amazon, etc.), and eventually being released to the entire Internet if the previous proofs of concept are successful. The proofs of concept would need to be done internationally. Perhaps the NIST Centers of Excellence (https://www.nist.gov/coe) might be a good place for the initial proof-of-concepts.

I'm sure I'm missing many other issues and challenges that will face Trust Assurance Services, but this chapter gave us some idea of what we are talking about and the challenges we face in implementing it.

Chapter Summary

This chapter covered the local and global Threat Assurance Services. It first covered the global Trust Assurance Service, including all of its components: server service, database, public allow lists, public blocklists, automation, human staff, investigations, appeals process, international liaison, and accreditation services. The local Trust Assurance Service was covered along with its required duties, including querying and reporting local data, finding out the trust stacks of other connections, and responding to queries from the global Trust Assurance Service.

Key concepts are:

- Trust stack
- Global Trust Assurance Service
- Public allow lists
- Public block lists
- Local Trust Assurance Service

Chapter 12 covers the last piece of the Internet high-trust ecosystem, the Internet Security Global Alliance.

Internet Security Global Alliance

The current state of Internet security is poor, and all the existing groups involved in trying to fix it are way too slow. None has a solution that would resolve most Internet security problems. This chapter envisions the group we need to implement better, faster, lasting Internet security standards. Most of this chapter is dedicated to discussing existing Internet security groups, because once you understand their problems, figuring out how the future, better group should be structured is easier.

Cybersecurity Standards

Cybersecurity standards are agreed-upon protocols, methods, guidelines, and best practices designed to protect users and devices from unauthorized access, exploitation, manipulation, and other cybersecurity threats. Standards, if broadly followed, are great as they allow agreement and interoperability among many different devices and entities. We have many cybersecurity standards, including HTTPS, TLS, Wi-Fi WPA/WPS, IPSEC, DNSSEC, WebAuthN, OAuth, and DMARC. Some are broadly followed, and everyone uses them. Others, like IPSEC and DNSSEC, are far less popular.

If you are trying to improve Internet security, you must do so using a standard approved by one or more controlling Internet security groups. A rigorous standards process ensures that the biggest flaws in the standard are found and removed during the review and approval process. If passed, it gives everyone a specification to build toward to ensure functionality and interoperability.

Most Internet security groups are made up of volunteers, either sponsored by their employers, sponsored by some other group, or self-funded. Most of the work is done in topic-driven *working groups*, which are trying to solve one or more problems about the topic of concern. Most Internet security groups allow anyone to join any working group, although participants have to agree to bylaws and can be kicked out of the group. It is not uncommon for members within a workgroup to have strong disagreements with each other, which results in competing working groups and standards.

Membership can be free or require an annual fee. Fees, if required, range from tens of dollars to more than $100,000, depending on the group. Sometimes, there are additional fees for in-person meetings. The higher the fee, the more likely it is that only large corporations and nation-states will be involved.

Many Internet standards are initially pushed as Requests for Comments (RFCs). An RFC document is authored by an individual or group of individuals to document their proposed standard. It often contains descriptions of the involved technology, defines terms, lists components, and details the involved technologies by packet type and bytes.

Note: Many early IETF RFCs were simply meeting notes. This method of formal documentation of IETF meetings using RFCs was reduced over time.

Most RFCs are released for peer review within the involved working group and are often available for review by anyone in the world. RFCs invite comments, considerations, and suggested improvements. RFCs can often go through several formal revisions and result in new dependent RFCs or new RFCs, which entirely replace the entire original RFC. Many RFCs, after years of review, become new official Internet standards. Others languish as historical documents, never to be implemented as an official standard. You can see the complete list of IETF RFCs here: `https://www.rfc-editor.org/rfc-index-100a.html`.

Note: RFCs are often staid, somewhat scientific-looking documents, but there are the occasional humorous ones. One of the most popular hilarious ones is `https://www.rfc-editor.org/rfc/rfc2549`.

Existing Internet Security Groups

Unfortunately, there is no single group that runs the Internet or decides Internet security. It would be great if it were so. Instead, Internet security is a distributed outcome that develops from many different groups to varying degrees of influence. I'm going to cover the most popular current groups.

Internet Engineering Task Force

Traditionally, it used to be that you would submit your great Internet security idea to the Internet Engineering Task Force (`https://www.ietf.org`) as a RFC. The Internet Engineering Task Force (IETF) was the earliest and largest standards organization for the Internet and is responsible for many of the early technical standards (e.g., HTTP, HTTPS SMTP, DNS, etc.) that made the Internet work. The U.S. government was the primary sponsor of IETF during the early days of the Internet, but it released control to broader world support in 1993. The IETF is probably still the most respected and mature organization to submit a new standard to, but it suffers from many issues, including a very long decision process. Although I'm sure it considers the long-waiting times as a feature, not a bug.

World Wide Web Consortium

Founded in 1994 by the creator of the World Wide Web, Tim Berners-Lee, the World Wide Web Consortium, or W3C (https://www.w3.org/), is the de facto standards-making body for everything web-related. The most prolific W3C standard is the latest version of HTML, called HTML5. They also designed and matured Cascading Style Sheets (CSS) and Extended Markup Language (XML). The W3C's version of the RFC is known as working drafts and recommendations.

The most prolific Internet security standard to come out of the W3C is WebAuthN, which is an open standard for authenticating users to web-based sites/applications/services using public-key cryptography. It is a core part of many trusted authentication standards, such as FIDO (Fast IDentity Online), and likely will have a large role in a future high-trust Internet ecosystem. FIDO-enabled USB keys and FIDO Passkeys use the WebAuthN standard. It is also possible to implement WebAuthN-style authenticators using Trusted Platform Module (TPM) chips.

Although the W3C is far from perfect, it's done a tremendous job in shaping and securing the web. The W3C is faster than the IETF, has more support and activity, and is delivering more new things. Still, at times, even though it's faster than IETF, some standards seem to move at a glacial pace. Some members have complained that W3C security standards seem to get watered down to be less effective over new versions.

NIST

The National Institute of Standards and Technology (NIST; https://www.nist.gov/) was formerly known as the National Bureau of Standards until 1988, when it was renamed NIST. Its role extends far beyond just cybersecurity, but it is the U.S. government agency that sets the cybersecurity standards, known as *Special Publications* (*SP*), required to be followed by U.S. government agencies and their contractors. Special Publications beginning with 800-series are usually cybersecurity recommendations and requirements. When NIST releases a cybersecurity guide, it is usually seen as a worldwide standard, and many other entities and countries frequently adopt its recommendations, even if not required.

NIST has a bunch of very influential cybersecurity standards and other entities, including:

- NIST Cybersecurity Framework (https://www.nist.gov/cyberframework)
- SP-800-63 Digital Identity Guidelines (heavily referenced in Chapter 7)
- SP-800-53 Security and Privacy Controls for Information Systems and Organizations
- NIST Post-Quantum Contests and Standards (https://csrc.nist.gov/projects/post-quantum-cryptography)
- NIST Centers of Excellence (https://www.nist.gov/coe)

NIST is what much of the world follows for cybersecurity standards and best practices. It frequently holds public "contests" for transparent open standard cryptography submissions (i.e., DES, AES, Post-Quantum), which become new future cryptography standards. Unfortunately, it has also been caught up at least twice in cryptography standard scandals (i.e., DES and Dual EC DRBG), which had the strong appearance of intentionally weakened or backdoored standards. Because of this, there are many who are skeptical of any security standard that NIST endorses. It's unfortunate, but NIST could help itself by staying out of scandals.

CISA

The Cybersecurity Infrastructure Agency (CISA) is the U.S. government's largest dedicated cybersecurity agency. It was the result of new legislation after 9/11, which merged 16 previous cybersecurity organizations into one. It is responsible for cybersecurity and other critical infrastructure protection across the United States. Its core mission originally focused on protecting government entities, but it has broadened to protect all U.S. organizations and entities better. It has dozens of very successful programs and spends a lot of its focus on establishing private-public partnerships to help improve cybersecurity for all. CISA is often the first U.S. government organization to warn everyone else about a popular or growing cybersecurity threat, like a particular ransomware gang or a popularly-exploited vulnerability. Here are some other notable programs:

- Known Vulnerability Exploited Catalog (https://www.cisa.gov/known-exploited-vulnerabilities-catalog)
- Public Exploit Announcement List (https://public.govdelivery.com/accounts/USDHSCISA/subscriber/new?qsp=CODE _ RED)
- Secure-by-Design (https://www.cisa.gov/securebydesign)
- Stop Ransomware (https://www.cisa.gov/stopransomware)

CISA has easily been the most successful U.S. cybersecurity agency, and the work that it does benefits the world. It works hand in hand with the other similar "Five Eyes" programs located in the United Kingdom, Australia, New Zealand, and Canada.

If there is a major ding against CISA, it is that it legally cannot compel non governmental entities to implement best cybersecurity practices. It makes recommendations and doesn't have much enforcement capabilities. It takes new laws from Congress to allow CISA to compel any requirement for any agency, and those don't happen that often.

NSA

The National Security Agency (NSA) is often called the "U.S. Spies" because a major part of its mission is spying on foreigners and their conversations. As part of that mission, they eavesdrop and record trillions of conversations (including involving many Americans) a year. The NSA is believed to have the largest number of full-time employees and contractors of all U.S. intelligence agencies. As part of its mission, it participates in the NIST cryptography process because of its recognized cryptographic expertise. It is also believed to be the central reason for the previously mentioned weakened and backdoor cryptographic standards that NIST released.

What the NSA learns from spying sometimes results in CISA announcements and recommendations, although it is also frequently blamed for withholding information to the public about vulnerabilities it knows about, even when the vulnerabilities are being actively exploited by themselves or our adversaries. There is a secret U.S. committee involving multiple U.S. government intelligence agencies and military leaders who meet to discuss which NSA-known vulnerabilities to keep secret and which to reveal to the related vendor so the vulnerability can be mitigated.

Note: Award-winning author James Bamford has written exclusively on the NSA, its mission creep, and areas where it is found to break the law. If you want to know about the NSA, Bamford's books on the NSA are the ones to read.

International Organization for Standardization

The International Organization for Standardization (or ISO) is an independent, non governmental, international standards organization comprised of representatives from the national standards organizations. Many of its cybersecurity standards, such as ISO 27001, are the international standard for information security. Many country and industry group cybersecurity standards are based on ISO standards. Some companies spend a significant amount of money and resources being accredited as having met particular ISO standards, for without, they would have fewer customers and business.

ANSI

The American National Standards Institute is, as Wikipedia states, "a private nonprofit organization that oversees the development of voluntary consensus standards for products, services, processes, systems, and personnel in the United States. ANSI also coordinates U.S. standards with international standards so that American products can be used worldwide. Most of its work does not involve the Internet or cybersecurity; however, ANSI ISO/IEC 27033 (`https://blog.ansi.org/iso-iec-27032-2023-cybersecurity-guidelines/`) is their official guide on cybersecurity standards.

IEEE

The Institute of Electrical and Electronics Engineers (IEEE) was formed in 1963 as an organization for engineers. The IEEE Computer Society covers computer topics, including cybersecurity standards. It has many well-attended conferences, publications, and awards. You will see many Internet security standards with IEEE in their name. For example, Wi-Fi is IEEE 802.11, IEEE 802.1X is network access control (covered in Chapter 10), and IEEE 802.1AR-2018 is secure device identities.

ACM

Found in 1947, the Association for Computing Machinery (ACM) is the world's largest scientific and educational computing society, particularly focused on academics and research. Its publications and journals are considered gold standards in the cybersecurity industry. The top technical innovators are given the title of distinguished fellows, and the list (`https://en.wikipedia.org/wiki/List_of_fellows_of_the_Association_for_Computing_Machinery`) reads like a Who-Who of computer giants. ACM, along with the IEEE, gets involved in setting some cybersecurity standards.

Government Organizations

Every country has one or more official government agencies or militaries setting cybersecurity standards for its members. The United States has the Department of Defense, Defense Information Systems Agency (DISA), and corporate-focused entities like the Securities and Exchange Commission (SEC). In the European Union (EU), the General Data Protection Regulation (GDPR), which governs the default rights and digital privacy of EU citizens, is probably their best-known cybersecurity law.

States and regions often have their own cybersecurity standards. In the United States, California and New York, because of their economic dominance, tend to create new state laws that often get adopted in more states and even at the federal level.

World Economic Forum

The World Economic Forum (https://www.weforum.org) is a non profit, non governmental organization that focuses on issues as applied to the national and global levels. Although best known for its annual financial "Davos" meeting, it contains members who work on everything, including cybersecurity. I belong to a WEF working group covering the quantum topic. It produces reports on quantum computers and makes recommendations to its members.

Political Laws

Of course, national governments often create and pass laws that impact cybersecurity standards. In the United States the best known is probably 2002's Sarbanes–Oxley Act of 2002 (or SOX), which made corporate executives personally accountable for ensuring their financial reporting was accurate, which meant stronger cybersecurity practices. The Health Insurance Portability and Accountability Act of 1996 (HIPAA) created cybersecurity standards for healthcare organizations and fines for those entities that are found lacking.

Government Industry Groups

The U.S. government has stood up many industry groups, which also have specific cybersecurity standards. These include the Federal Energy Regulatory Commission (FERC), which covers traditional energy infrastructures like electricity, oil, and natural gas. The Nuclear Regulatory Commission (NRC) covers the nuclear power industry. The Environmental Protection Agency (EPA) and CISA are charged with keeping our water safe.

Vendors

The very largest vendors, such as Google, Microsoft, and Amazon, are behemoths that can set new de facto cybersecurity standards simply because they implement them at scale. Google, running the world's most popular Internet search engine, is probably the leader. It frequently joins working groups, announces new standards, and tells the world when they need to comply. At times, it's a very welcome relief to get some big Internet problems solved, and other times, it can be frustrating for other people as one corporate entity sets new computer security standards by itself.

Multivendor Consortiums

Sometimes, multiple vendors see a cybersecurity risk to their industry and form a multivendor consortium. The Payment Card Industry Data Security Standard (PCI-DSS) is probably the best representative of this. PCI is a consortium of the major credit card vendors (Visa, Mastercard, American Express, Discovery, etc.). Their DSS contains hundreds of security controls every vendor processing a credit card transaction must have in place to process credit card transactions. Merchants found to be out of compliance can be fined or even prevented from processing credit card transactions. Unfortunately, PCI-DSS requirements only apply to larger merchants, and the vast majority of stolen credit cards come from non covered merchants.

Fast Identity Online (FIDO) Alliance (`https://fidoalliance.org`) is a multivendor consortium dedicated to replacing passwords with strong, phishing-resistant forms of authentication, such as multifactor authentication (MFA) and Passkeys. Members include the largest corporations, such as Google and Microsoft. Some people complain that FIDO is not an open standards body, but some of their standards, like WebAuthN, are open standards.

Dedicated Independent Groups

There are hundreds of independent groups set up to improve cybersecurity.

The Cloud Security Alliance (`https://cloudsecurityalliance.org`), or CSA, is a great example. Initially set up to cover emerging cloud security topics only, its popularity quickly spread to many other cybersecurity topics not only associated with cloud computing. For example, I belong to the CSA's Quantum Safe Secure working group. I was the major author of their white-paper, called Practical Preparations in a Post Quantum World (`https://cloudsecurityalliance.org/artifacts/practical-preparations-for-the-post-quantum-world`), covering how organizations need to prepare for sufficiently capable quantum computers.

There are many independent groups full of subject matter experts which focus on particular Internet security technologies. For example, the Internet Identity Workshop (https://internetidentityworkshop.com/) focuses on making more security identity and authentication solutions, which are key to better securing the Internet. There are a ton of industry groups full of vendors working to better secure the Internet as it relates to what they do. A good example is the Bank Policy Institute (https://bpi.com/). In general, they have often have fairly good connections and lobbying resources with various government agencies and politicians. They can help push new standards through the government faster than other groups.

Center for Internet Security (CIS, `https://www.cisecurity.org`) is one of my favorite groups that truly gets cybersecurity a bit better than the rest. It's famous for a couple of things, including its Critical Security Controls (`https://www.cisecurity.org/controls/cis-controls-list`), benchmarking, hardened images, and thought leadership. I especially love CIS's understanding of how to map cybersecurity risks to threats and controls. No one does it better.

Main Problems with Existing Orgs

I could be forgetting 20 other important groups, but you probably already see part of one of the biggest problems. There are too many groups. No one group is in charge. Most groups aren't even dedicated to Internet security. Most are full of part-time volunteers who simply don't have the time to push or evaluate new standards aggressively. Here are some of the problems with the existing groups:

- Slow in getting new standards passed (5–10 years is not unusual).
- Limited span of control.
- All are focused point problems and not the larger, underlying problems.
- Members often make dozens of recommended changes to any proposed standard, slowing it down (i.e., "death by a thousand cuts").
- Some groups charge money for their standards.
- Requirements are never risk-ranked.
- Staff by too many volunteers and not enough paid staff.
- Corporate sponsorship invites conflicts.
- Consensus agreement often waters down standard.

Conventional thinking is that in order to get a new security standard passed and implemented, you have to have a huge organization, like Google or Microsoft, support it first. If you have a new cybersecurity standard you want to push, you have to get their attention. Unless they have a bad problem and need your solution, they probably aren't listening. But if you have an idea for a cybersecurity standard that fixes one of their big issues, they may decide to adopt and support it. They will get it pushed into a working group, participate in early proof of concept projects, and become an early adopter. Many of today's cybersecurity standards have occurred this way.

As listed, there are many problems that make existing Internet security standards harder to create and implement. But out of all of these, speed is the biggest problem. New hacker techniques show up all the time. Unfortunately, it can take defenders years to a decade to adequately respond well enough to put down the threat. Then, attackers start using another method and the whole exploit/defend lifecycle begins again. Figure 12-1 below gives an example exploit/defense cycle.

Any new and improved Internet security group needs to be architected for speed to lessen the timeline of the exploit lifecycle.

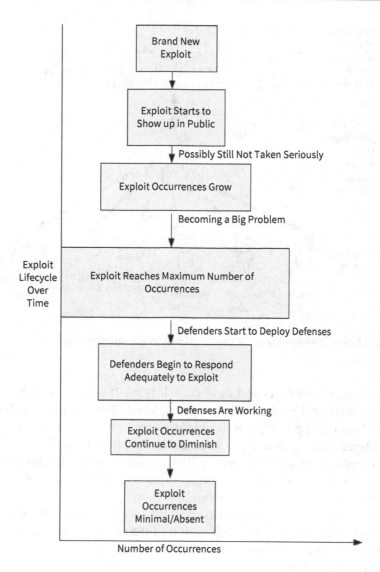

Figure 12-1: Example exploit/defense cycle.

Internet Security Global Alliance

We need a brand new dedicated group whose only mission is to quickly pass new cybersecurity standards. I call it the Internet Security Global Alliance. The Internet Security Global Alliance should be a private/governmental-sponsored technical group with full-time paid Internet security experts who look at existing

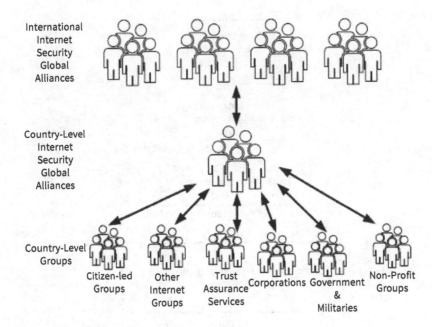

International
Internet
Security
Global
Alliances

Country-Level
Internet
Security
Global
Alliances

Country-Level
Groups

Citizen-led
Groups

Other
Internet
Groups

Trust
Assurance
Services

Corporations

Government
&
Militaries

Non-Profit
Groups

Figure 12-2: Example Internet security global alliance cooperation groups.

Internet security problems and develop solutions. It would be architected for speed and technical proficiency. Like the global Trust Assurance Service, it should be funded by participants. It should get input from various other Internet groups (those covered and those not mentioned), the global Trust Assurance Service, corporations, governments, militaries, and non profit organizations. It could help coordinate all the disparate, disorganized groups dedicated to trying to solve the various facets of the overall problem.

The Internet Security Global Alliance would have authority over each of its involved nation-states, and each nation's Internet Security Global Alliance group would interface with the other nations. Figure 12-2 above shows example relationship dependencies.

The Internet Security Global Alliance should have the following responsibilities traits:

- Focused only on Internet security.
- Supersedes all other groups for creating new Internet security standards.
- Built for speed.
- Focuses on underlying problems (instead of point issues).
- All standards are open standards and free to use and download.

- Any resulting recommendations and requirements are risk-ranked.
- Help global Trust Assurance Service investigate big cybersecurity events.
- Paid staff of subject matter experts.

If done correctly, this new Internet security group should correct the existing problems and fix Internet security problems in a better, more timely fashion.

Chapter Summary

This chapter covered the existing Internet security groups, their inherent problems, and the new Internet Security Global Alliance and how it should be structured to better serve Internet security.

Key concepts are:

- Cybersecurity standards
- Request for Comments
- Working groups
- Internet security groups
- Internet Security Global Alliance

Chapter 13 creates a threat model for the specific technologies introduced in Chapters 7 through 12.

Challenging the Solution

Threat Modeling

This is the second threat model of the two presented in this book. The first was in Chapter 5, threat modeling the overall theory of a high-trust Internet ecosystem in a perfect world with a perfect solution to test and see if the solution's defenses would work to significantly improve the security of the Internet. It concluded that a high-trust Internet ecosystem with a verified user identity and the other supporting trust components covered in more detail in Chapters 7–12 could significantly reduce Internet crime. This chapter is a another threat model of the various technologies presented in Chapters 7–12.

Threat modeling is normally done as part of the design process but is presented here after the technologies were presented in Chapters 7–12 for readability purposes. For many readers to understand the threat model, I had to first define the main design features, terms, and technology before discussing the threat model of the design. However, in reality, threat modeling comes first as part of the design.

I also recognize that this short chapter is not a full, formal threat model. A full, formal threat model over all the involved technologies would likely create a report over 100 pages long, far too long to place in this book. The threat models presented in this book are summaries and highlights of a far larger threat model that would be needed in the real world.

Technology Summary

Let's re-summarize the technologies involved in a high-trust ecosystem experience for trust assurance levels 4 and 5 (Higher and Highest (these are formal names)). Remember, trust assurance levels 0–3 are essentially the same as today's Internet and aren't evaluated here, but it's assumed the threats and risks would be far greater for them than Levels 4 and 5.

An Internet high-trust ecosystem would include the following components:

- Safe and trusted devices
- Trusted operating systems
- Verified identities
- Trusted applications
- Trusted actions
- Trusted networks
- Trust assurance service
- Internet security global alliances

The High-Trust Ecosystem Process

The high-trust ecosystem process at levels 4 and 5 would look similar to this experience:

1. The device hardware and firmware boots up and checks itself for unauthorized modification, using hardware-enforced (e.g., TPM) values.
2. After the hardware and firmware pass the integrity, the boot sequence would be passed off to the BIOS/UEFI process. All of that process would be hardware-enforced as well.
3. Once passed, the boot process is handed off to the active OS. The OS secure boot sequence would be processed and confirmed.
4. The user would log in using a phishing-resistant form of MFA associated with a trusted identity. This would become the default identity associated with each service/application unless otherwise instructed by policy or the user. Users can use different identities/personas for different sites/services/applications/sessions.
5. Trusted applications would be launched, each to their own hardware-enforced security domain, managed by an application control program, using security-bound access control token cookies (if involved).
6. Secure configurations of the OS and applications would be confirmed by local agents.
7. The trust of the network would be assessed, confirmed, and reported.
8. All of these statuses would be queried by the local trust assurance service and be reported to the global trust assurance service as part of the user's trust stack values.
9. When the user initiates a new connection/session, it will be tied to a particular minimum required trust assurance service level (0–5) and verified identity combination. The other side of the connection must meet or exceed the user's requirements and vice versa in order for the connection to succeed.

10. If another user/device/site/service/application attempts to connect to the user to initiate a new connection, the same rules apply. Both sides of the connection will set minimum trust assurance levels that must be met or exceeded before the connection can continue.

11. When the user connects to a site/service/application to interact with content/event/transaction, the user can see what other users were involved with the content/event/transaction and make a decision of how and whether to interact.

12. All identity and trust assurance level transactions are handled by the user's local trust assurance service, working in coordination with the global trust assurance service.

Much of this would happen without end-user interaction, based upon defaults and previous policy settings. If the user needs to be involved or make a trust decision, the user's local Trust Assurance Service will visibly display a prompt to the user and ask for a decision.

Involved Internet Security Solution Technologies

The following new technologies are envisioned for the Internet security solution:

- Local Trust Assurance Service
- Global Trust Assurance Service

Services and their requirements would be documented by the global Trust Assurance Service team. Different OS and app vendors can create local Trust Assurance Services as long as they meet global Trust Assurance Service requirements and are reviewed and accredited by the global Trust Assurance Service. All involved vendors should be globally registered with a globally unique developer ID, and involved services should be globally registered with a unique trusted application verifier (as covered in Chapter 9). No communication should be accepted by the global Trust Assurance Service from an unaccredited local Trust Assurance Service or from a node on the block list.

Both these services would communicate primarily over HTTPS and use application digital certificates and trusted device IDs. The local Trust Assurance Service network communications would be controlled by an access control list/ firewall to allow only communication between local Trust Assurance Services and its assigned global Trust Assurance Service. The local Trust Assurance Service should be designed and coded using secure development lifecycle methodologies, code, and tools. Any connections from a local Trust Assurance Service to a global Trust Assurance Service should be checked by the global service to ensure the local service does not originate from a device ID on the block list before performing the requested action. The services should be threat modeled during design, code reviewed, penetration tested, and put on bug bounty programs with adequate funding.

The following technologies are minor to moderate extensions of existing technologies and/or just needed to be more pervasive than they are today:

- Verified identities
- Hardware-enforced device identities
- Hardware-enforced device secure booting
- Hardware-enforced OS secure booting
- Hardware-enforced security domain isolation
- Application control program
- Trusted applications
- Trusted actions
- Trusted networks

Each of those technologies would need to be secured and threat modeled by their relevant vendors.

Potential Threats

Part of threat modeling is imagining common types of threats that would attack your security defenses. In general, the threats are split between intentionally malicious attackers and/or their malware programs and otherwise legitimate users trying to circumvent the involved technologies for one reason or another.

Here are the common threats/risks for the Internet security solution presented in this book:

- Intentional malicious attackers or their malware programs not using new Internet security solutions.
- Intentional malicious attackers or their malware programs using new Internet security services to appear more trusted than they are.
- Intentional malicious content with transformed email addresses or URL links using different character sets to appear as something, not on a block list (covered in a moment).
- Hackers intentionally use items (e.g., URLs, email addresses, phone numbers, etc.) that are on the global allowed list, hoping to use the previous decisions of trust to push maliciousness.

- Intentional malicious attacker or their malware program using one or more trusted devices as a "jumping-off point" for hacking activities.

- Intentional malicious attackers or their malware programs intentionally exploit new security solutions to appear safer and more trusted than they are.

- Intentional malicious attackers or their malware program causing DoS or DDoS attacks against the involved technologies.

- Intentionally malicious attackers or their malware programs trying to overwhelm (DoS, DDoS) global trust assurance service or trusted identity provider with numerous fraudulent submissions.

- Intentional malicious attackers or their malware program trying to poison global Internet assurance service with fraudulent entries.

- Intentionally malicious attackers trying to exploit other users' use of new Internet security solutions, including malicious modification of legitimate user's services.

- Intentionally malicious attackers or their malware program stealing legitimate user's trusted identity.

- Intentionally malicious attackers or their malware program being able to take control of an otherwise legitimate trusted device, OS, or application.

- Compromises against the underlying standard technologies (e.g., cryptography, MFA, etc.)

- Account takeover.

- Attacks by adversarial nation-states by fraudulent submissions at each country's top-level global trust assurance service.

- Adversarial nation-states not participating at all.

- Attacks against the hardware technologies involved (e.g., TPM, Secure Enclave, etc.).

- Physical threats . . . malicious attackers stealing or physically damaging involved devices.

- Otherwise, legitimate users intentionally trying to bypass or exploit new security technologies for personal reasons that do not involve intentionally harming others.

- Interfacing with legacy devices and technologies not capable of interacting with the newer technologies of the Internet security solution.

- New unknown threat, attack type, or technology.

The question is, how well do the various security solutions described in Chapters 7–12 prevent these sorts of threat scenarios?

STRIDE Threat Modeling

I will again use the STRIDE threat model for this chapter. Re-summarizing the STRIDE threat model presented in Chapter 5:

- **S**poofing
- **T**ampering
- **R**epudiation
- **I**nformation disclosure
- **D**enial of service

As first shown in Chapter 5, Table 13-1 shows the mapping between the STRIDE model and the different initial root access causes shown in Chapter 2.

Now, let's threat model each of the new and extended technologies as if they were being used at trust assurance levels 4 and 5 (Higher and Highest) using the STRIDE model.

Spoofing

Spoofing includes social engineering, impersonation/authentication attacks, and insider attacks. For social engineering, typically, a fraudster is pretending to be a person, brand, or entity that the potential victim might otherwise trust

Table 13-1: Mapping STRIDE to 14 Initial Root Access Causes of Hacking

STRIDE TAXONOMY	INITIAL ROOT ACCESS CAUSES TAXONOMY
Spoofing	Social Engineering, (Technical) Impersonation/Authentication Attacks, Insider Attacks
Tampering	Software and Firmware Vulnerabilities, Intentionally Malicious Programs/Instructions/Scripting, Data Malformation, Network Traffic Malformation, Third-Party Reliance Issues (supply chain/vendor/partner/etc.), Insider Attacks
Repudiation	(Technical) Impersonation/Authentication Attacks, Insider Attacks
Information disclosure	Eavesdropping/MitM, Side Channel Attacks, Information Leaks, Third-Party Reliance Issues (supply chain/vendor/partner/etc.), Insider Attacks, Brute Force/Computational, Human Error/Misconfiguration
Denial of service	Physical Attacks, Insider Attacks
Elevation of privilege	Software and Firmware Vulnerabilities, Intentionally Malicious Programs/Instructions/Scripting, Data Malformation, Insider Attacks

more than the attacker. In impersonation/authentication attacks, the attacker steals the victim's access control token (cookie), which acts as a bearer token and allows the attacker to pretend to be the victim of a site/service/application to which the victim has previously authenticated. Insiders often try to use other co-worker's login credentials to perform malicious acts so they won't be immediately traced to the insider attacker.

The Internet security solution presented in this book is specifically created to fight digital spoofing. Trusted identities will be harder to spoof and can be marked as compromised by the global Trust Assurance Service if associated with rogue behavior. IDs associated with rogue behavior will be placed on block lists, either permanently, for repeated rogue behavior reports, or for a time-limited period. Users who have their trusted IDs or device IDs stolen can have them permanently revoked if they cannot regain control or have them marked with higher assurance if they regain control for a long period of time without being associated with repeated rogue behavior.

Links reported as malicious to the global Trust Assurance Service will be placed on the block list. A huge challenge to this is the fact that most malicious links exist only for less than 10 minutes before they disappear or are removed. This will challenge any large-scale operation because it will likely often take more than 10 minutes to review a submitted link and confirm that it is malicious. By the time the reviewing tool or human confirms that the link is malicious and puts it on the block list, the link is no longer available. Where a global block list might help in spotlighting the legitimate services related to these malicious links (e.g., the DNS services, the web hosts, etc.) that are constantly associated with rogue links. They can be marked by the global Trust Assurance Service as No or Low trust by default, so participants receiving a link from the service can treat it as such. It would also give increased incentives for the DNS service and web host to be more diligent about allowing attackers to use their services to provide rogue links. Social engineers like to create look-alike links. These can be reported to the global Trust Assurance Service by participants who spot them early and block them, preventing further victims.

The higher assurance levels of a high-trust ecosystem require that a user's trusted identity be tied (i.e., bound) to a hardware-enforced device ID. Trusted identities coming from new devices not previously registered with the global Trust Assurance Service will be marked with lower trust than trusted identities coming from the same, previously registered device IDs.

Attackers could attempt to spoof a high volume of trusted identities and device IDs. However, both identities and device IDs are created using digital certificates from trusted Certification Authorities (CAs). If the attackers have a hard time generating fraudulent IDs without access to a trusted CA's signing certificate, if compromised (this does happen), the compromised signing certificate can be easily revoked, making all IDs signed by the same certificate invalid.

Attackers will for sure take over legitimate user IDs and devices and attempt to accomplish rogue behavior from the compromised device. When the rogue behavior is noticed by other victims, the IDs can be reported to the global Trust Assurance Service. The attacks against the original legitimate devices and identities would be harder to pull off because of the high-trust ecosystem.

Impersonation/authentication attacks will be harder to accomplish with trusted identities with high and better assurance levels because the identities are bounded, and anti-theft mechanisms allow access control token cookies to be security bound. Insider attacks that attempt to use co-worker credentials will be tougher to accomplish because of device-bounded trusted identities.

It is common for hackers to "encode" email addresses or URL links using different character sets to send potential victims to malicious locations after the rogue addresses and URLs bypass inspection services because they aren't recognized or decoded correctly into their eventual plaintext form. For example, the plaintext URL, `www.google.com`, can also be typed into a browser as `http://172.217.2.196`, using its underlying IP address. Another example, `www.knowbe4.com` can be represented by ASCII encoding as `https://%77%77%77.%6B%6E%6F%77%62%654.%63%6F`. Many detection tools and scanners don't understand encoding and treat all entries as plaintext. So, even though the email address or URL may be equivalent to some previously reported rogue email address or URL, the scanner doesn't recognize it, and a service may not recognize that the address or link it is looking at is already on a block list. Consequently, attackers routinely use these types of encoding tricks to bypass content inspectors and block lists. Both the local and global Trust Assurance Services will have to be programmed to understand encoding and encoding tricks.

In general, a high-trust ecosystem, as described in this book, will make digital spoofing harder to accomplish.

Tampering

Tampering includes vulnerabilities, intentionally malicious programs/scripts/instructions, data malformation, network traffic malformation, some types of insider attacks, and third-party reliance issues.

Most types of tampering should be harder to accomplish because of trusted IDs bound to hardware-enforce device IDs. If someone tries to tamper with something, the connection can be blocked before the tampering occurs, or at least blocked afterward to prevent future mischief from coming from the same trusted identity or device ID.

There is the possibility that an attacker attempts to tamper with the chip involved with hardware enforcement (e.g., TPM, Secure Enclave, etc.). However, these cryptographic chips are designed to prevent many types of tampering attacks. Some will randomly slow down after too many invalid accesses, for example, or completely "brick" the device so that the chip and device both become inoperable.

An attacker could attempt to delete, tamper, or bypass the local Trust Assurance Service. However, there are many critical system files that vendors make it difficult to do, at least permanently. For example, Microsoft protects many critical Windows system files from easy tampering. They are protected against easy modification by strict access control permissions that cannot be easily bypassed by even a local administrator or local system (the two most powerful accounts in Windows). If an attacker is successful in modifying or deleting them, they are either immediately replaced with a valid copy or at some short periodic time interval.

An attacker could attempt to modify their image in memory or to "hook" an interrupt that interfaces with the service instead. Malware writers frequently do all sorts of shenanigans to gain control of the operating system in a way that gives the malware early control. Again, Microsoft has spent decades successfully fighting those sorts of attacks. Today, it is more difficult than ever for an attacker or malware to modify or delete critical systems files (although not impossible). Alternatively, however, an attacker could simply choose a system that does not use or have a local trust assurance service installed.

An attacker could try to interfere with the statuses and values that a local Trust Assurance Service collects. For example, a hacker could try to implant a false device ID or insert a fake trusted application ID, that the local trust assurance service then reports to the global trust assurance service. The Local Trust Assurance Service should be designed as securely as possible to prevent tampering. Ultimately, it's impossible to prevent all tampering with the values and what the local Trust Assurance Service reports. The primary control is the possibility of the global Trust Assurance Service marking the reported values, along with other associated attributes, like IP address, as No or Low trust.

Exploiting software and hardware vulnerabilities should be harder for two reasons. First, there should be fewer unpatched software and hardware vulnerabilities to begin with because critical patches are checked for at the trusted device level or the trusted network level. Second, anyone trying to exploit an unpatched vulnerability will have to identify themselves by Real ID and a hardware-enforced device ID.

However, there are some types of vulnerability exploitations, like SMS-based "background pushes" that are very hard to prevent (see `https://help.pushwoosh.com/hc/en-us/articles/360000364923-What-is-a-Device-token` and `https://www.braze.com/docs/user_guide/message_building_by_channel/push/push_registration` for more details.) But in these types of exploits, the exploit is being pushed upon the device in a way that likely would not be detected by any local Trust Assurance Service and would be pushed by the trusted device vendor. It would be very difficult for any detection system to detect and prevent that type of exploitation.

The Internet security solution isn't as resilient against third-party reliance issues, as these usually involve a compromised third party, which is then used to compromise the primary intended target. These attacks would come from trusted identities and trusted devices that are managed by the third-party. Still, the Internet security solution should make compromising the third party in the first place more difficult to do (for all the reasons listed in Chapters 7–12), and if an attack is noticed as originating from a trusted third party, that connection and third party can be reported as engaged in rogue behavior to the global Trust Assurance Service and blocked not only for the current victim but other potential victims targeted under the guise of the same third party.

Repudiation

Repudiation involves someone denying they were involved in a particular event or transaction. Having Real IDs and trusted devices should diminish reputation issues as it will be easier to determine who was or wasn't involved in a particular transaction or event. There is always the chance that the person who is claiming it wasn't them having their Real ID stolen and used, but since it should be bound to particular hardware-enforced device IDs, this should be harder for an attacker to do. Every event and transaction should be readily traced back to a particular Real ID and device ID.

Information Disclosure

Information disclosure attacks include eavesdropping/MitM, side channel attacks, information leaks, third-party reliance issues (supply chain/vendor/partner/etc.), insider attacks, brute force/computational, human error, and misconfigurations.

One of the biggest challenges of any global registration system is how to prevent participants from trying to learn too much information from the global system. An attacker could try to enumerate trusted identities and device IDs. The local Trust Assurance Service should be designed so that it can be used only to enumerate the other participants in attempted active connections. The global Trust Assurance Service needs to be designed to prevent high-speed checks from device IDs not previously registered. If a bunch of requests come in from a new device that is found to be involved in malicious activity, it can be put on the block list.

Another concern is about legitimate users or attackers trying to learn about identity attributes they were not given use to view. The attribute enumeration method designed in Chapter 7, where each individual attribute and set of attributes is given its unique, unpredictable URL, which only the user and the trusted identity provider know, should prevent unauthorized attribute enumeration.

Misconfigurations should be diminished because trusted devices and trusted applications require attestation to appropriate configurations. Appropriate configurations would have to be defined by the application vendor and enforced by the local Trust Assurance Service (if possible).

Online brute-force/computational attacks should be diminished as the attack would likely be coming from an untrusted source and be noted as rogue action, and the attacker's source address could be put on a block list by previous victims. Offline brute-force/computational attacks would likely not be stopped other than the initial exploit to gain the initial needed information to crack should be harder to get.

Privacy Violations

Privacy violations are a special class of information leak where an individual's personal information is obtained by unauthorized parties. This is of particular heightened concern regarding nation-states and internal and foreign groups they are against, such as protesters, political opposition, and the press.

Because high-trust ecosystem participants would be intentionally identifying themselves (using Real ID) and using hard-coded device IDs, they would be more readily identified by anyone who is trying to identify them. This is especially problematic in nation-states that want to identify and punish adversarial groups. This would certainly be a problem in countries with long histories of human rights violations, such as Russia, China, Iran, Saudi Arabia, and North Korea. But even countries purportedly more associated with stronger human rights and free societies, such as the United States, have been found guilty of violating human rights and invading the privacy of investigations without appropriate authorization. The high-trust ecosystem model would provide an attempted anonymity identity type, but there is no guarantee that someone using it has true anonymity, and it is likely in a high-trust ecosystem to truly have guaranteed anonymity. This is likely the biggest risk to a new high-trust ecosystem, and it needs to be designed as best as it can to prevent authoritarian privacy violations.

Denial of Service

Denial of service (DoS) attacks can be accomplished by a single attacker node sending either a single malformed network packet or more than one network packet targeting a particular service. If a service has an undiscovered/unpatched vulnerability, it is sometimes possible for a single packet to "hang up" a service until the service or system is restarted. Distributed Denial of Service (DDoS) attacks usually involve multiple nodes under the direction of the attacker, trying to overwhelm the target service with sheer volume.

DoS/DDoS attacks can also occur at the application level when the attacker submits a large, overwhelming number of legitimate or malformed requests to the involved services. As examples, an attacker could submit a very large number of requests to:

- Global Trust Assurance Service asking for various trust assurance level values across the trust stack spectrum for multiple clients (both existing and/or non-existing)

- Asking Trusted Identity Service Providers for identity verification for multiple identities (both existing and non-existing)

- Local Trust Assurance Service of a particular target to overwhelm the service

- Global or local Trust Assurance Service trying to overwhelm and slow down its response while a fraudulent service, or other fraudulent packets, try to interrupt and/or participate in legitimate requests

Each service will have to be designed to best withstand DoS and DDoS attacks at all levels. At the global level, this is something that is routinely handled by many existing global services and sites, even against the largest, sustained attacks. Locally, though, it would be more difficult for local services to withstand very large DDoS attacks. To help, the default fallback position for any application or service relying on the local Trust Assurance Service would have to default to a No trust value if the service was unable to deliver the legitimate value in a timely manner.

The global Trust Assurance Service can be designed to be resilient against DDoS attacks, much like today's DNS system. Hackers have often tried to take down the global DNS system and have partially succeeded in varying degrees of success. Ultimately, however, at least so far, no hacker has significantly impacted the global DNS service for a long time. I would expect the global Trust Assurance Service to be similarly resiliently designed.

If nodes participating in a sustained DDoS can be identified (those that have completed the TCP handshake), they can be blocked from contacting involved services (i.e., placed on the block list), either permanently or for some period of time.

Other Attack Types Not Mitigated

There are many types of attacks and edge cases that would not be mitigated by these Internet security solutions. Current solutions do not address physical attacks where participating devices are stolen, damaged, or destroyed. The best defense against physical attacks would be simply denying a malicious user the use of a trusted device that was reported as stolen by placing it on the block list. Additionally, using a strong form of authentication, such as device-bound phishing-resistant MFA, would make logging on to the stolen device more difficult.

Physical side channel attacks and human errors would not be stopped by this Internet security solution. Wireless attacks using unlicensed frequencies, like electromagnetic interference (EMI), would not be mitigated. Shared logins will always be problematic.

Scammers who don't mind identifying themselves would not be mitigated. Many scammers are friends, relatives, community leaders, and even business CEOs (e.g., Bernie Madoff, Enron CFO, etc.). Even though they often know they are likely to be (or have a high risk of being) eventually caught and arrested, they still do the scam. Other types of cyberattacks accomplished by people and groups who don't mind being identified, such as adversarial nation-state attacks or terrorists, will not be fully mitigated.

I'm sure I'm missing lots of potential threats and risks, but this is what I came up with during the writing of this chapter. If this vision of Internet security ever comes to pass, a more thorough and complete threat model will have to be accomplished (during the design phase).

Threat Modeling Results Summary

This chapter's threat model looked at the designed technologies covered in Chapters 7–12. The summary results shown in Table 13-2 repeat most of the findings listed previously in Table 5-2 in Chapter 5. The only new finding and category is the last row, Privacy Violations.

Substantially Mitigated means the attack method would be perfectly (100%) defeated or substantially be mitigated to 1/20th or less of its current occurrence/damage in the near-perfect solution world. **Partially Mitigated** means the attack method would be mitigated down from its current levels,

Table 13-2: Modeling Results Summary

ATTACK TYPE	SUBSTANTIALLY MITIGATED	PARTIALLY MITIGATED	NOT MITIGATED
Spoofing, Social Engineering (70%–90% of attacks)	X		
Software and Firmware Vulnerability Exploitation (33% of today's attacks)		X	
Insider Attacks		X	
(Technical) Impersonation/ Authentication Attacks		X	
Elevation of Privilege Attacks		X	
Intentionally Malicious Programs/ Instructions/Scripting	X		

(continues)

Table 13-2: *(continued)*

ATTACK TYPE	SUBSTANTIALLY MITIGATED	PARTIALLY MITIGATED	NOT MITIGATED
Tampering	X		
Data Malformation	X		
Network Traffic Malformation	X		
Repudiation	X		
Information Leaks		X	
Eavesdropping/MitM	X		
Denial of Service Attacks	X		
Brute Force/Computational Attacks		X	
Human Error/Misconfigurations			X
Third Party Reliance Issue (supply chain/vendor/partner/etc.)		X	
Side Channel Attacks			X
Physical Attacks			X
Island Hopping		X	
Privacy Violations			X

but not to 1/20th or below. It could also mean that some forms of this attack type are substantially mitigated while others are not. **Not Mitigated** means the attack type is 100% not stopped or not even to 19/20ths of what its former levels were.

The biggest risk in a real-world implementation, besides privacy violations, is the number of participants and nodes that cannot (i.e., legacy) or will decide not to participate. The latter group is knowingly choosing not to take advantage of higher trust and remain at what is essentially the same level of trust given across today's Internet — which isn't much. Many people opting out would likely be trying to protect their personal privacy. This would not be the worst outcome. They would stay at the same level of trust and safety as they have today and not be worse off. The only risk to a non participating individual would be not being able to communicate with others who are participating and who choose not to communicate with non participants because of the increased risk.

Chapter Summary

This chapter did a threat model assessment of the Internet security solution using the proposed technologies. It started by re-summarizing the solution, potential threat scenarios, and STRIDE threat model, followed by assessing each threat type against the real technologies. If the new and extended technologies are appropriately designed and threat-modeled, they will be highly resistant to attack. In turn, they would significantly mitigate many types of Internet crime, including spoofing, malware, tampering, data malformation, network traffic malformation, repudiation, eavesdropping, and denial of service attacks.

Key concepts are:

- High-trust ecosystem process
- STRIDE threat modeling analysis

Chapter 14 covers common questions about the proposed Internet security solution.

14

Common Questions

"If I were to try to read, much less answer, all the attacks made on me, this shop might as well be closed for any other business. I do the very best I know how — the very best I can; and I mean to keep doing so until the end. If the end brings me out all right, what is said against me won't amount to anything. If the end brings me out wrong, ten thousand angels swearing I was right would make no difference."

– Abraham Lincoln

"Propose to a man any principle, or an instrument, however admirable, and you will observe the whole effort is directed to find a difficultly, a defect, or an impossibility in it. If you speak to him of a machine for peeling a potato, he will pronounce it impossible: If you peel a potato with it before his eyes, he will declare it useless, because it will not slice a pineapple."

– Charles Babbage (considered the father of modern computers)

"One experiment is worth a thousand expert opinions."

– Unknown, similar, but not identical attributions, to Albert Einstein, Wernher Von Braun, and Adm. Grace Murray Hopper

Those are some of my favorite quotations regarding critics. I've been presenting my Internet security solution for almost two decades now. I have gotten a lot of criticism. Fortunately, I can take it. I actually want critics. Over the years, critics have made my earlier ideas better. Some of my best friends and mentors are among my strongest critics. A good idea should stand up to criticism, invite it, and become stronger for it.

However, I do think the intention of the criticism is important. I'd rather my critics give me useful criticism that points to a structural problem that I can see if I can mitigate. However, many of my critics just wholesale hate my ideas (I get it) or dismiss them without intellectual arguments. But they never come up with any solution that will significantly fix Internet security even as they lambast my own.

But out of all that criticism comes good common questions and statements.

This chapter discusses some of the most common questions and statements I get along with my answers. Its intent is to help readers better understand my plan.

We Don't Need to Fix Anything

This is a common statement, especially from privacy-minded individuals. The idea is that even though Internet crime is pretty bad (as covered in Chapter 1), society and the world are functioning well enough, and the risks of implementing a high-trust ecosystem aren't worth the cost.

I will admit that when I first heard this argument, it caught me off guard. I mean, how can anyone think that we should just let Internet crime stay as bad as it is? With that said, the first time I heard this statement was nearly two decades ago, and here we are nearly two decades later, and things are still running along. There hasn't been a big Internet collapse. Societies are still moving forward, GDPs are still improving, employment is still improving, and most of us compute without being worried about being hacked every day.

My answer: Hackers and malware are already taking down entire companies, hospitals, and cities and literally killing people. But more importantly, Internet crime is getting worse every year, and nothing on the foreseeable time horizon is likely to stop that descent. I've been watching it get worse for over 36 years, and it gets worse year after year. It never gets better. So, even if we could live with what we have today, we will likely eventually get to a place where society finally rebels and forces us to do something different. Why not be proactive? Or let's vote on it. Even if you don't want to fix anything, let's ask the majority of Internet users if they would want less Internet crime. I think the vast majority will be on my side. Additionally, if you don't want to participate in significantly reducing Internet crime using my solution, you have the option to continue participating as you do today with no changes. The only penalty is that other connections that do want higher levels of trust may not want to connect to you. But you and every other like-minded person can keep continuing to use the Internet as it is today.

The Solution Is Too Complex

Many reviewers have said my solution is too complex.

My answer: I agree. But every part of the solution I have proposed fixes a particular part of the problem. If you can come up with a less complex solution that significantly fixes Internet crime, let's do that instead. Less complexity is better when it can accomplish the same goals. At the same time, sending rockets to space is complex because it involves complex challenges. Same here. Fixing the Internet's security issues isn't easy.

Further, much of what my Internet security solution proposes already exists (e.g., secure boot, device IDs, etc.); we just need to make it more pervasive across more devices. Other solutions are minor to moderate extensions of existing technologies. Only a few things, notably the local and global versions of the Trust Assurance Service, need to be invented brand new from scratch.

But I'll vote for any less complex system that solves Internet security over my own. Less complex systems are easier to implement, less likely to be compromised or bypassed, and are more likely to be implemented. One of the major problems with my system is that it's too complex. I'd love to solve that problem by simplifying my solution or even using someone else's solution.

Why Isn't Everyone Using Qubes?

I have promoted the Qubes OS (`https://www.qubes-os.org`) since its creation in 2012 by cybersecurity luminary Joanna Rutkowska. She is an absolute cybersecurity visionary pushing boundaries and thought leadership more than most. I was immediately attracted to Qubes OS hardware-enforced hypervisors (called a *xen*), which allowed every OS and application to run in its own hardware-enforced isolated security domain (called a *qube*) on the same computer and be controlled from the same single desktop. It's very thoughtfully done and more mature than any other publicly available OS.

Qubes' main goal is to keep the OS and applications isolated from one another so that if one xen is compromised by an attacker or malware program, it doesn't easily get to other applications and parts of the OS. Today, it is far too easy for an attacker to take over a user's single application (say, Internet browser or email client) and leverage that initial access to take over the entire operating system, learn all login credentials, and if the compromised device belongs to a corporate network, take over the whole network. It's the way hacking is done today. As far as I know, no computer running Qubes has been successfully used to take over the whole machine or network by a real-world attacker, although now that could be more due to its scarcity of use by people than its inherent security projections.

After I promoted Qubes OS, many people asked why more people don't use it. After all, it's free; it's been around for more than a decade, and it has all these security protections. Well, for one it's based on Linux. As much as I and so many other people love Linux, Linux is not as easy to set up and use as Windows, iOS, or Google Chrome OS. In fact, when I buy a new computer and install Qubes on it, it typically takes me days of troubleshooting to get it working. Just trying to get your standard network drivers can take days and seem nearly impossible. I know many users who simply just gave up because they couldn't get it to work.

On top of that, once you're in, much of the complexity of having such a complex OS is readily apparent to the user. You have to understand brand-new concepts such as templates, disposable VMs, global clipboards, and applications, which are really whole OSs. These are things that a person running Windows or Apple iOS simply doesn't have to bother with or learn. Users can't readily buy a ton of devices with Qubes pre-installed. Using Qubes usually means buying a device with another OS and then installing Qubes over it. That almost always takes lots of effort and troubleshooting. Once you get Qubes up and running, all the default OSs are installed or Linux-based, and if you don't know Linux, it's a new learning curve. Linux and Qubes are truly wonderful, but it does take a bit of cobbling and troubleshooting that the average user would probably want to avoid. It isn't for the average user.

With that said, if you want the most secure generally available OS on the planet, it's Qubes, hands down. Qubes is very close to what we need for the Trusted OS and Trusted Apps compared to any other OS. The question is if Qubes will become so much more user-friendly that more people use it before the other more popular OSs (e.g., Windows, iOS, Chrome OS) pick up its incredible hardware-enforced security domain isolation, which they are all moving closer to over time. It's a race to the finish. And if I was a betting man . . . and I am . . . my best guess would be that the more popular OSs get to hardware-enforced isolated security domains faster than Qubes OS becomes super popular. Why? Because Qubes OS has been around for 12 years; it is awesome — security-wise, and yet 12 years later, it remains used by small percentage of people. And the very popular OSs continue growing in use and popularity faster than Qubes, by pure numbers alone.

Why Are Governments Involved?

Many people are naturally distrustful of any government, and many times, rightfully so. Trust assurance levels 4 (Higher) and 5 (Highest) are identical, except level 5 is controlled and managed by the nation-state that it is over. This is to recognize that legally the highest level any "global service" can go is really to the nation-state level. It's also important to recognize that governments often have the strictest requirements regarding who can operate devices on their networks, and thus, there needs to be a special callout group for governments and agencies that operate under them. If you don't like governments involved, never go above trust assurance level 4.

It's also important to note that while I think nation-state governments need to be involved in trust assurance level 5, I don't think the overall Internet security solution as I propose it in this book should be led by the government. For one, governments are too slow. For two, governments have their own interests and have been shown to support solutions in their favor even when they contradict the overall large public good. This is the reason why governments learn about zero-day vulnerabilities and don't tell the rest of the world about them so they can be fixed until they have lost most of their value to the government. Or why the NSA/NIST has been caught at least twice intentionally weakening public cryptography (e.g., DES and Dual_EC_DRBG). I don't begrudge governments for operating in their own interests, but I recognize that their interests are not always aligned with the best interests of everyone else.

Any pervasive Internet security solution needs to be citizen-led so that the solutions that are best for most people are considered and pushed. Governments should be involved, but only in so far as they can help push the citizen-led initiatives better and faster. And, of course, I think trust assurance level 5 should be led and controlled by the various nation-states simply because it reflects the existing levels of trust in our real-world society.

Why Is Your Anonymous Identity Called Attempted Anonymity?

In early versions of my Internet security solution, I used to call it Anonymous or even Guaranteed Anonymity. Its current name recognizes that true guaranteed anonymity is very difficult to have. You certainly can't get it using low-trust identities, anonymizing services, and anonymizing services like TOR. I'm not sure how many TOR-using criminals have to be arrested before they realize they really aren't anonymous.

Your identity is leaked in all sorts of ways, including the device you use, the apps you use, the ad surveillance networks that track everything you do, location services, and Internet browser cookies. Much of what you do on any device that has an IP address attached to it is used to track what you do and where you go. Most of the sites, services, and applications you use to track everything you do, store that data, and sell it to others. Here's an article I wrote on "surveillance capitalism": https://blog.knowbe4.com/you-really-are-being-surv eilled-all-the-time.

If you want to truly be anonymous on the Internet, it takes major lifestyle changes and major inconveniences. You have to buy devices for cash (or let other people buy them for you) and use privacy-guaranteeing devices, VPNs, and applications. If you are interested in how to have more anonymity, see this article I wrote: https://www.linkedin.com/pulse/quickly-creating-using-us b-boot-images-roger-grimes-ko7be.

Just know that unless you take very extreme measures, nothing you do on the Internet is truly anonymous.

Will Your Solution Impact Consumer Surveillance and Ads?

Yes, although not that much. As stated, nearly every device, site, and app you visit tries to track what you do and where you go. They often sell that information (supposedly anonymized) to people who want that data. Often, the buyers are people looking to target particular types of customers to maximize sales opportunities. Consumer surveillance usually tracks your activity back to the identity involved in the activity.

My Internet security solution, which allows users to use any identity and persona they want with any particular site/service/session/application/connection, will also be tracked to the identity associated with that particular identity/persona, just like it is today. The difference is that a world with my solution will likely have far more identities for each user that are being used all the time. If you use those identities and personas regularly, most of the consumer surveillance sites will be able to track who is who and who owns which ID. It's not going to be hard for them to track you to the IDs you use. One possible caveat is that you can also choose the Attempted Anonymity ID when using apps that conduct consumer surveillance, which might give you some information protection.

Privacy Concerns

As covered in the previous chapter, privacy concerns loom large. Many people worry about increased nation-state surveillance of all its citizens or maybe just the citizens it deems adversarial. This is a major valid concern and one that I don't have a good answer to. I can just say that using Attempted Anonymity will give you the same level of anonymity that you have with today's Internet. Alternatively, you can choose not to participate in the proposed Internet security solution at all. However, if most other people participate, it is likely that the non participants will stand out more. It might be even easier for a government to spot and punish non participants.

It seems the countries most popularly associated with decreased human freedoms are already requiring Real IDs for at least some of their citizens. Here are examples: https://restofworld.org/2023/weibo-legal-display-name-infl uencers/ and https://denuo.legal/en/insights/news/240821/. This growing trend might reinforce the problem a Real ID high-trust ecosystem might invite.

The only benefit I can see to my system is that your identities and which ones you decide to use with particular services/sites/sessions/applications are a bit more in your face with my solution. Your identity management can become more active, and you can be more aware of what identity you are using and when, which might help you stay out of government crosshairs longer.

What About the Non-Internet Scams?

What about all the scams that don't use the Internet, such as SMS, in-person, or even end-to-end encryption apps like Signal? Would my Internet security solution help them? Possibly.

Let me give you a recent example: `https://krebsonsecurity.com/2024/12/how-to-lose-a-fortune-with-just-one-bad-click/`. In this example, a man is contracted over the phone by someone claiming to be Google tech support. The phone number (falsely) appeared to be a real Google support number. The fake Google tech support person said the victim's Gmail account had been taken over, and this is especially concerning for the victim because they have cryptocurrency protected by that account. He then got a related email with a form from `www.google.com` stating that there was a problem with the victim's account and that a tech support person had been assigned to help.

The fake tech support person told him he would soon receive a prompt asking him if he was trying to recover his account and instructed him to click Yes. The victim then got a pop-up pushed-based MFA prompt asking the victim to confirm that he was trying to recover his account. He clicked Yes, and unbeknownst to the victim, this action allowed the attacker to take control of his account and steal $500,000 in cryptocurrency. Huge loss.

So the scam started on the phone, then moved online, and included a form from `www.google.com`. If you're not aware of these types of scams, it can be difficult to stop them. My Internet security solution could have possibly given the victim more clues. First, the phone number the user was called from could have been more easily validated as the real number instead of the fake one the attacker supplied. Second, when the attacker used Google Forms to send the victim a fake form that truly came from `www.google.com`, in my system, that form would have been attached to the attacker's identity when they created the form. The victim may have been able to notice that the attacker was using an @gmail email address (personal) and not the corporate Google email address domain, @google.com. Additionally, the phone number and email addressed by the attack could have possibly been reported by a prior victim and been on the global Trust Assurance Service's block lists. None of these things could have been true, or they all could have been true. The idea is that my Internet security solution has a stronger chance of giving potential victims clues about what is going on to protect them better.

The high-trust ecosystem attempts to authenticate each connection/event/transaction to the Real ID of the person creating the connection/event/transaction. Thus, if the attacker is using Google Forms, the attacker's ID and assurance level across the trust stack can be stored with the transaction where potential victims can evaluate it. If the attacker sends another email or link to support the scam further or to get payment, the high-trust ecosystem can be involved even further.

This is especially important to think about when you realize that half of all scams don't use email or the general web. Instead, they use social media and instant message apps (https://www.thisismoney.co.uk/money/beatthescammers/article-14202913/More-half-scams-use-Facebook-Instagram-WhatsApp-target-victims.html).

Do You Think Your Solution Is the Only Solution or the Best Solution?

No. But I do think it is a comprehensive, workable solution tackling more of the issues around rampant Internet crime than any other that I know about. But I'm open to other solutions. I think there are other solutions that could be developed that are better than mine. My solution is fairly complex, and complexity and security don't normally go well hand-in-hand. A simpler solution that solves many of the same problems would be even more welcome by me.

I do know of other solutions, such as putting all OS clients into the cloud under the control of the vendor, say Microsoft, where they can be tightly controlled and easily patched, where malware can be prevented from exploiting them, and so on. But that doesn't fix any of the social engineering issues, which are far bigger than the OS and application exploitation issues. It doesn't fix compromised hardware, compromised network equipment, and a dozen other types of popular attacks. A solution that fixes the majority of Internet crime is likely to be complex if it's going to be successful.

If you have any criticisms or suggestions to make, feel free to send me an email to roger@banneretcs.com.

Chapter Summary

This chapter discussed many of the most common questions and statements I get from critics and provided my answers.

Key concepts are:

- Complexity is a real challenge.
- Governmental involvement is necessary.
- Privacy concerns are a real issue that needs to be solved.

Chapter 15 starts Part III, "Other Needed Solutions," discussing what other big solutions we need besides a high-trust ecosystem. Chapter 15 discusses secure coding.

Other Needed Solutions

Secure Coding

Since I've been keeping records (over 20 years), unpatched software and firmware have been involved in about 20–40% of successful attacks. According to Google's Mandiant in 2023, software and firmware vulnerabilities are involved in about one-third of all successful hacker attacks. So, it's still in its normal range of averages.

This chapter covers how to create more secure software and firmware with less exploitable vulnerabilities.

The relevant Google Mandiant link is `https://blog.knowbe4.com/hands-on-defense-unpatched-software-causes-33-of-successful-attacks`.

As previously threat modeled in Chapters 5 and 13, even a perfect-world high-trust ecosystem will not defeat all vulnerability exploits. If attackers can exploit vulnerabilities, they can often bypass all the other protections. Attackers will even be able to exploit weaknesses and vulnerabilities in the software and systems that provide and protect a trusted ecosystem.

It's not enough to provide faster and more timely patching. Attackers are frequently exploiting vulnerabilities the same day as they are announced, and more vulnerabilities were exploited ahead of their patches being available (i.e., zero days) than not in 2023 (`https://www.darkreading.com/cyberattacks-data-breaches/zero-days-wins-superlative-most-exploited-vulns`). That's something new. It's never happened before. But it points to the fact that we simply need fewer vulnerabilities in our code to start with.

We need our programmers taught secure coding, and employers need to require that their programmers have secure programming skills. It's been called many things over the years, including secure coding, software quality, security development lifecycle, and part of software engineering. I'll just call it *secure coding* for this book.

History of Secure Coding

The history of software insecurity goes back many decades. There are dozens of papers on software and computer security vulnerabilities during the 1970s and 1980s, including these: `https://seclab.cs.ucdavis.edu/projects/history/CD-1/`. In 1984, one of the co-creators of Unix, Ken Thompson, wrote a seminal paper on the trustworthiness of code titled "Reflections on Trust" (`http://genius.cat-v.org/ken-thompson/texts/trusting-trust/`). He summarized it by stating, "You can't trust code that you did not totally create yourself."

What he also said at the time is that you can't even fully trust the code you wrote because it could contain vulnerabilities that hacker "vandals" take advantage of. He footnotes a 1974 paper on software security paper entitled "Multics Security Evaluation: Vulnerability Analysis" (`https://csrc.nist.gov/pubs/conference/1998/10/08/proceedings-of-the-21st-nissc-1998/final/docs/early-cs-papers/karg74.pdf`).

The Carnegie Mellon University Software Institute (`https://www.sei.cmu.edu/`) was sponsored by the U.S. Department of Defense in 1984 to create and teach a discipline of secure software. It still is one of the few universities to teach secure coding.

Author Gary McGraw wrote the first of his many books on software security in 1998 (`https://www.amazon.com/Software-Fault-Injection-Jeffrey-Voas/dp/047118381`). Michael Howard and David LeBlanc, co-workers and friends of mine from Microsoft, started writing books on secure coding in 2001 (`https://www.amazon.com/Writing-Secure-Code-Michael-Howard/dp/0735615888`). My mentor and friend, Loren Kohnfelder, wrote the latest seminal work on secure coding that I'm aware of, which is entitled *Designing Secure Software: A Guide for Developers* (`https://designingsecuresoftware.com`).

This is to say that there has been plenty of writing and instruction on secure coding. Unfortunately, only a few percent of programmers have heard what secure coding is, and even fewer actually do it.

What Does Secure Coding Include?

Secure coding includes all the education, policies, tools, and methods that are used to reduce the number of vulnerabilities and exposure to vulnerabilities when developing software and firmware code.

Education

All developers (and anyone else in the development delivery chain, such as managers) need to be taught secure programming, including common vulnerabilities, common exploitation techniques, access control, least privilege, and fail-safe defaults. All developers should understand the CIA (confidential, integrity, availability) triad that drives the cybersecurity industry. Programmers need to understand authentication, access control, authorization, impersonation, delegation, accounting, auditing, and logging.

SANS puts out a Top 20 (`https://www.softwaretestinghelp.com/sans-to p-20-security-vulnerabilities/`) or Top 25 list every year or two. Most vulnerabilities fall within these same two dozen mistakes. A few programming mistakes, like buffer overflows and memory-type mismatches, account for more than half of all vulnerabilities. CISA states (`https://www.cisa.gov/news-events/news/urgent-need-memory-safety-software-products`) that 70% of vulnerabilities in Microsoft and Google software and services can be traced to one problem—memory type mismatches. They can all be mitigated by programmers using memory type-safe languages like Go, C#, Ruby, and Python. Here's a complete list of memory type-safe languages: `https://read write.com/the-nsa-list-of-memory-safe-programming-languages-has-been-updated`.

Much of the needed education would teach developers things such as never "hard-coding" credentials in their code, even when simply testing the code. It's too easy to forget and leave them in, only for them to be exploited once the code is in production. Programmers need to be taught the high risk of uploading their code to public repositories (like GitHub) or reusing other people's code without thoroughly reviewing it. There are the types of vulnerabilities where education is the primary mitigation.

Use More Secure Tools and Programming Languages

Programmers need to use more secure tools and programming languages. We've already discussed how using certain types of programming languages, such as memory-type safe languages, can result in fewer vulnerabilities, and this is also true of the tools that programmers use. Both tools and programming languages need to be designed with secure coding in mind, have secure defaults, have enforced memory protections, and ensure that developers will create fewer bugs.

Threat Modeling

All programmers and roles within the development pathway should be taught about how to threat model and forced to do it during the design phase of their project. The best requirement would be to make all developers release their threat models to the world for review and feedback. No vendor that I'm aware of does this today, but doing so would inspire confidence in the vendor and their products. Dare to dream!

> **note** The only publicly available threat model I'm aware of is FIDO's 2021 Security Reference Model document (`https://fidoalliance.org/specs/common-sp ecs/fido-security-ref-v2.1-rd-20210525.html`). Unfortunately, it hasn't been updated since it was originally released, even though the FIDO standards have been updated. Still, it's the only public example of a threat model that I can point to.

Good Cryptography

Every good cybersecurity defense is full of good cryptography. We need developers to understand why good cryptography is needed…what it means to say it's good cryptography and learn when to implement it. Developers need to understand symmetric encryption, public key cryptography, digital signatures, hashing, and random number generators. Programmers need to understand that they should never "roll their own" and instead always use standard, well-tested cryptography and key sizes. Programmers need to make their programs crypto-agile so they can have their cryptography updated without having to replace the entire program. And start to replace quantum-susceptible cryptography with quantum-resistant (i.e., post-quantum) cryptography.

Banned Functions

There are many programming instructions and functions that are known to involve an unnecessarily high percentage of vulnerabilities, such as the STRCPY (i.e., string copy) function in the C language, and should not be used. Here is a list of banned functions in the C language according to Microsoft: `https://lea rn.microsoft.com/en-us/previous-versions/bb288454(v=msdn.10)`.

Programmers should be taught what the banned functions are, including why they are higher risk, and told of the correct alternatives to use instead. The languages that have these banned functions should remove them from being used or let the developer know they are high risk and suggest safe mitigations. Code review tools should flag them and not let any code with them to be checked into the source code repository until they are removed.

Code Review

All code should undergo both human and automated security code reviews, at the code level and also in formal security design reviews. Automated tools can catch the easy stuff, but well-trained humans can always catch what the automated tools miss.

Penetration Testing

All services and applications should undergo penetration testing (pen testing), both in automated forms and by human pen testers. Programs should undergo "fuzz testing," where various, nearly random, inputs are tried against any fields accepting inputted information to see if it can cause a problem or vulnerability. The vendor should have an in-house team that is tasked with pen testing any developed programs or services before they are released followed by an external pen testing team. External testing teams often find vulnerabilities missed by the internal team.

Bug Bounties

Every developer should have an external-facing bug bounty program. A bug bounty program is one where anyone can participate in trying to locate security vulnerabilities in an enrolled program and get paid by the vendors depending on the severity of the bug found. A finder's fee is paid to the person who finds and correctly reports the bug. There are many popular public bug bounty programs, such as HackerOne (`https://hackerone.com`). Many vendors, such as Google and Microsoft, offer their own bug bounty programs as well. Every vendor that produces software, services, or firmware code should have an adequately funded bug bounty program.

Faster Patching

All software and firmware should have easy, automated patching routines so that they do not require end-user interaction (more on this in Chapter 16).

Secure Defaults

All software and firmware should have secure defaults. If a security decision is posed to the user, it should default to the safest choice if the user ignores or just hits Enter. History has shown that most users simply take the defaults, so if the vendor defines the correct defaults, everyone will be safer.

Roles and Actions

Sophisticated software with different types of users needs to be defined with the appropriate roles (such as admin, manager, user, etc.), and each role should have one or more allowed actions (i.e., Trusted Actions) defined. Every role should have the least privilege permissions necessary to perform the role.

Logging and Alerting

All programs and services should include good security logging, which should be enabled by default, along with alerts sent to the user or administrator when malicious actions are detected.

There is a whole lot more that defines secure coding, but this is a great start.

CISA Secure By Design

The Cybersecurity Infrastructure Security Agency (CISA) has a program called Secure By Design (https://www.cisa.gov/securebydesign). It's an initiative that works with (or even somewhat pressures) vendors to take a stronger ownership approach to secure coding. CISA wants to encourage vendors to take more security ownership of their products, including everything we discussed. CISA's program particularly focuses on:

- Secure design
- Memory-type safe languages
- Using MFA
- Logging
- Single sign-on (SSO)
- Reducing default passwords
- Increasing patching

Hundreds of vendors have signed up so far, and it's a promising start.

We Need to Teach Secure Coding

We can't expect our programmers not to put vulnerabilities in their code if we aren't teaching about them. But, almost no university, college, or programming curriculum includes secure coding in their curriculum, even though Carnegie Mellon University has been leading the way since 1984. Less than a handful of programming curriculums include any education on secure coding, much less require it for a student programmer to pass.

This is a shame and inexcusable. Every programming curriculum should include an entire semester course dedicated to secure coding. Surprisingly, most of the professors and programming curriculum developers I contact don't agree. Even those who do agree that secure coding needs to be taught say they can't think of what they could remove from existing curriculums to replace them with secure coding. Surely, there must be something less important that can be replaced. If not, let's extend the programming curriculums. Did I mention that vulnerabilities are involved in 33% of successful exploits today?

There have been some individual nascent attempts to develop secure coding curriculums. Carnegie Mellon Institute has had a secure coding curriculum since at least 1987. They offer graduate degrees in security coding and certificate programs (https://www.sei.cmu.edu/our-work/secure-development/index.cfm). But these curricula and certifications really haven't taken off beyond Carnegie Mellon University.

Professor Daniel J. Bernstein (https://en.wikipedia.org/wiki/Daniel_J._Be rnstein) became infamous for teaching a secure coding course at the University of Illinois, where students had to find 10 new vulnerabilities to pass the course (https://www.cnet.com/news/privacy/students-uncover-dozens-of-unix-soft ware-flaws/). No students found 10 vulnerabilities while taking the class, but together, the class found 45 new vulnerabilities and created quite a stir. There are lots of non-credit "certificate" courses taught by various universities and programs, but they aren't required, don't count toward graduation, and generally aren't well attended (because they aren't required).

The Association for Computing Machinery (ACM), introduced in Chapter 12, has a working group, CS2023 (https://csed.acm.org/security/), charged with creating a secure coding curriculum outline along with lecture hour estimates for the security elements of a proposed guideline for undergraduate Computer Science (CS) class. It is called CS2023-SEC, and you can read more about it here: https://csed.acm.org/wp-content/uploads/2023/09/SEC-Version -Gamma.pdf. It's a decent start, but it is missing a few topics, like post-quantum cryptography and crypto-agility, and it's taking too many years to be released as a final recommendation. But it's all we have regarding a possible national curriculum recommendation at the moment. Even when it's fully released there is no requirement for any programming curriculum to include it.

Example Suggested Curriculum

Here's a list of topics that I think should be covered in any secure coding curriculum. Much of this was taken from Loren Kohnfelder's book:

- Introduction to secure coding
- Threat modeling
- Secure design, secure defaults
- Mitiga tions
- Secure coding
- Trust modeling
- Cryptography
- Access control
- Least privilege
- Secure by default
- Fail secure
- Security reviews and testing
- Patching and updating

- Cryptography
- Why, when, where
- Standards
- Don't create your own
- Crypto-agility
- Post-quantum cryptograhy
- Common secure coding errors and attacks
- Untrusted input
- Type mismatches
- Memory access vulnerabilities
- Timing attacks
- Serialization attacks
- Inadequate error exception handling
- Arithmetic errors
- Logging and alerting
- Database security
- Website security
- Secure APIs
- Secure coding languages and tools
- Security reviews and testing
- Security development best practices

Any curriculum that includes these topics would be doing a great service to their students and the world in general.

We Need to Require Secure Coding Skills

I wondered for quite a while why more universities and programming curriculums don't teach secure coding. I mean, we have an ever-growing list of vulnerabilities, and they are involved in one-third of all successful compromises. It would seem there would be a big need for secure coding skills. And then it hit me. None of the job ads I see for developers and programmers has ever said a requirement for the job was secure coding skills. That's it. That's why programming curricula don't teach it...because if employers did require it, programming schools would teach it.

So, we've got a chicken-and-egg-type problem here. We need all employers of programmers and others in the programming chain to start to put secure coding skill requirements in their help-wanted ads. I don't write job descriptions or job ads, but I could see something like the following in a job ad under required or desired skills:

■ Secure software design skills

A job description might include phrasing similar to:

■ Position holder or candidate should possess secure software design skills to minimize security vulnerabilities, including threat modeling, software code reviews, the use of secure defaults, strong cryptography, and other knowledge to minimize commonly known security vulnerabilities

More than likely, any job description or ad would need to make secure design skills a desired skill versus a required skill because there simply aren't enough programmers with these skills. Let's change that starting now.

We need more education, improved secure coding languages and tools, and vendors requiring that their developers have secure coding skills.

Chapter Summary

This chapter discussed secure coding, what it means, and what we need to do to have more of it, including education, secure programming languages, secure tools, and vendors requiring that their development teams have secure coding skills. We certainly need developers threat modeling during the design phase and hopefully sharing that threat model with the public. Security reviews, code reviews, penetration testing, and bug bounties can only make software and firmware products more secure. Without a strong, secure coding ecosystem, hackers and their malware creations will find a way to penetrate our trusted ecosystem in significant percentages.

Key concepts are:

■ Secure coding

■ Memory-type mismatches

■ Banned functions

■ Bug bounties

■ Need to teach secure coding

■ Need to require secure coding skills in job requirements

Chapter 16 will discuss a related subject, patching.

Better Patching

As previous mentioned, at least 40,291 public vulnerabilities were found and announced in 2024. That's 10,000 more than in 2023 (`https://www.cvedetails .com/browse-by-date.php`). Chapter 15 discussed how we need better, more secure coding to minimize the number of software and firmware vulnerabilities. But no matter how much better developers get, there will always be some exploitable vulnerabilities that will need patching. This chapter covers how we can significantly improve patching.

Problems with Current Patching

There are a lot of problems with the way we currently patch beyond that we just have so many to do.

Patching Is Too Complex

Every OS, product, site, and service has its own method of patching. The OS has its own patching process. Our word processing apps have another. Every app on our computing device seems to have its own patching mechanism. Some automatically patch. Some don't. Some check for patches every day; and some never do. The average home user has more than 100 applications to patch. The average corporate environment has many thousands. That alone is mind-boggling complex, but then when you add firmware, cable modems, routers, phones, and IoT devices, it gets even more complex.

I frequently ask audiences to raise their hand if they know if their cable modem or home Wi-Fi router is patched. I asked them if they even knew how to check. Usually, I only get a few people who say they know or can even figure out how to patch their home network equipment. Then, you have to add in phones, baby monitors, alarm systems, and vehicles. Who decides when to patch them? How could you even tell if your phone, car, camera, or baby monitor had a known, public, exploitable vulnerability that the vendor had not yet patched?

It's even worse in corporate environments. Many times, there are so many teams involved with a particular server, site, or project that people aren't sure who is supposed to patch or what to patch. It can quickly lead to a lot of unpatched things. Many systems today run on virtual machines, which may or may not be active and patchable when you check. New virtual machines are easy to create and usually need a lot of patches. It's very easy to revert a patched virtual machine to an earlier, more unpatched state with the click of a mouse.

In today's world of containers, where the application can be isolated from the OS and further isolated from the hardware, complexity is added, which makes it harder to patch. Many of our systems run in the cloud. Who patches those? Does the cloud vendor patch some of it? Who is responsible? If the cloud vendor is responsible for patching, how timely do they do it?

If you own an appliance, you, as the owner, usually can't patch the appliance. Only the appliance vendor can do that. You're at their mercy. And in my 36-year career, I've never seen an appliance that was fully patched and contained no vulnerabilities.

Dependencies abound. Unpatched dependencies abound. Whether you're running on-premises software or software in the cloud, it can be difficult to figure out if the dependencies you rely on are fully patched. This type of problem was brought to life by the 2021 Log4j vulnerability (`https://en.wikipedia.org/wiki/Log4Shell`), which is considered the most critical and widespread vulnerability in the history of computers (although Spectre and Meltdown could have been worse if exploited). Unpatched log4j instances potentially impacted hundreds of millions of implementations.

However, the worst part of the Log4j vulnerability is that a large percentage of impacted instances were instances with dependencies the people running it didn't even know about. You might think that your product, site, or service didn't have the log4j vulnerability, but what you didn't know was that some program or feature inside the product included it. Or some ancillary adjunct program or service you hired to maintain it, like a backup product or security client software, was using it. You didn't know the thing you were using was using it and the vendor didn't tell you. The dependency issue risk was really publicly brought out by the log4j vulnerability. Today, it's not unusual for customers to ask vendors for dependency reports, known as a *software bill of materials* (SBOM). So, you may think you're patched, but are your dependencies' dependencies patched?

Even if you're trying to do it right and patch everything in a timely manner, it can be difficult to do consistently over time. How hard is it to patch correctly? Well, we all know we need to patch to prevent malicious hacking, and yet decades later, unpatched software and firmware are still involved in about one-third of successful exploits. That's after we tried everything we could to patch correctly.

Patching Focus Is on OS and Popular Apps

When we think of patching, most people focus on patching the OS and the most popular application software. For example, most Microsoft Windows users mostly focus on patching Windows and maybe Microsoft Office. And yes, years ago, the OS and the most popular application software were attacked the most and needed most of the patching. It used to be that Microsoft Windows got attacked the most, and that's still true, but it's a much smaller percentage than it used to be. Today, it is very common to see Apple, Linux, and Google products on the actively exploited lists. There are dozens of Android vulnerabilities routinely exploited, and even iPhone exploits are starting to appear on the actively exploited list.

Most of the software I see on the actively exploited lists today most people have never heard of. The most routinely exploited software these days has less recognizable names like MOVEit, Cleo, XSream, and Synacor Zimbra Collaboration. Network equipment like firewalls, routers, network-attached storage devices, appliances, and load balancers are among the most exploited products. It's common to see chipsets, programmable logic units (PLCs), and other industrial control systems on actively exploited vulnerability lists. There are dozens of firmware entries on actively attacked lists. There are dozens of Internet of Things (IoT) entries, like Internet-connected cameras. All of this is much less popular in sheer numbers than OS and general applications that people seem much better at patching, but just as likely, or more likely to be exploited. Today, if you get exploited, there's a great chance it happened because of something you never heard of or were not keeping your eye on as strongly. Times have changed.

Patching Not Done in a Timely Manner

The Cybersecurity Infrastructure Security Agency (CISA) recommends that all critical vulnerabilities need to be patched within two weeks. Many organizations have a hard time meeting that requirement. It's actually the rare organization that has everything fully patched in a timely manner. A sizeable percentage of vulnerabilities with an available patch were exploited for the first time in the targeted environment many years after the patch was first released. The victim hadn't applied the patch even though it had been available for years. I get it. Patching perfectly is hard.

No Patching

With every vulnerability patched, some non minor percentage of instances will never be patched and remain forever vulnerable just waiting for a hacker to discover it. Why? The excuses include:

- The user or admin turned off auto-patching and never re-enabled it.
- There is some sort of corruption that prevents the patch from applying correctly.
- The product does not have auto-patching.
- The product has auto-patching and has downloaded the patch but is waiting for the user to approve a prompt before applying, and the user never sees the prompt.
- The patch management program's inventory function doesn't correctly detect the product or detect it as needing to be patched.
- The system with the unpatched product is turned off when patch checking is done.
- A virtual machine instance is patched, but the user "reverts" the image to fix some sort of other sort of problem and doesn't realize they removed the patches, too.
- The product that needs to be patched is in a non default location on the system, so it's never found by the patch management program as an instance that needs to be patched.
- Old legacy instances are still in use, but no one is actively managing it.

The latter problem is very common. For example, perhaps some consulting group installed a new cash register system for a family restaurant, and at some point in time, the restaurant decided they didn't need to pay the ongoing support bill anymore. The restaurant thinks the cash registers are working just fine, but no one at the restaurant has an idea that the cash registers are running an operating system and ongoing patching needs to be done.

Regardless of the reason, some non minor percentage of vulnerable instances never get patched, leaving the impacted organizations at risk for future attacks.

Operational Interruption

Patching can cause the involved device or software to become inoperable. It isn't very common, but it happens. Oftentimes, inoperability happens because of some unforeseen third-party interaction the vendor could not have easily foreseen or because malware is causing an issue. Other times, the vendor makes a programming mistake, and applying the update causes the inoperability problem. Sometimes, the problem just means the app involved crashes, and sometimes, it impacts the entire device. The biggest example of this was the 2024 Crowdstrike upgrade debacle (`https://en.wikipedia.org/wiki/2024_ CrowdStrike-related_IT_outages`). It impacted 8.5 million computers, caused them not to be able to boot, and impacted entire industries, such as the airline industry. Although rare, these sorts of inoperability issues make users hesitant to patch and especially to allow auto-patching.

Faster Exploitation

Hackers are able to exploit unpatched instances (connected to the Internet) faster every day. A decade or two ago, it took months to years before an attacker would start to significantly target a particular exploit. These days, hackers "reverse-engineer" the patch minutes after it is released, create exploits that target the specific vulnerability, and begin scanning for vulnerable instances. They can use their own custom-made vulnerability scanners or use any of the publicly available ones, like Shodan (`https://www.shodan.io`). With any type of scanner, hackers can usually find thousands to tens of thousands of exploitable victims within hours of a patch release.

Suppose I'm an attacker trying to break into a particular target organization, but during my initial scan, I find out that the target organization has no unpatched software or firmware. If I have the time and patience, I can just catalog the software and firmware I found during my scan, wait for an involved vendor to announce a new patch, and then attack the target faster than they can patch it. The hacker can come up with an exploit in minutes. It usually takes most organizations days to weeks to patch. In today's world, CISA's advice of allowing up to two weeks to patch a critical vulnerability just isn't aggressive enough.

Zero Days

Zero days (0-days) are vulnerabilities that are exploited by attackers and are either not known by the involved vendor (or publicly released by the vendor) and not known by the public. Zero days used to be used somewhat sparingly by those who used them the most (e.g., professional penetration testers, nation-states, and commercial surveillance vendors).

> **note** Currently, commercial surveillance vendors are responsible for more zero days than any other source.

But that changed over the last few years, and in 2023, as previously stated, more exploits were accomplished by zero days (`https://www.darkreading.com/ cyberattacks-data-breaches/zero-days-wins-superlative-most-exploited- vulns`) than non zero days. It remains to be seen if this trend will continue, but it's a Rubicon crossed that can never be taken back.

All of this reinforces the idea that we need fewer vulnerabilities to start with (i.e., secure coding) and faster patching for the vulnerabilities that still get by. We've known for decades that patching is a top way for hackers to compromise environments (only second to social engineering), and yet one-third of successful attacks still involve exploited vulnerabilities. Something significant needs to change.

Better Patching

We absolutely need fewer bugs in the first place (Chapter 16), but we also need better patching. There are things we can do to improve the process drastically, including what I propose below.

Rewrite Software and Firmware to Be More Patching Friendly

The best and really only long-term answer is to make all software and firmware easier to patch. That would, sadly, take a complete re-engineering of the OS and applications involved. Right now, the patching process is complex not only for end-users and administrators but also for the vendors who are trying to apply those patches. It really is difficult to get it right, especially with so many inherent dependencies. However, if we really want to fix patching—making it easier and faster—we need to look at re-architecting OS and applications to allow it. The longer we go without doing this, the worse everything will be.

More Auto-Patching

Such a large percentage of users do not ever patch one or more products that it is clear that we need more pervasive auto-patching that does not require human intervention. It needs to be enabled on every product by default and randomly downloaded and installed during off-time hours. Auto-patching should be enabled by default but also be allowed to be disabled and scheduled, especially for businesses that really need to control when the patch is applied. Downtime can literally mean lives or millions of dollars lost.

Easy-Reverting

It should be very easy for any patch to be reversed. To be pervasive, this would likely involve a complete re-architecture of OS and applications to allow it. If a system becomes problematic or inoperable because of a patch, there should be an auto-reverting mechanism. Some products already have this today, but we would need it to be more across-the-board and pervasive.

Patch Only What Needs to be Patched

Even without any of the improvements in patching listed, users and administrators can better handle patching by only patching what is needed. Although at least 40,291 separate vulnerabilities were announced in 2024, only 1% of them were ever exploited by real-world attackers against real-world computers. The rest of the publicly announced vulnerabilities were just the ones we talked about, demonstrated, and researched. We really don't need to patch everything, just the 1% that hackers are actively abusing or are likely to abuse.

Known Exploited Vulnerabilities Catalog

In 2021, CISA introduced its Known Exploited Vulnerabilities Catalog (`https://www.cisa.gov/known-exploited-vulnerabilities-catalog`). It lists every known exploited product vulnerability that real-world attackers use against real-world organizations. If it's on the list, it's being exploited. Since 2021, there have been 1,239 exploits (as of 12/24/24) placed on the list. There have been 113,943 publicly announced vulnerabilities during the same period. That means real-world exploited vulnerabilities are barely over 1% of the overall list. It's a lot easier to patch 1% of the problem than 100% of the problem.

You can subscribe to CISA's Known Exploited Vulnerabilities Catalog (`https://public.govdelivery.com/accounts/USDHSCISA/subscriber/new?topic_id=USDHSCISA_136`) list and get an update anytime they add a new vulnerability to the list. It's updated every day when there is a new exploit to add. Since 2021, I average about one or two KEVC alert emails a week on average.

Suggested Patching Priority

We all need to patch what is being actively exploited. After that, it's what is most likely to be exploited in the near future. Here is what I think should be the optimal patch management prioritization order should be (shown in Figure 16-1 below).

Any vulnerability identified by CISA in their Known Exploited Vulnerability Catalog and in your environment should be patched ASAP! Do not wait. Do not pass Go. Look for it, test the patch, and then patch the involved product. Bad actors and computer worms are hoping you will take your time. I think CISA recommends patching known public exploited vulnerabilities within 2 weeks, but why wait? The risk of exploitation is likely higher than the risk of extended operational interruption due to something related to the patching.

I do understand waiting a day or two after a patch comes out before you apply. If a patch is going to cause any widespread problems, usually the problems are found and publicly known within the first day or two. If you haven't heard of any significant operational issues caused by the patch, you're usually safe to apply. Of course, you are supposed to test all patches before you apply, just in case.

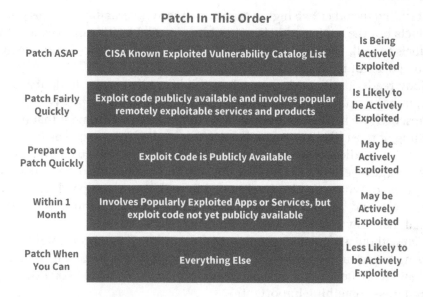

Patch In This Order

Patch ASAP	CISA Known Exploited Vulnerability Catalog List	Is Being Actively Exploited
Patch Fairly Quickly	Exploit code publicly available and involves popular remotely exploitable services and products	Is Likely to be Actively Exploited
Prepare to Patch Quickly	Exploit Code is Publicly Available	May be Actively Exploited
Within 1 Month	Involves Popularly Exploited Apps or Services, but exploit code not yet publicly available	May be Actively Exploited
Patch When You Can	Everything Else	Less Likely to be Actively Exploited

Figure 16-1: Suggested patching prioritization order.

Usually, if a vulnerability is fairly pervasive and public "exploit code" shows up "in the wild," there is a very good chance that public exploit code will be used by bad people to exploit victims. Not all publicly available source code ends up with the related vulnerability being exploited by an attacker. But if the involved device/application/service is popular, that increases the chances that it will be exploited. If the device/application/service can be remotely exploited without any end-user input, that significantly increases the odds that it will be exploited.

Most attacks today are "client-side attacks." This means it requires a user to be involved (e.g., click on a link, download and execute malicious content, etc.) to kick off the exploit. Client-side attacks are involved in far more attacks than truly remote-only attacks, but because they need a user to start the process, this makes them far less likely to succeed than truly remotely exploitable vulnerabilities.

If you do not know if something is remotely exploitable or if the likelihood of it becoming exploitable in the near future is low, when and if it becomes publicly available, look for the vulnerability's CVSS (Common Vulnerability Scoring System) score. There are many vulnerability-tracking sites that list a vulnerability's CVSS score, including `https://www.cve.org/CVERecord`. Many vendors, like Microsoft, also list the CVSS scores of the vulnerabilities they announce on their website. Not all vendors include the CVSS risk rating in their vulnerability announcement, but they should. Any CVSS score of 8.0 or higher is something that needs to be patched fairly quickly.

If the exploit code is available but the product isn't super popular, it's a little less likely to be attacked immediately. Still, you want to patch these things after first tackling the other two higher priorities. If the vulnerability involves popular products but the exploit code is not publicly available, it's time to patch these products as well. Then and only then, after these four higher-priority categories, do you go about trying to patch everything else.

Many readers might ask themselves if it is not just easier to do it all, all at once, rather than picking and choosing which patches to apply. Well, yes and no. Yes, because if you are covered by a compliance requirement that involves patching, it most likely says you have to apply all "critical patches in a timely manner," regardless of whether they are being actively exploited or not. So, you have to forget everything I said here anyway and just use the recommendations as a guide of what you absolutely need to make sure you patch 100% every time, above and beyond your normal patching cadence. I think most readers will fall here anyway.

Even without a regulatory requirement, many patch managers might wonder if trying to pick and choose which patches to apply is a good way to go about it. Would it not be easier to just patch everything all at once so you do not goof up and miss something important?

Well, in theory, yes. In a perfect world, we would apply all needed patches in a timely manner. But we have supposedly been trying to do that for decades, and decades later, unpatched software is involved in one-third of successful attacks. So, for various reasons, we, collectively as a global society, do not seem to be doing a great job at patching everything all at once. Commonsense tells me that patching 1% of 40,291 vulnerabilities should be easier than trying to patch 100% of 40,291 vulnerabilities, but your mileage may vary.

This is my take on the subject. No matter which strategy you take…selective patching or patching everything…make sure you 100% quickly patch what CISA says is being actively exploited. In the midst of whatever you are required or trying to patch, carve out some extra special attention to patch the things that attackers are actively using to break into devices and networks.

Doing significantly better cybersecurity is not really a matter of buying new, shiny tools. It is better to concentrate on the things that are far more likely to lead to malicious compromise, first and best, before you worry about all the other things. Being a patching pro is mostly about focusing on the right things first and best. Go be the best pro you can be! Subscribing to and following CISA's Known Exploited Vulnerability Catalog list/service is a great place to start.

Cloud Services Are Easier Patching

It's becoming clear to me that cloud software-as-a-service (SaaS) products—products and services existing solely in the cloud are making patching easier for a bunch of reasons. For whatever reason, there seem to be fewer vulnerabilities on cloud products than on on-premise products, even for the same product and functionality. It's common for me to read that a particular vulnerability exists on an on-premise product but not on its cloud companion. I suspect it's because the cloud version has fewer legacy concerns, has less legacy code, and is built with newer, more code-secure languages and tools.

Second, the vendor can more easily apply any needed patches to their cloud products than all their clients can. When a cloud product needs to be updated, the cloud vendor can just apply it all at once or, more likely, test and apply it across banks for servers so that there isn't any downtime. There are going to be far fewer third-party interactions involved in causing unexpected downtime. There is going to be less of a chance of malware causing problems. Usually, cloud upgrades can be more quickly reversed if needed or if something starts to go wrong. You rarely hear of a cloud product down at all for any patches, and if downtime is needed, it isn't long. It is clear that the cloud is making it easier and faster to patch.

Most cloud products are servers and services focused on serving clients. Over time, you can expect that even our clients and OS will start to be cloud-based. A great example is Microsoft's Cloud PCs (https://support.microsoft.com/en-us/windows/introduction-to-cloud-pcs-71c6370b-8da4-4e8d-9b42-48b6542bf463). There is a strong likelihood in the future that every client OS will simply be an image stored in the cloud somewhere. We turn on our hardware device, the client OS image, applications, and configuration download to our devices in a second or three, and we start using our devices and applications as we normally do. However, being stored in the cloud by default should mean easier patching and many other stronger security controls.

Chapter Summary

This chapter covered the big problems with today's patch management, followed by ideas that might improve it in the future. These ideas include re-architecting OS and software to allow easier and faster patching, pervasive auto-patching, easy reverting, and cloud-based products. We are going to need improved patching to go along with our high-trust ecosystem if we are going to significantly minimize cybercrime.

Key concepts are:

- Current problems with patching
- How to better patch
- CISA Known Exploit Vulnerabilities Catalog

Chapter 17 will discuss the international agreements we need to better mitigate Internet cybercrime.

Getting International Agreements

As we covered in Chapter 3, the main problem that allows Internet crime to be so rampant is that we cannot identify, stop, or arrest Internet cybercriminals. There are other systematic problems, but that is the main one. Criminals love being criminals on the Internet because they are rarely caught and punished. It's all reward with very little risk.

Even if we could identify hackers better, most cybercriminals conduct their crimes from countries other than where their victims are. Law enforcement, lawyers, and court systems in one country (where the victim is) often can't force the other country (where the hacker is) to do anything about it. Internet crime will stay rampant as long as we can't agree globally on what is and isn't a crime that should be enforced by all countries. This chapter is about the need to get good, strong, enforceable international cybercrime agreements. We are possibly almost there, at least in theory.

Note: I'm not a lawyer, and anything I state in this chapter could be wrong. With that said, I tried to get things correct as best as I could.

Cybercrime Law Basics

In most countries, there are two main types of laws: criminal and civil (torts). Criminal laws are enforced by the government and law enforcement and may lead to the offender being fined and/or imprisoned (and possibly worse). Civil suits can be brought by anyone, including government agencies, against someone or an organization for breaking a law, violating a regulation, or being unethical. Civil suits can result in fines and required actions but generally cannot result in imprisonment. People found innocent in criminal trials have been found guilty in related civil trials and vice versa.

Most countries have one or more criminal laws defining what is illegal when using a computer. In the United States, the federal law that is most often used to prosecute cyber criminals at the federal level falls under what is known as Title 18 (`https://en.wikipedia.org/wiki/Title_18_of_the_United_States_Code`). The Computer Fraud and Abuse Act (CFAA), 18 U.S.C. § 1030, is the primary federal statute under Title 18 for prosecuting cybercrime, including malicious hacking. But there are many other federal laws that can be used at the federal level, including:

- Electronic Communications Protection Act
- Digital Millennium Copyright Act (DCMA)
- CAN-SPAM Act of 2003
- USA Patriot Act

There are also many other national regulatory acts that may also apply from a legal standpoint, such as HIPPA, PCI-DSS, SOX, etc., and laws and regulations from the FCC, SEC, NERC, FISMA, GDPR, etc., although these laws and regulations usually penalize organizations and their leaders for not following prescribed cybersecurity requirements. They usually aren't used to prosecute malicious hackers.

States often have their own criminal and civil laws regarding cybercrime, although, again, most of the newer laws are directed at making legitimate organizations and their leaders adequately fight cybercrime and protect consumer privacy. But many are similar to federal laws against cybercrime, and some, like N.Y. Penal Law § 156.10, are even broader than federal statutes. There are also many state laws enacted to protect consumer privacy, usually led by California and New York in the United States. There can even be "lower" laws passed at the county, city, region, or smaller geographic region that may apply.

In serious criminal cases, there is usually a complainant; evidence is collected, the relevant broken laws are identified, a decision to prosecute is made, and the defendant is arrested/charged and prosecuted. The case may or may not go to trial. Most cases are settled before going to court. If the case is going to court, there may be an arraignment hearing, and bail may be required, and if so, may be posted. There can be one or more pre-trial motions and preliminary hearings.

Criminal cases can also be applied to foreigners in and outside of our country if domestic laws are being broken against U.S. citizens or organizations, although the entire process is significantly more difficult and expensive. Most of the time, it is nearly impossible to successfully prosecute someone in another country unless the two involved countries have a legal understanding and both countries are working in good faith to uphold that agreement. For example, the U.S. Department of Justice has identified dozens of Chinese, Korean, and

Russian cybercriminals over the last few years and created warrants for their arrest and multi million-dollar rewards for information leading to their arrest, but rarely are foreign criminals arrested or the rewards paid.

Perfect International Cybercriminal Law

In a perfect world, every country would respect every other country's cyber-criminal laws and hold their own citizens accountable. But this is difficult to impossible in practice. For one, not every country agrees on what is or isn't illegal. For example, in some countries, pornography is illegal. In other countries, pornography is not. If a foreigner in a country that doesn't outlaw pornography visits a pornography site located in a country that does outlaw pornography, would it be right to demand the arrest of the foreigner in his own country where they are not breaking the law? In some countries, pictures of a woman in a bikini or with her head uncovered on the Internet would break the law.

Nation-state interests are also a concern. Most capable nation-states spy on and hack other nation-states. It is very unlikely that a nation-state employee or contractor would be arrested by their own country for following the instructions of their own nation-state and interests. Adversarial nation-states, in general, don't like enforcing the laws of other adversaries even when the crime committed by their citizens is illegal under their own laws.

In a perfect world, all countries (there are 193 or 195 countries right now, depending on whose source you rely on) would agree on what is and isn't considered cybercrime, say:

- Ransomware
- Denial of service attacks
- Password-stealing trojans
- Child pornography
- Theft of money or cryptocurrency
- Unauthorized eavesdropping, and so on

They would even agree on which nation-state actions are considered legal and acceptable and which would be considered acts of war. Each country might decide which industries are considered especially protected, such as water, power, and healthcare. It would be a sort of digital equivalent of the Geneva Conventions.

> **note** The U.S. government defines 16 critical infrastructures: https://www.cisa.gov/topics/critical-infrastructure-security-and-resilience/critical-infrastructure-sectors.

The agreement would define rules of evidence, legal cooperation, and the conditions for extradition. In total, it would describe how the countries of the world would cooperate to prosecute cybercrime that crosses national borders.

UN Convention Against Cybercrime

This exact sort of agreement has been trying to be established for more than 20 years. Every time it looked like it might happen, it was defeated or neglected. In my career, I've read about some magical forthcoming international agreements on cybercrime that were soon coming up for a vote many times. Usually, these international cybercrime agreements were proposed at the United Nations (UN) by one or more member states.

And every time, multiple major countries voted down what was under consideration. Many times, the objecting countries were the United States, Russia, or China. It's felt that if these three countries did not support an intentional cybercrime agreement, the law would be largely ineffectual because these three countries have the lion's share of hackers attacking others and also being hacked by others. Oftentimes, reliably, if the United States supported something, Russia and China did not, and vice versa. So, for decades, we got nowhere.

Then, at the end of 2020, the French were able to get 43 nation states to agree on an international cybercrime agreement (https://front.un-arm.org/wp-content/uploads/2020/10/joint-contribution-poa-future-of-cyber-discussions-at-un-10-08-2020.pdf). None of the big three nation states joined, but it kept hope alive.

> **note**   A previous agreement known as the 2019 Budapest Convention was defeated.

Finally, on December 24, 2024, the UN adopted a resolution entitled the *United Nations Convention Against Cybercrime; Strengthening International Cooperation for Combating Certain* (https://documents.un.org/doc/undoc/ltd/v24/055/06/pdf/v2405506.pdf). It's huge news! It's the first international cybercrime agreement to have been negotiated in more than 20 years. It's not perfect and has plenty of critics, but it is our first agreement on this issue in a long time, so I'll take it.

The Convention defines illegal cybercrime acts, creates cyberwarfare standards, discusses how to exchange evidence, outlines protection for victims, and attempts to safeguard human rights. This latter point is particularly contentious and almost defeated its passage. There are widely held beliefs by many nation-states, legislators, companies, and organizations across the spectrum that the wording of the Convention could be used by nation-states to legally spy on their citizens and the citizens of other countries (called *extraterritorial* surveillance), commit human rights abuses, and prosecute cybercrime researchers.

The UN members involved in crafting the Convention inserted some minor language concerning the Convention not being used in those ways and stated that any member found to be using the Convention in that way would face retribution. With that statement, the United States changed its initial opposition to support the bill, mainly because it will significantly increase the number of countries that will respond to its legal warrants for arrest involving cybercrimes. Still, there is still significant opposition to reaffirming the Convention as many don't think that authoritarian governments will do anything to respect human rights concerns. In 2025, the UN Convention against Cybercrime will open for signature at a formal ceremony in Hanoi, Viet Nam, and it will become official international law 90 days after being ratified by the 40th signatory. This is very likely to happen.

We've still yet to see how this will play out. For example, will Russia actually start arresting all the ransomware gangs? Will China start to arrest all the intellectual property thieves? Will it be against the law for nation-states to do Stuxnet-like worms, take out power structures, and so on? It took decades to get our first serious cybercrime international agreement. Will it be used as a cudgel to commit human rights abuses? Will cybercrime researchers be arrested? Will it hold up in practice?

We will see.

What's Still Missing?

Besides the missing defined privacy protections discussed, the main component missing is a link to an Internet security group, like the Internet Security Global Alliance, which contains all the technical people and expertise needed to significantly secure the Internet. The UN is political and led by politicians. Each country is following the technical requirements as proposed by their sponsoring governments. Each government is following the technical lead of its various technical government-led and government-sponsored researchers and groups. It doesn't include all Internet security researchers. It's not even guaranteed to include the best solutions. Because it's a government-led political process, it's always going to be swayed in the direction of government interests (which are often significantly swayed by big donors and companies).

An optimally secured Internet would be directed by technical experts who are then supported by politicians (and not the other way around). In reality, the process is always going to be led by politicians, especially at the global level. And any "technical" group is going to be full of politics and biases. But in a perfect world, the technical experts would see the challenges and develop solutions, and the politicians would help carry them out. Linking an international technical group that leads the process, like the Internet Security Global Alliance, with all its dedicated subject matter experts, would likely make a better outcome.

Still, I have to say I'm happy to see our first international cybercrime agreement in decades.

Chapter Summary

This chapter covered why we need international agreements, explored what the perfect international cybercrime agreement would look like, and discussed the just ratified UN Convention on Cybercrime.

Key concepts are:

- Cybercrime law basics
- UN Convention on Cybercrime

Chapter 18 ends the book by summarizing all the technical concepts and presents things you, the reader, can do.

18

What You Can Do

"Never doubt that a small group of thoughtful, committed citizens can change the world; indeed, it's the only thing that ever has."

– Margaret Mead

This chapter re-summarizes the Internet security solution and then covers what you can do to help make the Internet a significantly safer place.

Putting It All Together

For one last time, here is the high-trust Internet security solution.

High-Trust Ecosystem Components

The high-trust Internet security solution involves a lot of components, as shown in Table 18-1 below, along with whether the relevant technologies are ready, need to be technologically extended, or invented.

note A few of these components have two values, because different sub components will require different technology improvement efforts.

Most of these components already exist, are ready to go technology-wise, and just need to become far more pervasive. There are a handful of others that need some moderate technology extending. All that needs to be done is that we

Table 18-1: High-trust ecosystem components and technology readiness

COMPONENT	READY OR MINOR EXTENSION	MODERATE EXTENSION	NEW
Trusted identity providers	X		
Trusted identities	X		
Bound identities	X		
Identity attributes		X	
Trust assurance levels		X	
Real ID	X		
Trusted Platform Module, secure enclave, etc.	X		
Device secure boot	X		
Trusted device ID	X		
Location services	X		
OS secure boot	X		
OS security domain isolation	X	X	
Trusted OS	X		
Globally unique developer IDs	X		
Globally unique application IDs	X		
Secure coding	X		
Self-checking applications		X	
Secure configuration	X		
Trusted applications	X	X	
Application control programs	X		
Security-bound cookies	X		
Better patching		X	X
Trusted actions			X
Node compliance	X		
Trusted network		X	
Local Trust Assurance Service			X
Global Trust Assurance Service			X
Internet Security Global Alliance		X	

all agree that these things need to be standard and pervasively used in a way that allows us to get significantly better Internet security. Only a few things (e.g., Trust Assurance Services and related packet protocols) would have to be invented and newly deployed.

Example High-Trust Ecosystem Scenario

You power up your trusted device that has a hardware enforcement chip (e.g., TPM, secure enclave, etc.) with device secure boot. The trusted OS boots up using OS Secure Boot. You log on using one of your trusted identities. You can then assign any of your trusted identities to one or more trusted applications and sessions (or they are assigned by default). When you connect to another site/service/connection or someone connects to your device, the local trust assurance service ensures that both sides agree to a minimum trust assurance level before continuing the connection. Any new connections are reviewed for trustworthiness and to see if they are already on a global block list. Any email addresses or URLs sent to you or that you view are automatically submitted for review to the fully funded global trust assurance service. All sites/services/ connections are wrapped in color to indicate their trustworthiness. Any malicious connection/identity/site/service/session can be submitted to the global trust assurance service for review.

Here is a brief summary of the technology improvements needed.

Trusted Identity Providers

Many global identity providers already function reliably at scale, such as ID.me (https://id.me/), U.S. Common Access Cards (CACs), and even Facebook when they request Real IDs to be involved. However, they would need to be modified to operate at different standard trust assurance levels, be approved by the global trust assurance service, have new attribute storage areas, and be able to handle Real IDs.

Trusted Identities

We already have many phishing-resistant multifactor authentication (MFA) solutions, like FIDO, that we can attach to our new high-trust identities. We just need to make both high-trust MFA solutions and other similar strong high-trust identity solutions more pervasive.

Bound Identities

Many identity types, such as FIDO, already require binding to the device, sites, and services where they are used. We just need identity binding to be more the norm than the exception.

Identity Attributes

The concept of identity attributes is nothing new, but we need at least three things. First, identity attributes need to become more pervasive, especially among high-trust identities. Second, Trusted Identity Providers need to ensure that attributes associated with identities get as much attesting as the rest of the identity. Third, each trusted identity provider would need to create a site and service dedicated to attributes so that relying parties can request one or more attributes, as allowed by the trusted identity holder, by the submission of a custom HTTPS URL link to the involved attribute(s).

Assurance Levels

Assurance levels are already something widely known and used in the identity community, especially around Public Key Infrastructure (PKI) and digital certificates. The moderate extension would be globally recognized trust assurance levels (0–5, No, Low, Medium, High, Higher, and Highest) and everything identity-wise and the high-trust ecosystem coalescing around these values and agreed-upon definitions.

Real IDs

We already have Real IDs in the real world (e.g., required at U.S. airports for travel) and required on the Internet by various sites and services. ID.me is an example of a Real ID credential service provider. If your Facebook account is taken over and you want to recover it, one of the first things Facebook will do is request your Real ID to begin the recovery process. We just need to make them more pervasive and make more sites and services understand and use them.

Trusted Platform Module, Secure Enclave, and so on

Lots of devices already have these types of chips. All Microsoft Windows 11 devices have a TPM chip. All Apple devices have a Secure Enclave chip. We need every device connecting to a network or the Internet to have a cryptographic chip dedicated to hardware-enforced cryptography. We need these devices enabled and used with secure boot processes.

Device Secure Boot

Like cryptographic hardware chips, we already have many devices with hardware-enforced device secure boot, which prevents unauthorized modification of the hardware's firmware, the BIOS/UEFI process, or the installed and bound OS. We just need to be on all devices.

Trusted Device ID

We already have a method for hardware-enforced trusted device IDs (like is defined in TPM version 2.0); we just need it to be more pervasive across all devices.

Location Services

We already have sites and services that are pretty good at detecting where a particular device is located, even when that device is using forged user agents and location-specific VPNs. In my testing, Google, in particular, is pretty good at location services, even when I'm intentionally trying to fool it. We just need to share and use that technology with more sites and services.

OS Secure Boot

Many operating systems have or allow OS Secure Boot, including Microsoft Windows and Apple iOS. We just need to ensure that it is hardware-enforced and more pervasive across all devices and OSs.

OS Security Domain Isolation

Many of today's most popular operating systems, like Microsoft Windows, are slowly moving toward better hardware-enforced isolated security domains for their OS and applications. Qubes OS has the best hardware-enforced isolated security domains of any generally available OS and is really the model for all the rest. We just need hardware-enforced isolated security domains to be more pervasive across more OSs and for even more of the complexity to be hidden from the end-user. It should just be the way all operating systems work.

Trusted OS

We already have operating systems today that are linked to device secure boot, have OS Secure Boot, and try their best to ensure that all starting critical drivers and applications are secured against unauthorized modification. We just need this to be more pervasive and more often enforced by cryptographic hardware.

Globally Unique Developer IDs

We already have this for the two biggest app stores, from Apple and Google. We just need to expand this to a global program.

Globally Unique Application IDs

We already have this for the two biggest app stores, from Apple and Google. Many operating systems require the same thing at the OS level. We just need to expand this to a global program.

Secure Coding

We have everything we need to do more secure coding—we just need to do it. Every university, college, technical school, and online programming course must include a requirement for secure coding education. We also need every employer of programmers to require secure coding skills and experience.

Self-Checking Applications

This field needs more research and solutions. We have studied it for many decades. There are many programs that check themselves, especially anti-malware detection programs. They work hard to ensure they are not compromised by unauthorized code and do a fairly good job at that goal. We need the best self-checking solutions to be more pervasive.

Secure Configuration

There are already many programs, usually for individual vendors, that analyze an OS and/or app's existing configuration and warn the user when insecure settings are detected. We need this to be far more pervasive and exist on every OS and application by default.

Trusted Applications

Trusted applications are programs that include all the previous application checks and are digitally signed by the developer/vendor. The vast majority of legitimate programs are already digitally signed today, but so, too, are many malicious programs. We need trusted programs to have all the previous application components mentioned (e.g., digitally signed, secure coding, self-checking, secure configuration) and also be reviewed and approved by the global trust assurance service. Applications submitted to the two biggest app stores, from Google and Apple, are already reviewed by those services before being released. However, we need to improve the approval requirements and make them global.

Application Control Programs

We already have many application control programs. They just need to be hardware-enforced and more pervasive.

Better Patching

Better patching, as covered in Chapter 16, will require substantial modifications to most OS and applications. At the very least, it will require that there be more pervasive auto-patching requiring less user input with easier reversion if the patch causes problems. But what we really need to do is redesign OSs and apps to allow easier patching.

Security-Bound Cookies

Google and other entities are starting to implement one or more security-bound cookies, which means authentication access control token cookies are bound to Internet browsers on a particular device. The existing technologies are currently perfect, but you can feel that these solutions and the improvements that will soon be made are going to finally significantly improve the problem of cookie and token theft.

Trusted Actions

In general, almost no OS or application does this. It requires that an OS or application be designed and written to understand the concept of trusted actions and that those trusted actions be registered with the application and potentially the local or global versions of the trust assurance services. This would be a huge lift across all applications to make this happen. From a technical perspective, this component is probably one of the hardest to achieve . . . not necessarily because it's technically difficult to achieve, but because it pervasively impacts the design and operation of every application it would be implemented on.

Node Compliance

Node compliance is generally known as network access protection and was a big deal a decade or so ago. It would not take much to bring it around again. The client software and processes are there. It would just need to be far more pervasive. For a few years, it used to be very popular. Every vendor had a network access protection solution if not two. But it never gained widespread adoption, as was hoped, and quickly faded as something most defenders did.

Trusted Network

The concept of local and global trust assurance services working together to determine what is or isn't a trusted network (e.g., trusted device ID, node compliance, etc.) isn't one that exists today broadly, although individual vendors do have something like it for their customers with various services and computer security clients. We just need this type of service to be far more pervasive.

Local Trust Assurance Service

This does not exist today and would need to be designed and developed from the ground up. Ideally, the global Trust Assurance Service and the Internet Security Global Alliance would define the requirements, functionality, and accreditation process. Then, various vendors would offer local Trust Assurance Services or install them on their devices, OS, or applications. This is going to be a hard design because it queries so much information about the local device, OS, apps, and networks, and reports it to the global Trust Assurance Service, as well as acts as the local query and query responder for related tasks and requests. Plus, it needs to be designed to be highly secure and resilient because malicious hackers will certainly try to undermine it constantly.

Global Trust Assurance Service

This does not exist today and would need to be funded, designed, and developed. It needs to be designed to be highly secure and resilient because malicious hackers will certainly try to undermine it constantly. It would not only function as a repository for related information but participate in tasks and requests related to individual participants. It would require significant funding.

Internet Security Global Alliance

This does not exist. However, we do have many nearly similarly existing entities (such as the Internet Engineering Task Force, the Cloud Security Alliance, or the World Wide Web Consortium), but we need a funded group tasked with subject matter experts, fully dedicated on better significantly securing the Internet.

Sure, none of the existing programs or components is perfect, without flaws, or directly ready for a high-trust Internet ecosystem. But many are far closer to being ready and used than away. Don't let those components being perfectly ready to stop us from doing something better. We can start using the programs and components now even as we improve them.

"Better to do something imperfectly than to do nothing flawlessly."

Robert Schuller

Be a Champion of Better Solutions

What can you do? Be like me and many others who are pushing for significantly better, broader Internet solutions. Stop listening to a security vendor's product tackling a specific point of issue and thinking that it will really matter. Every time a vendor comes up with a good specific point solution, the malicious hackers and their malware programs simply sidestep the resistance put in their direct path and quickly move on to something else that works better. Stop accepting mediocre, guaranteed-to-fail solutions. Push for better, broader solutions. Use upstream thinking.

Join a Working Group

Be like thousands of your co-workers and other leaders who are actively participating on a working group to fix a problem. There are dozens of groups, such as the aforementioned Internet Engineering Task Force, the Cloud Security Alliance, and the World Wide Web Consortium, that allow voluntary or sponsored participation. Instead of just reading or complaining about something, get actively involved. Be the man in the arena.

Make and Push Your Own Solution

The ultimate experience is to look at existing solutions, find their faults, and then make your own solution. Remember to use all the recommendations for creative thinking, such as fail fast and first principles thinking, along with threat modeling, to help design your solution. Perhaps you can come up with a far better solution than I have presented in this book. It's overly complex and has too many components. Design something simpler and easier to adopt. Be the designer of your own destiny. Be the person who changes the world.

Final Word

Thanks for reading and putting up with me along my personal journey of what I think it would take to make a significantly more secure Internet. It would involve more trusted devices, identities, OS, applications, networks, secure coding, and better patching, all implemented in a way that would be easy for users to use and implement. In its best possible solution, most of it would be invisible to the end-user, handled by defaults and configurations enabled by vendors.

We can make a better, more secure Internet. It isn't a technology problem. We've got most of the needed technology. It's a doing problem. When will we do what is needed to fix the Internet? What will it take? The parts and pieces that we need are mostly nearly ready to go, and it would not take long to make up the parts that need to be developed. When the world is ready for a more secure Internet with far fewer hackers and malware, we are ready.

No matter what you do, keep fighting the good fight!

Index

Page numbers followed by *f* and *t* refer to figures and tables, respectively.